CONVERSATION

CONVERSATION

ROBERT HOPPER

INDIANA UNIVERSITY PRESS
Bloomington • Indianapolis

The paper used in this publication meets the minimum requirements of American
National Standard for Information Sciences—Permanence of Paper for Printed
Library Materials, ANSI Z39.48–1984. ∞™

Manufactured in the United States of America

Library of Congress Cataloging-in-Publication Data
Hopper, Robert.
    Telephone conversation / Robert Hopper.
        p. cm.
    Includes bibliographical references (p.   ) and index.
    ISBN 0–253–32846–2 (cloth). — ISBN 0–253–20724–X (paper).
    1. Conversation. 2. Telephone. 3. Interpersonal communication.
    I. Title.
    P95.45H66 1992
    302.3′46—dc20   91–34116
1 2 3 4 5 96 95 94 93 92

We can read the world out of the phone conversation . . .

Harvey Sacks
April 11, 1972

CONTENTS

TABLES

FIGURES

We hear the sounds of telephone conversation so often that we usually forget to listen to their patterns:

> R: **Tom's not in the office right now**
> **can I have him return your call?**
> K: **Please, this is Kate Shopper in Retail**
> R: **Okay**
> K: **I'm at three three one one**
> **and I'm returning *his* call**
> R: **Okay.**
> K: **Th*an*k you**
> R: **Thank *you***
> K: **Bye bye**
> R: **Bye**

The sound of telephone conversation is the poem of North American industry, the voiceprint of western culture. This fragment of transcription looks like literary verse in its short lines that alternate dialogic voices and in its rhythmic repetition of words and phrases.

Like much telephone poetry, this brief exchange is laden with speakers' purposes. We immediately recognize this dialogue as a failure in the recurring game of telephone tag. Such recognation is easy for us because we are the people of the phone.

The telephone may be our most important communications medium. It is surely the primary electronic medium for interpersonal communication, but we rarely ask how telephones affect our interaction.

This book describes the everyday sounds of telephone conversation. I listen repeatedly to tape recordings of naturally occurring telephone talk and write what the partners say in a form that looks like play scripts. There are many transcribed telephone dialogues in this book. Like play scripts, these transcriptions come alive when you read them aloud.

Some special transcription markings indicate how the talk sounds. In the example above, italics indicate emphasis. This marking helps us *see* what telephone speakers *hear* in exchanged thank yous: that speakers perform the stress of a second thank you to contrast with that of the first one.

> K: **Th*an*k you**
> R: **Thank *you***

The speaker of the second thank you indicates by stressing the second syllable that the first thank you has been heard—and that the present utterance is the second half of a pair of thank yous.

The transcriptions in this volume show such tiny details to help you attend to the sounds of telephone conversation. These transcribing symbols should become evident to you without special study, but you may also wish to consult the transcription conventions in the Appendix.

This book is monologue; telephone conversations are dialogues. That puzzle explains some features of this book, such as the dialogues between chapters and the frequent use of quotations in the text. Single quotes ['Hello'] designate what a person has actually said in natural conversation. Double quotes cite authors and enclose hypothetical examples.

I hope you enjoy reading my long-distance call to you. We can make this book more dialogic if we continue the conversation in which it occurs. Let me hear from you.

Acknowledgments

The faculty and students at the University of Texas at Austin have provided me two decades of stimulating environment. Every sentence in this book has been simmered in the soup of class discussion. Thanks to the University Research Institute for paid research leaves in the spring terms of 1983 and 1989, to Project Quest and the IBM Corporation for the grant of three personal computers, and to the Charles Sapp Centennial Professorship in Communication (1983–present) for continuing research support. No officer of the University of Texas has ever limited my academic freedom nor suggested that anyone besides me should chart the progress of my research.

Robert Jeffrey hired me twenty years ago and has served as my able chair and dean every day of my teaching career. His support makes life safe for scholarship. Texas colleagues have given generously of their time to hear my perseverations on this project: Jurgen Streeck and David Payne (now at the University of South Florida) have provided invaluable interaction and detailed critique at each stage of construction. Rick Cherwitz has served as my conscience for philosophy (none without tears). Madeline Maxwell has been a dialogue partner about ethnography and discourse analysis. Mark Knapp has challeged me to show how telephone conversation enacts intimacy in relationships. Rod Hart and Kathleen Jamieson read preliminary drafts of the early chapters and provided valuable advice. Paul Gray and Lynn Miller have taught me that every human utterance is performed art. Richard Howard has taught me that the voice of poetry and the voice of conversation are one.

Numerous coauthors and collaborators are acknowledged throughout the pages that follow. To emphasize that this work is a community creation, I use the pronoun "we" to pose arguments and procedures—reserving the first-person pronoun for personal opinions and speculations.

Colleagues from around the world have discussed this book with me and have tuned my work with their own astute observations. Such colleagues are too numerous to list, but such a list would include Wayne Beach, Jim Bradac, Lori Brown, Bob Craig, Bryan Crow, Paul Drew, Kent Drummond, Kristine Fitch, Rich Frankel, Howard Giles, Phillip Glenn, Candy and Chuck Goodwin, Hanneke Houtkoop, Michael Hyde, Gene Lerner, Jenny Mandelbaum, G. H. Morris, Michael Moerman, Michael Motley, Tony Mulac, Robert Nofsinger, Mel Pollner, Sandra Ragan, David Sudnow, Karen Tracy, Rod Watson, John Wiemann, Don Zimmerman, and dozens of others.

The world's best ethnomethodologists and conversation analysts have taught me about their craft, blending instruction and friendship in that intense yet playful authenticity that typifies the foremost contemporary school of applied phenomenologists. In addition to those listed above: Harold Garfinkel, whose ethnomethodology is essential to this work, has been generous with his astute necromancy and unfailing humor. Anita Pomerantz, my first and fiercest analytic teacher, was also the first to encourage me in the present project. John Heritage was the first analyst willing to discuss theory with me.

Emanuel Schegloff's telephone researches inform nearly every page of this book. His uncompromising dedication to empirical investigation makes his the most cumulative work in contemporary human studies. His generous and gentle critiques of these works-in-progress prevented many errors. Gail Jefferson's practices of transcription illuminate every speech sample that appears here, and she has gone the extra mile to teach me this art. Jefferson's achievements as a transcriber combine revolutionary science with spellbinding concrete poetry. Her written analyses roam the margins of the unknown to provide resources to the rest of us. And her tireless efforts to keep alive the legacy of Harvey Sacks have allowed me to read his lectures in photocopy.

Student collaborators have followed my directions to perform the numbly numerous necessary tasks of assembling the collection of recordings and transcriptions into the permanent collection of the University of Texas Conversation Library (UTCL). These persons have performed above and beyond the call of duty for the UTCL: Cecilia Cordova, Roger Cude, George Daughtrey, Nada Doany, Kent Drummond, Phillip Glenn, Susan Koch, Jennifer Mandelbaum, Ray Thomason. For keyboard assistance, thanks to Janis Wright, Susana McCollum, and Janet Ng. Thanks to David Weber and Duff Wrobbel for advice about computers and a can-do orientation.

Every week since 1983, an intrepid group of curious learners have met in group listening sessions. These co-listeners have refined half-formed ideas: Larry Browning, Chia-hui Chen, Molly Conway, Margie Culbertson, Suzanne Daughten, Carol Diesel, Kent Drummond, Phillip Glenn, Dennis Grady, Juanita Handy Bosma, Michael Johnson, Charlotte Jones, Irene

Kacandes, Pamela Kreiser, Jennifer Mandelbaum, Madeline Maxwell, Patty Sias, Jurgen Streeck, Nathan Stucky, Ray Thomason, Duff Wrobbel. The Texas listening sessions provide my primary day-to-day colleagues.

These people, among many others, have contributed recordings to the University of Texas Conversation Library: K. Abramson, S. Braggs, Cancer Information Service at M. D. Anderson Hospital, Houston; B. Crow, R. Esslstyn, L. Ingram, L. Scott, A. Sims, N. Stucky, K. Tracy, and K. Tuerff.

Portions of some of my previously published works are summarized here with permission. None of these works appears whole here, and any reprinted portions have been extensively reedited. I acknowledge: *Communication Monographs, Human Communication Research, Western Journal of Speech Communication, Journal of Language and Social Psychology*, and *Research in Language and Social Interaction*; also these books: *Talk and Social Structure*, ed. Dede Boden and Don Zimmerman, Polity Press, 1991; *Conversation*, ed. Derek Roger and Peter Bull, Multilingual Matters, 1989; and *Communication and the Culture of Technology*, ed. Martin Medhurst, Alberto Gonzalez, and Tarla Rai Peterson, Washington State University Press, 1990.

Segments of the lectures of Harvey Sacks, as transcribed by Gail Jefferson, are printed with the permission of E. A. Schegloff. The Sacks lectures are soon to be published by Polity Press.

A drawing by Alexander Graham Bell is taken from the Alexander Graham Bell Family Papers, which reside in the Manuscript Division of the Library of Congress, Washington, D.C. Thanks to Mr. J. Flannery for his assistance in locating this document.

A portion of Amy Clampitt's poem, "Dancers Exercising," from her 1983 book, *The Kingfisher*, is quoted with permission of Random House, Inc.

Cordon Art–Baarn–Holland, and Collection Haags Gemeentemuseum, The Hague, granted permission to reprint M. C. Escher's "Drawing Hands."

Tribune Media Services, Orlando, Florida, granted permission to reprint a cartoon from the comic strip *Shoe*.

Spoken Arts, Inc., granted permission to print a segment of Ruth Draper's "The Italian Lesson," from a recording made during Ruth Draper's farewell New York engagement. Recordings titled: "The Art of Ruth Draper," in five volumes, may be ordered from Spoken Arts, Inc., 10100 SBF Drive, Pinellas Park, Florida 34666.

To Kay, Brian, and Christine, whose conversations care for me best and most often—I gratefully dedicate these leaves. Thanks for all the times you let me tap your phone, for continuing tolerance of pun-ishment, and for all the rest of it. And thanks to my six siblings, who continue to teach me what a speech community can be.

BEGINNINGS

One rarely searches for beginnings unless the present matters a great deal.

Edward W. Said
Beginnings

THE PEOPLE OF THE PHONE

> The telephone bell was ringing wildly, but without result, since there was no-one in the room but the corpse. A few moments later there was. Lionel Rackstraw, strolling back from lunch, heard in the corridor the sound of the bell in his room, and, entering at a run, took up the receiver. He remarked, as he did so, the boots and trousered legs sticking out from the large knee-hole table at which he worked, but the telephone had established first claim on his attention.

This passsage, which begins Charles Williams' 1931 novel, *War in Heaven*, illustrates the telephone's influence on us. The hero runs into his office to answer the phone. He sees the corpse's legs sticking out from under the table, but he does not investigate the murder till after finishing the telephone call. The telephone conversation takes priority in our daily lives.

We are the people of the phone.

"There is a weird power in the spoken word," wrote Joseph Conrad; and he was right. But there is also power in that contemporary harbinger of the spoken word: the ringing telephone. The telephone's atonal summons typifies our awkward age. When the telephone rings, we stop whatever we were doing and scramble toward the promise of conversation. Money, power, or pleasure may move us, but we do not run into our offices after them.

One nineteenth-century railroad baron reputedly installed sixty telephones in his home so that he could conduct commercial ventures from any location, even the bathroom. When asked whether he was a slave to the telephone, the man replied, "Nonsense, it's a slave to me!" Did he underestimate this medium? Do we?

Telephone speaking deserves study as a primary activity of contemporary living, especially in the urban West, where the telephone hosts a large portion of our daily interaction. U.S. citizens spent 3.75 trillion minutes on the phone during 1987, a twenty-four percent increase since 1980. The nation's population grew only seven percent during those years, so the telephone's growth outruns population (Hall, 1989).

Part of the telephone's practical significance is that it extends occasions for speaking. Using the telephone each of us can speak across distances, across social barriers, across barriers to mobility. Telephone conversation has occu-

pied breadbasket provinces of our semiotic lives. Its acoustic images knead
our consciousness. Therefore the consequences of failing to understand the
details of telephone speaking grow in importance. To describe telephone
conversation is to understand ourselves better.

Descriptions of telephone speaking are of practical concern if only because
of the phone's omnipresence in our lives. We live in telephone societies. Both
at home and at work, we respond to the telephone's rhythms as traditional
peoples have responded to rhythms of nature, summons of church bells, or
other taken-for-granted experiential boundaries. We measure out our lives in
call-length episodes—coffee-spoons of spoken interaction, fragments to
which we must lend coherence.

We expect to reach others quickly and to accomplish our goals. We plan to
telephone for pizza, then wish happy birthday to an aunt in Cleveland, place
an order to Chicago, and consult a colleague in Berlin before sitting down to
eat. Competent professionals presume the telephone's piggyback relationship with computers, fax machines, answering services, and other media.
The telephone lurks in the background of every mass media event from

Figure 1: Maze of Open Wires; Pratt, Kansas, 1909.
How do we assess the prices of telephone progress?
(Photograph courtesy of AT&T Archives.)

broadcasts of election returns to the stock market page in the daily newspaper.

We experience telephone conversation most every day, yet rarely do we study its sounds. Scholarly and political attention has been lavished upon electronic media of mass communication, but this has in no way been balanced by attention to the primary electronic medium for interpersonal communication. How did we become the people of the phone? What are the prices of this progress?

In spite of our wide experience with telephones, most of us experience recurrent, poorly understood problems with the medium. Ask any friend or colleague if they have pet peeves about the telephone. Allow time for tirades: against answering machines, against talking computers, against telephone solicitors, against telephone call waiting, against the fouled-up new phone system at the office, against people who tie up the phone with small talk, against people who get straight down to business with no small talk, against people who call too early or too late.

Most of us suffer from telephobias: Our call return slips pile up, we experience psychic distress as we place a call, we procrastinate making a call because we fear it's not the best time, callers worry whether to self-identify at the outset or to begin by guessing who answered the phone. Virtually everybody volunteers a phobia or a pet peeve about telephone speaking.

How should we treat these difficulties? Where is our basic map for this domain? There are books on talking back to your television, but few treat effective telephone use—except books for telemarketers. There exist high school and college courses to teach the public speech, but almost nobody teaches the skills of telephone speaking. We lack a pedagogy for this speech environment because we have not explored it.

There exists a technical literature on telephone engineering, and some institutional history about A T and T—especially since divestiture. There has been survey research and historical investigation about uses of telephones (Pool, 1976; 1977; Williams and Dordick, 1985). Some experimental studies compare face-to-face talk to sound-only talk (Rutter, 1987; Short et al., 1976). But none of these writings describes the sounds of telephone speaking.

The present volume should help you achieve increased critical awareness of your own speaking patterns. But the answers are not simple; do not expect a quick fix. There is a domain and a vocabulary to be learned.

We cannot describe telephone conversation in a single book, but we may begin. Beginnings are first steps from which other steps follow. We designate beginnings "in order to indicate, clarify, or define a *later* time, place or action" (Said, 1975, p. 8).[1] The present book describes these beginnings in telephone talk: historical beginnings of telephony, the beginnings of telephone calls, the start of speaking turns, and beginnings of episodes. In each case we find that to begin entails more than one speaker and more than one consequence.

Historical Beginnings of Telephone Conversation

The history of telephone use affects how we think about communication (chapter 2). In telephone conversation two people cast their voices across electronic distance. From telephone experience, we discover the centrality of speech to communication and the centrality of dialogue to interaction. Telephone experience is pure speech communication and very little else. This experience is one major basis for our contemporary understanding of communicative interaction.

Telephone Openings

The most obvious beginning in telephone conversation happens at the opening of each call (chapters 3 and 4). In the first few seconds of a phone call, participants chart an encounter's course.

UTCL A24.7 ((simplified))

⇒	OP:	**Afternoon it's Gwe:n**
	JAN:	**Yea I'd like to charge this to 713 442 4002.**
	OP:	**Thank you for using A T and T:.**
	JAN:	**Thank you**
		RING
⇒	MIMI:	**Hello**
	JAN:	**Mimi?**
	MIMI:	**Yes honey**
	JAN:	**Jan**
	MIMI:	**Hi darlin howr you**
	JAN:	**Fine how are you**
	MIMI:	**Awright sweetie pie**

This transcription fragment shows one caller opening two telephone encounters: one with a telephone operator and one with her grandmother. These two conversation openings are quite different from one another. In the first opening the answerer gives her name, but the caller does not. In the second, the caller supplies both names. In the first opening the caller states her business straight out; in the second opening the parties exchange 'how are you' inquiries. During the opening turns of the second call, Mimi shows intimacy with the caller by using three endearing terms of address: 'honey,' 'darlin,' and 'sweetie pie.'

The first opening shows institutional contact between strangers; the second opening displays relational history. Each pair of telephone partners enacts a relational state within a few seconds of speaking. At each telephone opening partners improvise a dramatic scene.

Turn Beginnings in Telephone Conversation

Telephone speakers, like stage actors, achieve smooth transitions between speaking turns. Stage actors, in fact, copy and idealize the practices of turn taking used by ordinary speakers. One speaks, someone else speaks, and so on in rhythmic cadence. When problems emerge, the rhythm grows irregular and more fraught with uncertainty about who will speak next. That mystery occupies chapters 5 and 6.

The central concept in this description is the *transition-relevance place*, or moment at which speakership is up for grabs. Most of the time during conversational interaction, one speaker has the floor, but at certain times speakership may be changed. Consider this obvious example:

> UTCL A24
>
> | MIMI: | Hi darlin howr you |
> | JAN: | Fine how are you |
> | MIMI: | Awright sweetie pie |

These speakers handle turn transitions smoothly, rhythmically, and pauselessly. The turn transitions do not happen just any time, but only when the previous speaker may be heard as finished speaking. Speakers' management of transitions between speaking turns is essential to telephone conversation. The study of turn beginnings also helps us understand relationships between language use and social power.

Beginnings of Interaction Episodes

Episodes are discourse units in telephone interaction bigger than individual speaking turns, yet smaller than the telephone call, including: stories, topics, and coherent lines of interaction. Episodes, like phone calls and individual speaking turns, must begin. Consider once more this example:

> UTCL A24 ((simplified))
>
> | | MIMI: | Hi darlin howr you. |
> | | JAN: | Fine how are you |
> | | MIMI: | Awright sweetie pie |
> | ⇒ | MIMI: | Muh Pawpa's alright |
> | | JAN: | Okay |
> | | MIMI: | I know that's why you're ca:llin |
> | | | (0.4) |
> | | JAN: | Are you *sure* |
> | | MIMI: | Yea:h he's- he's lying do:wn no:w |
> | | | ((topic of Pawpa's medical emergency continues)) |

Soon after this phone call begins, the partners start to discuss Pawpa's health. This topic begins in answer to the mundane question: 'How are you?' The answerer of the call answers first on her own behalf ('awright') then guesses that Pawpa's condition is the caller's concern. Thereby these partners move efficiently from greeting routines into a discussion of medical problems. The beginning of such episodes is discussed in chapters 7 and 8 of this book.

To summarize: for historical beginnings of telephony, openings of phone calls, beginnings of speaking turns, and beginnings of episodes, telephone conversation provides unique purchase for studying naturally occurring conversation. As we use the telephone, we do things that we also do in face-to-face conversation. Telephone speaking illustrates how speech works. We describe telephone speaking not only as one important speech environment, but also as a representative anecdote for all speech communication. Describing telephone conversation provides a pathway to understanding the human spirit, language, and social interaction.

Telephone Speaking versus Face-to-Face Speaking

Certainly telephone speaking is a frequent enough human experience to merit study, even if no other speaking were like it at all. However, descriptions of telephone speaking prove robust in generalizing to face-to-face conversation.

Telephone speaking differs from other speech on a number of dimensions. Compared with face-to-face speaking, telephone speech is like message transportation, is limited to sounds only, is limited to two persons, and begins at definite moments.

Differences

Telephone speakers cannot see one another, and their messages are limited to sounds that must find the other at some distance. As we note consequences of such contrasts, however, we also emphasize that telephone conversation's simplifications provide opportunities to describe it.

Message travel. Telephone speakers do not share a space but send messages to one another across distance. Telephone conversation highlights the similarities between communicative activity and message transportation.

Speech sounds. Telephone conversation is constrained to sounds, split from the rest of action. This differentiates telephone encounters and face-to-face encounters at the very beginning of each encounter (chapter 3) when telephone callers must recognize each other vocally, rather than visually. Given this limitation it is surprising just how much is left when only sounds remain. We do, in fact, recognize each others' telephone voices almost instantly. We do, in fact, interpret emotional nuances without visual data. These experiences raise one of the central themes in twentieth-century thought—the centrality of speech sounds to all human experience. To study the sounds of speech, split off from other phenomena, is to study what is most basic about speech communication.

Dyads. A telephone implies another telephone, and two speakers, split off from the rest of a speech community. Telephone conversation's limit to two parties[2] focuses our attention on what is specifically dialogic in conversation: how speech action emerges across partners' turns.

The two parties in a telephone conversation relate asymmetrically: one is the *caller* and one is the *answerer*. The caller acts, the answerer must react. This role imbalance, caller hegemony, is a defining characteristic of telephone conversation.

Openings. Caller hegemony is most obvious at the opening of each phone call. The caller knows whom she is calling, and why. The answerer picks up the phone uninformed on these issues. In the opening of the call, parties must identify each other and define the situation in which the dialogue will unfold. These opening moments affect what happens later.

Telephone call openings occur at distinct moments, when one party summons another into encounter. Face-to-face partners may meander in and out of conversing. Telephone partners' interaction remains a primary focus for both parties, whereas face-to-face speakers braid talk into other actions. Therefore, the opening moments of conversation, so resistant to study for face-to-face encounters, become describable in telephone conversation.

To summarize contrasts between telephone and face-to-face speaking: The telephone call begins at a definite moment when two parties must construct an encounter, setting context with only their voices. Each constraint on telephone conversation simplifies descriptive tasks. We need not consider multiple speakers, visual signs, nor indefinite moments of beginning. An audio recording of a telephone conversation displays quite precisely those signals available to the conversation's participants, which allows the study of

> conversation and its sequential organization without examining gesture, facial expression and the like. Telephone conversation is naturally studied in this manner, and shows few differences from conversations in other settings and media. (Schegloff, 1979a, p. 24)

The very contrasts between telephone and face-to-face conversation make the telephone an excellent site for the study of dialogic speaking.

Similarities

Given the contrasts noted above, one might argue that telephone speaking seems quite different from face-to-face speaking. However, face-to-face and telephone speaking remain more alike than different. Researchers have contrasted face-to-face speech events versus sound-only events in terms of various discourse features: turn lengths, interruptions, pause lengths and others (Short et al., 1976; Cook and Lalljee, 1972; Rutter and Stephenson, 1977; see review in Rutter, 1987). In each of these studies investigators predicted differences favoring face-to-face over sound-only conversation. Cook and Lalljee (1972) argue that since gaze seems important to turn-taking in face-to-face conversation, sound-only partners must take turns less efficiently. Rutter labels this communicative deficit *cuelessness* (1987, pp. 126-31), though his data scarcely support this characterization of telephone interaction. He repeatedly fails to find features to differentiate face-to-face from sound-alone speech: "By the late 1970s the conclusion was emerging that visual cues were rather less important for turn-taking and synchronization than had been thought" (p. 126). Cook and Lalljee state: "The results of the study are very disappointing" (214). They report only one of eight predicted differences between the conditions, and this was in the opposite direction from predictions.

More controlled comparisons may produce news, but researches designed to contrast telephone and face-to-face conversation have displayed instead their essential similarity. Telephone speaking's rich communicative ecology is surprisingly like face-to-face speaking.[3] To be sure, visual cues are absent, but what those cues accomplish in face-to-face encounters does not go undone. For example, in face-to-face conversation we use visual cues to recognize our acquaintances. In telephone conversation, identification work must be accomplished in speaking. But the functions of mutual identification remain similar in both environments.

We must not dismiss as trivial all differences between face-to-face and telephone speaking. The telephone medium does constrain encounters, especially their opening moments (chapters 2, 3, 9).

To summarize: Telephone conversation is worth studying on its own merits as a primary site of contemporary speech communication. Telephone conversation's constraints make it a felicitous environment for studying interaction. Finally descriptions of telephone conversation generalize to conversation in other contexts.

Conversation Analysis

The present inquiry follows the theory and method of conversation analysis, the only perspective that has compiled detailed descriptions of telephone talk. Conversation analysts ground descriptions of speech features in empirical evidence derived from repeated listening to tape recordings of naturally occurring talk. Levinson (1983) argues that conversation analysis is the outstanding empirical tradition in pragmatics, because its data remain open to any investigator's inspection. Any reader may test my claims by inspecting the transcriptions and recordings used as exemplars. The greatest benefit of basing this report in conversation analysis is the sense of detail this method makes available.

Many scientific approaches to speaking lose the sense of detail that ordinary speakers take for granted. The details that get lost in many techniques for data reduction may be preserved in conversation analyses:

> It's a credo of social science reasoning that we can suffer the loss of details while we build abstract models. . . . Possibly it needn't be. (Sacks, Fall 1971, lecture 2, p. 13)

In preserving delicious and artful details, conversation analysts align with dramaturgical approaches to communication (Burke, 1966, 1945, 1935; Goffman, 1959, 1974).

Dramatic Detail

All the world's a stage, life is like drama, largely because, in life as in plays, actions unfold across speakers' turns. A play script looks much like the transcriptions in the present volume. Here is one instance from Shakespeare:

> Twelfth Night, II:4
>
> ((THE CLOWN HAS JUST FINISHED A SONG REQUESTED BY THE DUKE))
>
> Duke: **There's for thy pains.**
> Clown: **No pains, sir; I take pleasure in singing, sir.**
> Duke: **I'll pay thy pleasure, then.**
> Clown: **Truly, sir, and pleasure will be paid, one
>   time or another.**

In this play as in everyday telephone conversation, speakers' turns are placed immediately contiguous to one another. When one actor stops speaking, the next actor speaks. Each next speaker does not allow a gap between turns; nor do the turns overlap. Rather, the actors place each turn's beginning precisely at the end of the last turn.

In the Shakespeare segment, each speaker's turn does part of its work by means of its sequential placement. That is, each turn shows relevance to its immediate moment of occurrence. The Duke's first utterance: "There's for thy pains," does its work largely by being placed after the Clown's song and by accompanying a gift of money to the Clown. The Duke describes the money as "for thy pains," and the Clown's following turn plays upon the word "pains." The Clown accomplishes irony in substituting a literal misreading of "pains." This utterance is funny in large part due to its sequential position. To be sure, the Clown speaks a meaningful grammatical sentence.[4] But this sentence is communicative (and comic) by virtue of its placement. The humor works because the word 'pains' appears in two successive turns. This humor is heightened by placing the pun in a turn when something like "thank you" could have been expected, and heightened by the repetition of its key word.

Telephone partners build lines of action across speaking turns much as stage players do. Transcriptions in this book rely on conventions of dramatic scripting. These conventions, of course, have themselves been adapted into drama from the ongoing human conversation. To conversation analysts ordinary encounters provide the primal scene of human society: mundane conversation is the primordial speech system.

> Conversation obviously occupies a central position among the speech-exchange systems; perhaps its turn-taking system is more or less explanatory of that centrality. (Sacks, Schegloff, and Jefferson, 1974, p. 701)

Given this perspective it seems curious that scholars have attended to conversation less than to oratory, institutional communication, or written literature. Debates, press conferences, classroom discussions, doctor-patient interviews and many other formats for speech communication are based upon principles of form inherent as speakers take turns in ordinary conversation. A play or debate is much like a conversation, except that speakers' turns are pre-allocated rather than being worked out on the scene by participants.

There is little mystery to how stage actors take turns in preplanned, memorized, and rehearsed discourse. Stage actors speak lines composed in advance by poets. In telephone conversation, however, speakers enact an undirected play (Pearce and Cronen, 1980, p. 120). As in a stage play, each telephone partner builds each speaking turn on the bases laid out in preceding turns.

Telephone speakers' turns are small events, events that may not engage conscious attention. By analogy, trees may not think about leaf-production, yet they grow orderly leaves. Birds may not think about aerodynamics, yet they fly. Sacks quips that molecules behave with marvelous precision, yet do not have very good brains (1989, p. 227). To assume that the ordering intelligence for a system of signs must reside in the brain of each individual speaker is akin to assuming that a molecule must know physics.

A speaking turn is something like a leaf. If we think at all of a leaf or a speaking turn, we think of it as a small part of something—not as something in itself. If you see a tree, you do not notice any particular leaf. But if you study a leaf close up, you may discover bilateral symmetry in its veined superstructure (Bateson, 1972). If you study parts of that same leaf under a microscope, you may observe forms that make each leaf, and by extension each plant, function. As the study of a single leaf may advance the study of life, microanalytic study of speaking practices advances the human sciences.

This book contains transcriptions of about an hour's worth of speaking. Each argument is supported by short fragments used as examples. Longer passages, from which many of the small fragments are taken, appear between chapters.[5] These duets and trios may be read, or performed, as found art.[6]

Small patterns merit artistic as well as scientific attention. Walt Whitman's *Leaves of Grass*, a poem that celebrates the ordinary speech as the great poem, takes its title from a small curiosity: What is the grass? William Blake's verses also celebrate tiny phenomena:

> To see a World in a Grain of Sand
> And a Heaven in a Wild Flower
> Hold Infinity in the palm of your hand
> And Eternity in an hour (complete poems, p. 490)

Blake writes that the description of a single flower or a grain of sand may inform us about the order of things; or to understand an hour might help us understand much larger units of time. These poets resonate with Sacks' (1984) claim that there exists detailed order at all points in the human conversation.

Sequence

As we describe speakers' improvisations of spoken interaction, we continue Austin's (1962) project of describing speech acts. But most of speech act theory remains monologic: each act is considered as a single utterance responsive to situation and convention. Conversation analysts show that many speech actions are performed across sequences of utterances, especially two-utterance sequences. Table 1 respecifies some labels for speech acts as utterance pairs. For instance, a question becomes a question in that it gets an answer. Actions get accomplished by interactive work of more than one speaker. In this interactive recasting of speech action, "requesting" becomes a request-acceptance pair, a sequence accomplished across two utterances. This sometimes blurs individuals' responsibilities for speech acts.

Table 1
Speech Acts as Sequences

Speech Acts	Conversation Sequences
question	question - answer
request	request - responses
offer	proffer - accept or reject
greeting	greeting - return greeting

Consider greetings. A referential speech act position (e.g., Searle, 1975; Bach and Harnish, 1979) holds that we greet by making an utterance that conforms to a conventional formula. In a conversation analytic hearing, greetings occur in pairs of turns that distinguish first greeting from second greeting.

Schegloff, 1979a, p. 55

	H:	H'llo:?
	R:	Harriet?
	H:	Yeah:
⇒	R:	Hi!
⇒	H:	H*i:*.

This example shows the opening turns of a telephone conversation. The turns indicated by arrows are greetings. These two turns distinguish first from second greetings. The second 'H*i:*.' is spoken with a stretched sound (shown by the transcription symbol ":") and vocally stressed (shown by italics). This contrastive speaking of 'H*i:*.' apparently marks it as the second 'Hi' in this pair of telephone greetings. A single speaker utters each greeting, but the greeting exchange is jointly produced.

   To further illustrate the importance of utterance sequence, consider how this telephone caller identifies the answerer:

Schegloff, 1979a, p. 54

	L:	H'llo
⇒	P:	Laura?
⇒	L:	Yeah
	P:	This is Pam.

The utterance pair indicated by arrows occurs directly after the opening 'hello' of a telephone conversation. Two short turns align on answerer's name. These two turns are first and second parts of a sequence. The first pair-part calls for its second, to the extent that if the second pair-part ('yeah') did not appear, this would violate an expectation. Such two-utterance sequences are labeled *adjacency pairs* (Schegloff and Sacks, 1973) to describe the sequential relevance of the two consecutive speaking turns to one another. These two utterances together comprise a unit of discourse. The speaker of the first part guesses at the name of the answerer. The guessing gets displayed in part by the upturn in vocal pitch (marked on the transcript by "?"). This pitch contour emphasizes the first pair-part nature of the turn by making the turn a question (calling for an answer) as well as a candidate identification (calling for a confirmation). These two descriptions do not conflict with each other, but collaborate.

   We have now illustrated the adjacency pair notion with two instances, greetings and identification. The two kinds of instances are quite different, though both may be described as adjacency pairs. In the greeting example, the first and second parts use the same wording, and intonation signals the distinctiveness of each turn. In identifications, the first and second parts use different words. Here, the second part is 'Yeah,' an expression of confirmation. Yeah is used for a wide variety of second-part tasks: to confirm guesses, to agree with assertions, or to assent to proposals. Yeah is a multi-purpose second pair-part. Consider the large number of acts that get completed by a second part like "yeah."

UTCL A24.9:1

JAN:	Are you *sure*
MIMI:	Yea:h

UTCL A10.4:2

JEN:	Billy's at swim practice I see:?
SKE:	Yeah

UTCL A32.3:1

GORDON:	You're Dawn D*a*wn's friend.
DAWN:	Ye(h)ah

UTCL A32.3:3

DAWN:	Out a state tuition's pretty ex*pen*sive=
GORDON:	=Uh yeah

UTCL F1.1:1

M:	. . . that's *really* ha*rd.
D:	Yeah,

The first pair-parts of these instances do varied tasks: asking questions, expressing opinions, telling plans, checking the other's identity. Yet each of them quite naturally elicits an agreeing 'yeah' in the second slot. The response set alerts us to something that these diverse first pair-parts have in common.

In environments allowing a second pair-part of "yeah" you might also find a small number of other responses: "no," "I don't know," and so on. A speaker who hears a first pair-part is like a student facing a multiple-choice test item: there are a small number of choices by which each response-slot may be filled.

Notice especially the contiguous placement of the second parts in each of the above instances.

UTCL A24.9:1

JAN:	Are you *sure*
MIMI:	Yea:h

Sacks (1987) describes second parts of adjacency pairs fitting to firsts according to *preferences for agreement and contiguity.* This term "preference" does not denote an individual's act of preferring, but rather the term denotes a structural characteristic of conversation:

> [I]f a question is built in such a way as to exhibit a preference as between 'yes' or 'no', or 'yes-' or 'no-' like responses, then the answerers will tend to pick that choice. . . . zillions of things work that way. (1987, p. 57)

If a first pair-part is built to expect a "no" answer, then the answer will be phrased negatively.

Sacks, 1987, p. 63 (NB:II:2:R:18)

A: **'N they haven't heard a *word* huh?**

B: **Not a word**

The display of agreement and contiguity in second pair-parts occurs in enormous numbers of everyday speech events.

Each second pair-part in the instances above is offered immediately after the first pair-part. A routine (or unmarked) second pair-part does much of its work by means of its contiguous placement after an apparent first pair-part. The two halves of adjacency pairs unfold in steady rhythm. A break in the rhythm between sequential first and second parts marks that moment as special, or indicates problems.

UTCL A32.3:1

	GORDON:	**Dawn, this is Gordon Turner**
⇒		**(1.4)**
	DAWN:	**Yeah?**
	GORDON:	**u- Your old Hilton friend**
		(1.0)
	DAWN:	**My old who?**

In this telephone opening the caller identifies himself, then there is a pause of over a second before the other party responds. This pause shows that something has not gone as expected. The utterances that follow confirm that the answerer did not recognize the caller. A pause after a first pair-part is a marked event in telephone talk. Suppose you call a friend and ask to borrow her walkman. If there is a pause after you make the request, you can guess you will not succeed.

Adjacency pairing provides a dialogic unit for the analysis of telephone conversation. Not every utterance partakes in adjacency pairing. Adjacency pairs are especially important at the opening moments of phone calls, or where partners encounter problems. At these moments, adjacency pair organization allows speakers to perform close coordination (Schegloff and Sacks, 1973).

Telephone partners use adjacency pairs to signal each other about failure to understand. When you do not understand, you say "Huh?" or "Who?" or you repeat part of what your partner said, with up-turning pitch at the end of the repetition:

> UTCL A32.3
>
> GORDON: u- Your old Hilton friend
>   (1.0)
> ⇒   DAWN: My old who?
>   GORDON: Hilton

Dawn signals Gordon that she is having a problem by repeating part of his prior utterance, altering the pronoun but keeping the word 'old,' then she adds the word 'who?' which—marked by up-turning pitch as a question—locates the problematic word in the prior utterance to have occurred right after 'old.' Gordon shows he hears Dawn's utterance, 'My old who?' as initiating repair, for he repeats just that trouble-source word: 'Hilton.' Gordon shows that he hears Dawn's turn as a first pair-part, a question whose answer is the missing word located by the placement of 'who' in the question-repeat. Schegloff, Jefferson, and Sacks (1977) term Dawn's utterance a *next turn repair initiator* (NTRI), and argue that NTRIs are strong first pair parts.

Schegloff et al. observe that NTRIs happen after a previous turn and a pause, that is, they are not contiguous to the turn they repair. Again, we find that a pause, or break in the rhythm, co-occurs with problems in telephone conversation.

To summarize: there are numerous two-utterance sequences in telephone conversation: greetings, questions and answers, offers and responses, and so forth. It frequently takes at least two utterances, spoken by two different persons, to get a speech action accomplished. Adjacency pair organization allows both telephone partners opportunities to signal alignment with any actions in progress.

Conversation Analysis Procedures

Conversation analysts conceptualize interpersonal communication as speakers' displays of interactive orientations to each other. Analysts discern these displays from evidence in tape recordings. Conversation analysts:
    record natural speech
    repeatedly listen to recordings
    transcribe
    describe.
Conversation analysis is especially applicable to the study of telephone speech. Detailed information on conversation analysis methods is available.[7]
Recording Natural Speech. Conversation analysis strikes an alliance be-

tween the telephone and the tape recorder. Audio tape recordings preserve precisely those message details that participants in telephone encounters make available to one another. The focus on natural speech guides data collection away from controlled settings.[8]

There are numerous technical difficulties associated with recording natural speech. Speaking humans may walk around a room or drive down a street while speaking. Telephone conversation is among the very easiest interaction to tape record. The participants stay at one location and speak into a device that can be easily connected to a tape recorder.[9]

Since 1983 I have collected voluntary donations of tape recordings of natural speech. About 250 hours of tape recordings, about half of which is telephone talk, comprise the University of Texas Conversation Library (UTCL). These recordings come from homes and workplaces in a variety of locations. Speakers come from various ethnic backgrounds, ages, and genders. About one tenth of the collection is spoken in languages other than English. I also use telephone transcriptions by Jefferson, especially her exquisite NB materials.

Repeated Listening. Repeated listening is the gristmill for empirical verifiability of conversation analyses. Any description is subject to replication or confirmation in replay of tape recorded speech events. Over the centuries few communication events have been available for repeated playing and reexamination. Sacks reports that he began to work with tape recordings because:

> I could replay them. I could transcribe them somewhat and study them extendedly. . . . [and] others could look at what I had studied and make of it what they could. (1967/1984, p. 26)

Atkinson (1984) compares analyses supported by replayed tape recordings to instant replays in televised sporting events. The fine points of interaction are "brought into sharper focus as the event is replayed" (p. 7). The replay process constrains and validates analysts' commentary:

> Replays of sporting incidents are almost always accompanied by a further commentary on the events we are seeing again, the object of the exercise being to supply a more detailed and informed analysis. But viewers can also see the sequence of events for themselves, and are therefore in a position to draw their own conclusions about what actually happened, as well as to judge the adequacy or otherwise of the commentator's description and analysis. (1984, p. 8)

The reader of this book, like the television sports consumer, enjoys some access to data. Conversation analysis improves upon most other forms of data presentation as instant replay improves announcers' commentaries. Your access to data constrains my claims and provides empirical grounding for observations. Conversation analysis invites a reader to inspect the analyst's descriptions of what appears to be going on with reference to exactly the same material as that to which the analyst's descriptions refer. (Atkinson and Drew, 1979, p. 26)

You need not replicate an experiment or complete specialized training in order to validate my results. You may check my claims against transcriptions—and against your own experience.

How does an investigator select those recordings that merit repeat listening? Sacks argued that issues of sampling are secondary: that there is "order at all points" in social interaction (1984, p. 22). This is why a child may experience a small, randomly-selected segment of interaction in a language community, yet be able to interact with others. Sacks' position is extreme: surely there may be systematic differences in communicative detail that are related to scenic facts: being in an elevator, or being a newlywed, or being a participant in court, or being French, or working on a moving van. Figuring out which facts respond to any single scenic characterization, however, is a considerable puzzle (See Schegloff, 1991; Mandelbaum, 1991, Beach, 1991).

Repeated listening is like conditioning exercise for an athlete or dancer. The sport/art/science cannot proceed without such work, but these practices do not, in themselves, guarantee adequate performance in a public arena.

Transcription. Transcriptions, the most obvious topographical feature of this book, retain the features of play scripts but add some additional signs to emphasize timing of turns and marked moments within turns. Moerman argues that these transcriptions

> represent, or render, events that occurred in the world; they provide an inexhaustible resource for your own, and future, interests. My descriptions, analyses, and claims are based upon the transcriptional evidence they cite. You can therefore evaluate them. (1988, p. 12)

Gail Jefferson, who designed this transcription system, has also been its primary practitioner for two decades. Jefferson has been generous in teaching me and many others to use these tools. The present inquiry follows Jefferson's system. The following extract illustrates some features that this system adds to written orthography.

UTCL CIS.255

C:	**I've been wanting to go on- on base to the doctor.**
A:	**Uh huh**
C:	**About my breasts**
A:	**Okay.**
C:	**And i- I caught that number and a- it-**

> I:'d rather ask somebody I can't s(h)ee
> in p(h)*er*son than go on ⌈ba(h)se
>   ⌊Sure a lot of

A:

> people feel that wa:y

These transcriptions show not only speakers' words, but also such extra-lexical speech objects as 'uh huh' and sounds that are cut off before their completion: 'i-.' Vocal *em*phasis is shown by italics of the stressed sounds. The stre::tching of a sound may be shown by colons. Pauses are shown by (.) and longer pauses show the pause length in tenths of a second. The brackets show overlap—moments when partners speak at the same time. Final punctuation indicates pitch contour, not grammar: a question-mark indicates rising terminal pitch, and a period indicates terminal falling pitch. In the extract above, the speaker embeds laughter within a word 'p(h)erson.' Readers who wish details on particular transcription symbols should consult the Appendix.

A willing reader may become used to reading the Jefferson symbols within an hour of experience. Reading transcribed segments aloud hastens this learning. A transcriber may learn to use the symbols in this system within two or three hours of practice. However, the system allows continuing refinement in what one hears.[10]

Describing Interaction and Reporting Findings. Conversation analytic findings take shape as inductive proofs structured around exemplars. We use exemplars much as linguists do but give precedence to utterances that have actually occured—while linguists commonly use hypothetical examples of utterances that could be said (Hopper, 1988). Analysts glean evidence from message details about what participants are doing. Schegloff and Sacks argue that

> insofar as the materials we worked with exhibited orderliness, they did so not only for us, indeed not in the first place for us, but for the coparticipants who had produced them. (1973, p. 290)

Conversation analysts describe empirical details displayed by participants to one another. Evidence for analyses must include details displayed in recordings and transcriptions. Recordings and transcriptions are incomplete copies of actual talk, but they seem relatively rich and replayable representations of many speech details. If a feature is audible in recordings of telephone conversation, it is likely to have been available to participants—especially telephone participants.

Conversation analysts prescribe a *methodical* restriction to displayed detail, not a claim that everything important is invariably displayed, nor an argument that every actor in every scene perceives everything accurately. To limit evidence to empirical details of messages allows verification of descriptions

(Pomerantz, 1990). To emphasize the importance of naturally-occurring examples in this book, I enclose instances of actual speech in 'single' quotes.

The proof model for conversation analysis aspires to *analytic induction*, or specification of features displayed in every case of a phenomenon (Znaniecki, 1934). This goal cannot be achieved, but the attempt lends conversation analysis an astringent empiricism.

Analysts may err in insisting on confirmation in every case. When one investigates naturally occurring phenomena, this criterion may be unrealistic.[11] Instead the analyst should be able to explain any exception,[12] and to show that the speakers treat each exception as exceptional.

Analysts disagree about the place of numerical tabulations and statistical hypothesis testing. Znaniecki denounces studies resorting to statistical enumeration.

> The statistical method substitutes for this real, objective interdependence of all the characters of an empirical datum a multiplicity of arbitrary mental combinations of characters artificially isolated from their empirical context. . . . Thus, the worst mistake of mediaeval scholasticism is here repeated: juggling with concepts instead of investigating reality. (p. 231)

Znaniecki argues that when analytic induction is combined with enumerative induction, it loses "most of its advantages" (p. 237).

This stance, however, leads certain psychological empiricists (Cappella, 1990) to misread analysts' claims as entirely preliminary to tabulation and hypothesis-testing. This claim is given a certain feasibility by the number of social-psychological studies that attempt such work beginning with conversation-analytic concepts. Studies of interruption reviewed in chapter 6 are perhaps the best example of this. Most of these studies are riddled with inconsistencies that keep them from advancing conversation-analytic theory. Is that because the analysis is quantitative or only because these quantifications are poorly grounded in conversational phenomena? The argument continues. I have worked enough in both social psychology and conversation analysis to see why there are some paradigm clashes here—though I do not claim to resolve all of them.

In this book we argue against premature enumeration but insist that analytic descriptions may be quantitative:

> The conversation analytic approach does not entail a principled rejection of quantitative approaches as such, but only of the unreflective application of quantitative techniques in a fashion that does not respect the nature of the subject matter. (Zimmerman, 1988, p. 412)

Zimmerman argues only against hasty or imprecise quantification. Jacobs (1988) argues that issues tied to frequency of occurrence can only be settled by enumeration. But how often is frequency of occurrence an important issue? Jacobs (1990) celebrates an "especially nice fit" between qualitative analysis and properties of conversation.

The most important principle here is that observations rest upon empirical evidence from the details of speech. A dichotomy between quantitative analysis and qualitative analysis, which does not work well in conversation analysis, is overshadowed by the standards of empirical adequacy. There are some distributional analyses in the current volume (see especially chapters 5 and 9), though these are exceptions.

To summarize: The current volume's descriptions of telephone conversations follow the paradigm and method of conversation analysis. This method is particularly appropriate for telephone speaking.

Plan of the Volume

Chapter 2 ties the historical beginning of the telephone to new apprehensions of spoken conversation in art and scholarship. Chapter 3 treats the first few seconds of each telephone conversation with a model of the telephone opening as four ordered tasks. Chapter 4 tests the model against differences of situation, relational history, and culture.

Chapter 5 moves to a smaller beginning: how speakers begin single turns at talk. Here we probe the mystery of how telephone speakers, who cannot see one another, take turns as efficiently as face-to-face speakers. Chapter 6 applies this approach to issues of competition for the floor.

Chapter 7 addresses beginnings of long episodes, such as stories and topics. Chapter 8 considers episodes of speech play from the standpoint of "frame analysis." Chapter 9 describes some crises in the present ecology of telephone speech: a telephone access war that plays itself out in the realm of the familiar new mini-technologies such as the answering machine and call waiting.

The present work sketches some details of a dynamic and troubled ecology: telephone conversation. In one volume, we can only begin to describe it. This volume works best if experienced at a certain leisure of pace, giving attention to details in the transcriptions. Between chapters appear brief fragments of telephone conversation, labeled by number of participants as "duets," "trios," etc. These transcriptions show many of the smaller examples *in situ*. They provide grounding for your inspection of my arguments. I hope you find these transcriptions edifying as well as informative. Transcription of speech—and the reading of such transcription—requires a combination of empirical science and poetry. Conversation analysis blurs familiar distinctions and prejudices: individual and group, beginning and middle, message and context, qualitative and quantitative, language and culture, science and art.

	A:	Cancer Information Service may I help you?
	C:	Uh yes ma'am I saw your advertisement on t v?
	A:	*U*h huh?
	C:	And I was just wondering if I could ask a
5		question
	A:	·hhh Sure which advertisement did you see:=
	C:	=On the cancer
		(0.3)
	A:	Which k*i*nd of cancer
10		(0.3)
	A:	Was it on sm*o*king or ·hhhh um (0.4) diet and
		nutrition ⌈an:d
	C:	⌊I just caught the last part
	C:	·h ⌈hhhh ↑I'm sorry⌉
15	A:	⌊O:h okay ·*h*hhh⌋ So y*o*u don't really
		⌈know⌉ what ⌈you⌉ saw ⌈huh huh huh hûh
	C:	⌊No ⌋ ⌊No ⌋ ⌊See n*o* what I was-
		wondering about because see I've been wanting
		to go on- on b*a*se to the doctor.
20	A:	Uh huh
	C:	About my br*e*asts
	A:	Okay.
	C:	And i- I caught that number and a- it- I:'d
		rather ask somebody I can't s(h)ee . . .
		((encounter continues 25 minutes))

THE REDISCOVERY OF SPEAKING

Doctrines must take their beginnings
from that of the matters which they treat.
Vico, *The New Science*

During the first decade of the twentieth century, Genevan scholar Ferdinand de Saussure delivered three courses of lectures in general linguistics. Previous philologists and grammarians had concentrated on ancient written texts, but Saussure urged his students to found a new science describing facts of speech. Saussure compared speaking to an electronic circuit, a model that echoes telephone conversation.

Today, we revere Saussure's lectures as a turning point in the history of thought, a moment of discovery. This discovery would have been impossible without the most important new communicative invention of Saussure's lifetime, the telephone that completes circuits between speakers. In this chapter, we consider the telephone as our century's electronic speech teacher.

The basic technology of human speaking may not have changed very much since we became humans. We discovered speech communication a very long time ago—in the sense that bees discovered flying a long time ago. However, so far as we know, bees have not yet *re*discovered flying in the sense that humans are presently rediscovering language and conversation.

During the past century, the century of the telephone, we have deduced that speaking is the central manifestation of human consciousness. Following Saussure, we now take acts of speaking as the empirical base for any communication theory. This conceptualization grows from our telephone experiences.

By now we are accustomed to claims that electronic media spearhead changes in society and consciousness. Such claims have been advanced about television, movies, and music. We have perhaps overlooked the social impact of the primary electronic medium for interpersonal communication. Meanwhile telephone experience creates a new consciousness about spoken language. The telephone teaches us that communication happens when speech travels between pairs of individuals. This lesson stimulates the twentieth-century turn to linguistic analysis. Ferdinand de Saussure's science of language and Sigmund Freud's talking cure share with Mark Twain's oral prose style the fruits of telephone experience.

But certain features of telephone experience remained mysterious to us until the 1960s, when the founders of conversation analysis combined the telephone with the tape recorder and tumbled down a rabbithole into conversation's micro-world. They discovered in ordinary speech an order more powerful and more detailed than we could have imagined.

The history of the telephone is tied to our rediscovery of human speaking.

Knowledge of Speech Leads to the Telephone

There are reflexive relationships between our understanding of speech communication and developments in telephone technology. At mid-nineteenth century, the telegraph had made the world smaller by making it possible to send a coded-written message between any two points where telegraph offices existed. Scientists believed that eventually the sounds of speech could be transmitted as Morse code was. Many electronics inventions pecked away at this problem.

Alexander Graham Bell, the inventor who finally won the telephone patents, was a relative newcomer to electronics and telegraphy. He was a speech teacher whose particular fascination was making it possible for deaf persons to speak aloud. Bell won a head-to-head inventors' race against electronics wizards Elisha Gray and Thomas Edison, who were both at the height of their productivity, and who both worked (sometimes collaborating) on the same instruments during the same period. Bell won the race because of his special knowledge of speech processes.

Bell's grandfather was a comic actor and a teacher of "methods to correct defective utterance" (Boettinger, p. 41). His father, Alexander Melville Bell, devised a precursor to contemporary phonetic alphabets. Bell's Visible Speech capitalized on the insight that the sounds of speech are systematically related to the positions of articulators in the mouth. Bell staged demonstrations of Visible Speech in his home. His son "Aleck" was his collaborator in demonstrations such as this one, for philologist Alexander Ellis:

> . . . on August 23 the round, rumpled figure of the great phonetician appeared at the door of 18 Harrington Square. Ellis himself told the story in a letter to the *Morning Star*. He gave the father "a most heterogeneous collection of sounds, such as Latin pronounced in the Etonian and Italian fashions, and according to a purposely rather eccentric theoretical fancy; various provisional and affected English and German utterances. . . . Cockneyisms mixed up with Arabic sounds, and so forth," including some sounds not amenable to any known alphabet. Young Aleck came in, took the paper and slowly, "echoed my very words. Accent, tone, drawl, quantity, all were reproduced with remarkable fidelity, with an accuracy for which I was totally unprepared." (Bruce, p. 42)

This demonstration prefigures those Alexander Graham Bell would later use to generate publicity for the young telephone.

Scholars recognized Visible Speech as an advance in picturing speech sounds (Bruce, p. 59). Visible speech seems to have a sign for each sound that speakers make, including "a wheezing cough, a checked sneeze, braying, shuddering, growling, grunting, and so *ad nauseam*" (p. 40). In this respect, Visible Speech exceeds the accomplishments of later phonetic alphabets and prefigures conversation analysts' transcriptions.

The therapeutic applications of Visible Speech became a central concern, even an obsession, to Alexander Graham Bell. His first solo employment occurred when he substituted for his father to teach Visible Speech to deaf children. This debut struck the light of an illustrious career as a lecturer, a teacher, a courtroom speaker, and a salesman. Bell's classes for deaf children were such successes that he

> repeated them in Northampton, Massachusetts, taught for some weeks in Hartford, Connecticut, and took pupils in Newton Lower Falls. He addressed a national Conference of leaders in deaf education at Flint, Michigan. The title of his address was "Speech." (Boettinger, p. 46)

Bell professed a strong connection between his vocation as a teacher of speech and the invention of the telephone. His two financial backers in the invention process were the parents of deaf students. His mother and wife were deaf.[1] His assistant, Watson, later observed that many of their experiments were performed at night because Bell was busy in the daytime

> teaching his father's system of visible speech, by which a deaf mute might learn to talk—quite significant of what Bell was soon to do in making mute metal talk. (Watson, p. 12)

Bell's approach to teaching deaf children began with Visible Speech but also involved time-intensive combinations of signing, spelling, reading aloud, and lipreading. These instructional experiences fed the quest for the telephone. Bell explained in an 1884 lecture that one critical breakthrough in the development of the telephone came through applying analogies to the human ear in the construction of a phonautograph (a forerunner of the sound spectrograph).

> I determined, therefore, to construct a phonautograph modelled still more closely upon the mechanism of the human ear, and for this purpose I sought the assistance of a distinguished aurist in Boston, Dr. Clarence J. Blake. He suggested the use of the human ear itself as a phonautograph, instead of making an artificial imitation of it. . . . I requested my friend to prepare a specimen for me, which he did. . . . [i]t occurred to me that if a membrane as thin as tissue paper could control the vibration of bones that were, compared to it, of immense size and weight, why should not a larger and thicker membrane be able to vibrate a

piece of iron in front of an electro-magnet, in which case the complication of steel rods shown in my first form of telephone . . . could be done away with. (Bell, in Prescott, 1884, pp. 69–70)

This ghoulish passage shows how Bell's observation of the ear's working parts provided progress toward the invention of the telephone.

Not only the development of the telephone but the way it was publicized drew upon Bell's training as a speech teacher. During 1877 and 1878, the inventor staged a series of lectures noted for their oratory. The "elocutionist, Bell" made his lectures "popular entertainments" (Casson, 1910, p. 51).[2] The central demonstration of each lecture occurred when Thomas Watson's voice arrived by telephone from some remote location. The telephone impressed listeners by making a distant speaker's voice identifiable to listeners. Prescott's early account of his own telephone experiences observed that

what strikes one the most is that the character of the speaker's voice is faithfully preserved and reproduced. Thus one voice is readily distinguished from another. No peculiarity of inflection is lost. (1884, pp. 85–86)

Prescott's claim is exaggerated; what he really could accomplish was vocal recognition. Today's telephone users have come to presume the availability and usefulness of vocal recognition by telephone. A century ago this experience was a novelty.

The experiments with the telephone were made by me upon the cable lying between Dover and Calais . . . (in spite of interference from Morse code and other noises on the wire) when all the three wires were working simultaneously, the telephone sounds were easily and clearly distinguishable above the click of the signals. I happened to know several of the party in France, and was able to recognize their voices. They also recognized mine, and told us immediately a lady spoke that it was a female voice. (p. 87)

By contemporary standards these are modest accomplishments: identification of a speaker's sex, and recognition of the voice of a known and familiar other whom you already expected would be speaking at this time.[3] Yet the fact that telephone voices could be recognized demonstrated the transportation of a vocal message. It also shows the voice's central status in human conversation—a fact we rediscover in telephone experience. In Chapter 3 we detail how mutual vocal recognition remains an important component of telephone call openings.

To summarize: the invention of the telephone fell to a third-generation speech teacher who devoted much of his life to the vocal conquest of the deaf person's solitude. Bell defeated superior electricians in the race to his invention because of his knowledge about the facts of human speech.

Today, Alexander Graham Bell's contributions continue to puzzle us. Bell's disciple deaf-educators espouse oral instruction of deaf children and stress vocal communication with hearing persons. This stance differs sharply from (presently more popular) approaches that stress sign languages and interaction within communities of hearing-impaired individuals. Meanwhile Bell's sideline, inventing the telephone, made him rich and famous in time to marry his deaf sweetheart. The telephone achieved its spectacular commercial successes without Bell. He sold his patents and never took much interest in the growth of the telephone companies that still bear his name.

Ironically, Bell's invention of the telephone may have been his most enduring and hostile contribution to the deaf people he taught so earnestly. The telephone creates an enormously important universe of discourse that systematically excludes deaf persons' participation.[4] The telephone's reliance on hearing makes deaf persons nonmembers by fiat.

After learning about speech spurred the telephone's invention, the telephone's use brought increased attention to the facts of speech. In the balance of this chapter we trace telephone experience in twentieth-century thinking.

The Telephone's Lessons

Experiences of telephone speaking teach its users about details of speech communication. Telephone experience heightens awareness of conversational processes and promotes conceptions of communication as a *two-party exchange of spoken signals that travel back and forth from party A to party B*. The telephone's lessons may be expressed as these propositions:

(1) Speech communication is the transportation of messages through channels.
(2) Speech sounds provide central components of communicative interaction.
(3) Speech communication is dyadic and dialogic.
(4) Speech events have definite opening moments.

Let us show how each of these notions is expressed in telephone history—saving for later the defects of these lessons as a general model for communication processes. It seems that in telephone communication these lessons add up to asymmetrical role specifications for telephone callers and answerers.

Communication Is Message Travel

Since Alexander Graham Bell's first drawings of telephones (Figure 2), we have grown used to diagrams picturing the travel of messages along wires, or "channels." Shannon's (1948) Mathematical Model of Communication, published in the *Bell System Technical Journal* (Figure 3), describes communication as the passing of a signal through a conduit that connects two speakers. Only what passes through this middle-place is communicative. As noted below, this supposition was also evident in Saussure's model of the "speech circuit." Did this metaphor become available precisely in experiences with telephones?

There were diagrams of communication across wire channels adjacent to the development of telegraphy, and also celebrations of the telegraph's speed. But with the coming of the telephone, the experiences of vocal immediacy across distances lent to telephone interaction an element of miracle. This miracle was celebrated in an 1889 publication:

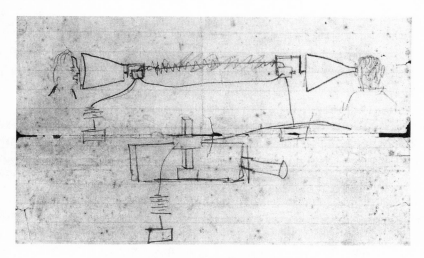

Figure 2: Sketches of the First Telephone
(Alexander Graham Bell, 1876)

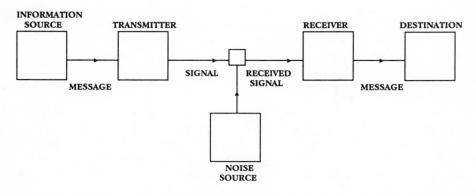

Figure 3: Mathematical Model of Communication
(Claude Shannon, 1948)

That Hello! . . . went down through the desk, down through the floor . . . then out into an underground conduit. . . . crossed rivers and mountains . . . and it caught a glimpse of Bunker Hill monument before it plumped into the city of baked beans and reached its destination in the ear drum of a man seated in a high building there. . . .

In about one millionth of the time it takes to say Jack Robinson, it was there. . . . It was as if by a miracle the speaker had suddenly stretched his neck from New York to Boston and spoken gently into the listener's ear.[5]

This early description begins with the word "Hello," which was already becoming the first word in telephone encounters. This passage celebrates the gentleness of the voice's arrival at a distant ear. As telephone conversation increases the sense of communication as transportation, it also increases its users' consciousness of voice in conversation.

Speech Sounds Are Central to Communication

Telephone conversation splits speech from the rest of action. To paraphrase McLuhan's aphorism, the telephone gives us an ear for an eye. The phone world is a world of sound only. Telephone speakers may gesture and move while talking, but this action proves unavailable to a telephone partner.

The telephone teaches us about the centrality of sounds to speech communication. Since we have relied on telephones, we have noticed that speech is the central ordering system for interpersonal communication (Ong, 1982; Dance, 1972; Modaff and Hopper, 1984; Schwartz, 1973). The impact of putting speech at the center of semiotics emerges when we contrast oral and visual signs. You can see a number of visual signs at once—a crowd of people or a row of trees appears to vision in an instant (Gurwitsch, 1964, p. 71). You can see somebody speak, smile, and wave an arm at the same time. But sound is linear; it strings signs out across time.[6] Splitting sound from the rest of communication emphasizes this linear emergent property of dialogic speech communication.

Speech Communication Is Dyadic

The phone is a medium built for two. The phone call cuts a dyad out of the speech community and wires it into an exclusive, private two-person mini-community. The telephone conversation creates an event intended for just two partners, and this helps us perceive dialogic artifacts. Much communication before the telephone was monologic. A letter or a public speech offers only limited opportunities to respond. On the telephone, we respond immediately: each next speaker's turn is critical to how telephone conversation works. The most important theorists of dialogue and interaction (e.g., Bakhtin, Mead, Buber) are post-telephone persons. A description of telephone conversation must be a description of dialogue. Bakhtin (1986, p. 72) situates his notion of dialogue in the fact of speaker change. Telephone participants signal attention and agreement in each next speaking turn. Telephone conversations unfold as speakers' turns string out into sequences and episodes. Playwrights capture this dramatic character of interaction in the form of their scripts—which look like telephone transcriptions.

Dyads seem simpler to conceptualize than multi-party encounters: the limit to two parties entails that telephone utterances are designed primarily for the ears of the partner. A dyad is little affected by shifting alignments between speakers and overhearers (Goffman, 1964). Consequently, the dyad forms the basis of twentieth-century communication models proposed by Saussure, Shannon, Wendell Johnson, Wilbur Schramm, David Berlo, and others. In our time, since the invention of the telephone, the dyadic conversation has joined the oration and the sentence as a central exemplar of human speech communication.

The telephone's restriction to dyads is not absolute. Party lines and extension phones have long made multi-party conversation feasible. But the dyad remains the basic format for the overwhelming majority of telephone conversations.

The boundary around the telephone dyad also creates new venues for overhearing. In face-to-face speaking any number of participants may enter into (or observe) an encounter. The telephone bystander does not have the same sort of access. A Mark Twain sketch, published in 1880, decries the experience of overhearing just one end of a telephone conversation.[7]

You can overhear a face-to-face conversation by accident, but if you overhear a phone call you are eavesdropping. The rapid spread of the telephone, much of it employing "party lines," gave rise to a society-wide fascination with eavesdropping.

> *The World's Work* reported in 1905 that a farm wife who had telephone service just a few months was asked how her family liked it and replied, "Well, we liked it a lot at first, and do yet, only spring work is coming on so heavy that we don't hardly have time to listen now." (Brooks, pp. 116–17)

The early telephone listener may become a consumer of the poetic details of overheard talk. In excluding all but one other, the telephone creates an aural keyhole—a technology for overhearing, as well as hearing, conversations. Anyone present at one end of a call can scarcely avoid overhearing half a conversation. Any user of a party line may overhear considerably more. These overhearing experiences objectify the facts of conversational interaction.

Telephone Openings

Phone call beginnings are more distinct than those in face-to-face encounters. If you fish with friends, or do the dishes with your daughter, you may drift in and out of conversation. In those environments you speak as you do other actions, and communicative action cannot be rigorously segregated from the rest of life. Much action has semiotic properties. There is no benefit for attending to which details of action are specifically communicative.[8]

But the telephone provides experience in pure speech communication. Telephone participants do virtually nothing but communicate with their partner. Before (or after) the call they are not interacting with that partner. This contrast splits communicative interaction temporally from other things we do. Hence telephone experience teaches us what is specifically communicative about spoken interaction.

A telephone call starts and ends at definite moments, whereas face-to-face talk is braided into other action. If you encounter a friend on the street, your gaze and body movement show recognition before speech begins (Goffman, 1964; Kendon and Ferber, 1973; Schiffrin, 1977). In telephone talk, however, there are *definite moments* near the start of an encounter in which our speech signals recognition. These definite beginnings of telephone encounters contrast communicative activity with other action—allowing communication to be conceptualized in its own right. Early telephone users experienced abrupt and interruptive telephone openings. An anecdote published in 1897 concerns a male suitor who had just spent an hour in futile attempts to tell a lady of his feelings:

> "Excuse me for a moment, Mr. Featherly," she said, "I think I hear a ring at the phone." And, in her queenly way, she swept into an adjoining room.
> Presently she returned and his mad passion found a voice.
> "I am sorry, Mr. Featherly," she said, "to cause you pain, but I am already engaged. Mr. Sampson, learning that you were here, has urged his suit through the telephone."[9]

This tale slurs a woman's fickleness, but it also shows that the telephone may interrupt an ongoing conversation, and even affect its course.[10] This tale tells a universal experience. Who has never been interrupted by the telephone? When these interruptions occur, cannot they intrude into the most urgent encounters? Will not the party who answers the phone likely say something like "excuse me?"

The characters in this story, and its readers, have already become people of the phone. They already know from experience how telephone beginnings work. The story relies upon gender stereotypes for its humor, but it relies on telephone experience for its formal organization.

Caller's and Answerer's Roles: Caller Hegemony

The story of the telephone marriage proposal indicates advantages that a telephone caller enjoys over the answerer and the bystander. The story's caller, Mr. Sampson, wins the lady's hand, defeating his copresent rival. The party put on hold, Mr. Featherly, loses the prize to the telephone user. The contrast between the names of these parties shows that the writer sees this decision as fated: the strong suitor (Sampson) uses the medium that most favors a caller's projects. The weak suitor fails to keep up to date and trusts the time-honored technique of calling on his sweetheart in person. To call in person is to trust the natural emergence of sentiment formation in the course of conversational copresence. Featherly shows up first and demonstrates his sincerity by putting his body where his mouth is. He hopes that local circumstances of the encounter will provide occasions to which he may fit his proposal.

The telephone proposal arrives as a bolt out of the blue. The telephone caller's purpose penetrates. Mr. Sampson calls only after he learns of his rival's visit. He expects that the telephone can coopt the present party and get quick results.

This parable shows not only Sampson's victory over Featherly, but also his hegemony over the answerer who may have accepted the proposal against her will. Ronell (1989) argues that when we answer a telephone

> the call is precisely something which we ourselves have neither planned nor prepared for nor voluntarily performed. . . . "It" calls against our expectations and even against our will. (p. 31)

The caller (Sampson) has a plan that overwhelms the answerer's lack of plans. Surprise operates in the caller's favor. The answerer already says "yes" by answering:

> . . . you're saying yes, almost automatically, suddenly, sometimes irreversibly. Your picking it up means the call has come through. . . . You don't know who's calling or what you are going to be called upon to do, and still, you are lending your ear, giving something up, receiving an order. (Ronell, 1989, p. 2)[11]

It is sometimes claimed that the telephone is a social leveller because anybody can call anybody else. However, the telephone unlevels the playing field of human discourse by favoring any caller's project at the answerer's expense. Mr. Sampson may not turn out be such a good husband, and the lady expresses no sentiment that favors him. Yet she accepts his proposal. The fable illustrates caller hegemony: a systematic power imbalance between telephone callers and answerers.

Sacks argues that telephone use has developed social roles for appropriate conduct of caller and answerer:

> you cannot, for example, as a possible Called pick up the phone, you say "Hello" and they say "Is Mary there?" and you say "This isn't Mary" and hang up, and Mary's sitting next to you. So plainly, persons who take on Answering take on a series of obligations. The obligations vary, depending to some extent on what Caller demands, Callers often demanding very elaborate things from Answerers, to whom they have no relationship otherwise in the world. (Spring 1972, lecture 3, pp. 9–10)

The answerer's role includes the obligation to speak first, which entails vulnerability to be recognized by a still-unrecognized caller and to assent to whatever the caller asks. Sacks argues that the caller's role includes first chance to show recognition of the other and first chance to launch preliminary inquiries such as "what are you doin"—inquiries that may intrude into the answerer's privacy. Caller also gets first chance to introduce the call's first topic. Caller and answerer are asymmetrical roles, and the obligations attached to these roles make telephone talk socially problematic.

Is there a relationship between the answerer's one-down position and the institutional deployment of women within such telephone-answering roles as operator or receptionist? Can women retain gracious tonalities in repeatedly-dominated setting; does feminine socialization prepare one for such work? Do callers prefer to dominate women or find it confusing if a man takes on a one-down role such as that of institutional answerer? Does the telephone augment sexual inequalities? If so, it may augment inequalities due to class, education, ethnicity, and so on (Rakow, 1988).

In a related vein, Ronell argues that the notion of "phony" originates in the inauthentic telephonic relationship between caller and answerer:

> The phone phones . . . establishing the phony, the shady Other, like the moon, whose identity and therefore also ours is held in suspension . . . performing and inducing fraud. (p. 45)

Caller hegemony waxes strongest near the opening of the phone call. We return to this theme in chapters 3, 4, and 9.

To summarize: The telephone is our century's speech teacher. Telephone users gain special knowledge about communication and sociality that is like things about writing that a user of word processing knows. The vulnerability to interruption by phone is a bit like the word-processing user's vulnerability to accidental file erasure. A present-day story in which a character loses a computer file may be best appreciated by computer users. Routine experiences with a medium allow such vulnerabilities to be exploited in fiction.[12]

Below, we consider fictional and scholarly instances from the first generation of telephone users.

Telephone Talk in Fiction

Telephone experience enhances its users' appreciation for the details of spoken experience. This is reflected in the development of the "colloquial style" in American literature, which includes "greater concreteness of diction," with corresponding emphasis on "dialect pieces and in fictional dialogue" (Bridgman, 1966, p. 12). The colloquial style "comes from one book by Mark Twain called *Huckleberry Finn*" (p. 5). That novel appeared in 1884, just four years after Twain published a satire depicting his family as telephone users. Perhaps the colloquial dialogue in *Huckleberry Finn* owes not only Twain's Missouri childhood but also his adult telephone experiences.

The telephone displays details of speech. Consider this dialogue that appeared in the publication *Tit-Bits* in 1897:

> Halloa Fletch! Do you hear me?
> Yes.
> This is Sid. Thought I'd call you up.
> Glad to hear from you, Sid. How are you?
> First-rate. How's things?
> Oh, nothing especially. Hadn't anything to do, you know, and thought I'd call you up.
> (Pause)
> Yes. (Another pause.) Everything going on about as usual in the old town?[13]

This sketch jibes people who would call each other up with nothing to say. Such encounters may be celebrated as triviality. Yet, this scene's humor springs from accurate observation of telephone conversation's details—observations that prefigure the transcriptions in this book. Each new paragraph in the sketch shows speaker change, and pauses are allocated their own line in the dialogue, showing that they do not belong within the turn of either speaker.

This sketch also captures details of Schegloff's (1986) canonical telephone opening (chapter 3). Here we show Schegloff's illustration of that form alongside the first lines of the 1897 sketch about two bumpkins.

	Schegloff, 1986, 115	Fletch and Sid, 1897
R	Hello	
C	Hello Ida?	Halloa F! Do you hear me?
R	Yeah	Yes.
C	Hi,=This is Carla	This is S. Thought I'd call you up
R	*Hi* Carla.	Glad to hear from you, S.
C	How are you.	How are you
R	Okay:.	First-rate
C	Good.=	
R	=How about you.	How's things
C	Fine.	Oh, nothing especially...

Schegloff describes the parts of a canonical opening as summons-answer, identification-recognition, greeting-greeting, and exchange of "how are you?" inquiries. These features in Fletch and Sid's dialogue[14] show a keen ear for conversation's details. The experience of talking on the phone teaches these details. In 1897, North American society was convulsed in a craze of telephone adoption, which created a community of readers to appreciate this humor.

The telephone teaches its users about details of conversational speaking.

Scholars are subject to the same cultural curricula as other readers and writers.

The Telephone's Echo in Scholarship

The linguistic turn in contemporary thought may be rooted in the experience of the telephone. Scholars presently consider spoken language to be the central ordering system for human activity. Ferdinand de Saussure, whose lectures[15] launched modern linguistics, semiotics, structuralism, and communication theory, posited a model, shown as Figure 4, that prefigures Shannon's diagram. Like the Shannon model, Saussure's representation shows two parties speaking to one another. Speech is pictured travelling

A   B

Figure 4: Pictorial Representation of the Speaking Circuit
(Ferdinand de Saussure, 1915)

along wire-like lines. Shannon's lines explicitly represent telephone wires. In Saussure's model the lines *"look* suspiciously like telephone wires" (Harris, 1987, p. 216). Saussure, like Shannon, explicitly distinguishes between sources and encoding.

There are circumstantial links between Saussure's approach to language and his experiences of telephone use. He lived the middle third of his life in Paris during the very years that saw that city become festooned in telephone wires. In Saussure's *Cours de Linguistique Generale* (delivered in 1907–1910, first published in 1915), Figure 4 bears the quasi-electronic label: "circuit:"

> il faut se placer devant l'acte individuel qui permet de reconstituer le circuit de la parole (p. 27).

> We must place ourselves in front of (in the presence of) the individual act that allows us to reconstitute the speaking circuit.[16]

What leads Saussure to compare speaking to a dyadic circuit, if not his experiences of telephone conversation? We begin to speak on the telephone only when a circuit is completed. What travels on that circuit is the spoken voice. Saussure's diagram of the "circuit de la parole" prefigures the information model and also resembles Bell's early drawings of telephones. Each diagram shows a dyad connected by an electric conduit. The conduit takes the message to a waiting ear.

Telephone experience, available for the first time to persons of Saussure's generation, stands behind this approach to the sounds of speech. Saussure criticizes thinkers who emphasize writing over speech.

> The object of study in linguistics is not a combination of the written word and the spoken word. The spoken word alone constitutes that object. (Harris trans., pp. 24–25)

Linguistics before Saussure concentrated upon writing. Saussure's *Cours* proposed a science of speech. As Saussure noted the centrality of the spoken word, he also described spoken signs as "linear."

> Unlike visual signals (e.g. ships' flags) which can exploit more than one dimension simultaneously, auditory signals have available to them only the linearity of time. The elements of such signals are presented one after another: they form a chain. (Harris trans., pp. 69–70)

The experience of telephone conversation suggests the linearity of signs in spoken interaction.[17] When interaction is truncated into sound, then the sequential structures of interaction are laid bare. Speech occurs in sequence, one sound at a time: "any unit acquires its value simply in opposition to what precedes, or to what follows, or to both" (Harris trans., p. 121).

Saussure's insights show a consciousness in transformation, a transformation that grew from the telephone. The telephone had come about because a speech teacher invented a new electronic device for speech communication. This machine carries pure speech—speech split off from the rest of action. Telephone experience reframes the possibilities of interaction and locates speaking at its middle place. We could not hear speech speak until the telephone blew its cover. The telephone forces speech to experiential attention.

Saussure's lectures, for all their pellucid vivacity, offer only partial solutions to the problem of modelling telephone conversation. He espouses a conventionalist view of meaning and a literalist bias toward monologic communication. Scholars who follow Saussure encounter these problems by emphasizing dialogue—an emphasis also grounded in experiences of telephone conversation. The linguistic turn which claims Saussure as a parent has grown toward a master trope of conversation.

The Linguistic Turn and the Human Conversation

Issues that used to be discussed as problems of metaphysics, epistemology, psychology, or research method are now examined in terms of speech and language. In one characterization, the *linguistic turn* is studying any phenomenon "X" by studying the word "x" and related words (Rorty, 1967, p. 4). Rorty applies this term to an anthology of analytic and ordinary language philosophers, but it applies as well to certain writings of Heidegger (1962), Wittgenstein (1953), or Derrida (1967), who variously ground inquiry in language.

Heidegger wrote that any attempt to understand human experience must "take linguistic considerations as its starting point" (1962). Freud, who invented the talking cure, also put language at the center of human psychic experience: "we shall have no hesitation in letting ourselves be guided by linguistic usage" (1930/1961, p. 40). The linguistic turn touches every branch of human studies.[18] To understand human experience or thinking, we must describe language. But what is language?

This century's answer is a precipitate from telephone experience. The theorists cited here have lived during the first years of telephone use. Freud, in the work cited above, decries contemporary technologies, using the telephone as one example:

> During the last few generations mankind has made an extraordinary advance in the natural sciences and in their technical application and has established his control over nature in a way never before imagined. . . . One would like to ask: is there, then, no positive gain in pleasure, no unequivocal increase in my feeling of happiness, if I can, as often as I please, hear the voice of a child of mine who is living hundreds of miles away. . . . [but] If there had been no railway to conquer distances, my child would never have left his native town and I should need no telephone to hear his voice. (1931/1961, pp. 38–39)

The rediscovery of speaking follows the trajectory of the linguistic turn toward conversational pragmatics. The telephone is a co-author of these discoveries.

As twentieth-century thought unfolds, thinkers amend Saussure's notion of language as an abstract conceptual structure into models based in interactive conversation. Kenneth Burke describes the human condition as

> . . . the 'unending conversation' that is going on in history when we are born. Imagine that you enter a parlor. You come late. When you arrive, others have long preceded you, and they are engaged in a heated discussion, a discussion too heated for them to pause and tell you exactly what it is about. In fact, the discussion had already begun long before any of them got there, so that no one present is qualified to retrace for you all the steps that had gone before. You listen for awhile, until you decide that you have caught the tenor of the argument; then you put in your oar. Someone answers; you answer him. . . . However the discussion is interminable. The hour grows late, you must depart. And you do depart, with the discussion still vigorously in progress. (1941/1973, p. 94)

We are guests of an ongoing spoken conversation, or as Oakeshott writes,

"We are the inheritors of a conversation" (p. 196). Speech-in-language involves us in primordial activity.

Conversation analysis, the approach we follow here, arises in an intellectual ecology of poststructuralism and discourse analysis.[19] This tradition repeatedly grapples with how to account for the structures of naturally occurring dialogue.

The Monologue View and the Dialogue Hearing

One embarrassment to the linguistic turn and its pragmatic offshoots has been its reliance upon monologic (often written) documents. These documents fail to account for intricacies of human conversational interaction. We must replace the written sentence as the primary unit of analysis with the spoken utterance (Volosinov, 1930; Bakhtin, 1986, p. 72; Schegloff, 1982; Hakulinen, 1990).[20] And we must describe dialogic sequences of utterances—patterns of form that connect utterances by different speakers into structural units.

To a *monologue view*, communication consists in transportation of a message from point A to point B. Effective communication is high-fidelity monologue: as complete, clear, and undistorted as possible.

Telephony brings a *dialogic hearing* of speech. While telephone communication is, perhaps more than ever, identified with transportation of signs, the signs now alternate in speakers' turns. Clarity and completeness recede in favor of aptness and keeping the floor open.

Bakhtin (1986, pp. 68–73) attacks Saussure's diagram of the speech circuit as picturing only monologue—a message-flow from an active speaker to a listener who decodes the meaning of the message. However, actual listening is inherently responsive. Listening to an utterance, one

> simultaneously takes an active, responsive attitude toward it. He either agrees or disagrees with it . . . augments it, applies it, prepares for its execution, and so on. And the listener adopts this responsive attitude for the entire duration of the process of listening and understanding, from the very beginning—sometimes literally from the speaker's first word. Any understanding of live speech, a live utterance, is inherently responsive. (1986, p. 68)

Bakhtin argues that responsive listening is poorly described by models emphasizing decoding. Listeners respond more than they decipher. Bakhtin argues that speaker change provides the mechanism for response, and that *two-party dialogue provides a paradigm case of speaker change* (p. 72). In all these particulars, Bakhtin builds upon Saussure by describing a speech situation modelled upon experiences of telephone speaking, which is dialogic precisely in the alternation of two speakers' utterances.

Bakhtin also prefigures the conversation analytic notion of adjacency pairs in his list of activities done as rejoinders, or responsive utterances:

> Rejoinders are all linked to one another . . . question and answer, assertion and

objection, assertion and agreement, suggestion and acceptance, order and exe-
cution, and so forth. (p. 72)

Bakhtin lists here several forms of adjacency pairs and notes a similarity in
the rejoinder (or second pair-part) turns of these sequences (chapter 1).

The special role of response in oral interaction is illustrated by Schwartz's
(1973) title: *The Responsive Chord*. Schwartz, who has pioneered the tape
recording of sounds in their natural environments, claims that sounds key
human responsiveness. He adds that we hear sounds in the context of
surrounding sounds:

> We expect to hear a space between telephone rings. If I record a telephone
> ringing and then cut out the space between rings, so that I have one continuous
> ring, a listener would have great difficulty identifying it. (p. 32)

Schwartz evokes a Saussurian notion of linearity, the notion of the hearing of
sounds in sequence. Melded to Bakhtin's insistence on dialogue, the notion
of the sequential hearing of speech helps us to focus on utterance sequences
as units of response.

To consider communication as response-centered spoken dialogue based
in speaker change turns us toward the growing conviction that there is
something primordial about patterns of ordinary human conversation. The
more ordinary a conversation, the more banal its sounds, the more playful
its course, the more basic its tracery of the forms of human experience.

Although Saussure insisted that we study the facts of speech, his own
analyses described only single words and sounds selected to exemplify an
idealized uniformity among speakers of a language. This idealization retains
current defenders. For instance, Chomsky (1965) insists that natural speech
includes so many imperfections that it cannot provide useful data for theories of grammar.

> A record of natural speech will show numerous false starts, deviations from
> rules, changes of plan in mid-course, and so on. . . . Observed use of language . . .
> surely cannot constitute the actual subject matter of linguistics. (1965, pp. 3–4)

Chomsky presumes that linguists know the ways that language is ordered,
and other things humans do must be disorderly. Against this view, Goodwin
(1980) argues that certain apparent speech perturbations may be deployed
systematically for interactive purposes. Goodwin shows that certain sentence *restarts* are not false starts at all, but resources that speakers use to
secure a listener's attentive gaze. Schegloff (1979b, p. 282) argues that much
in current theories of syntax may be subsumed into theories of syntax-for-
conversation.

Human conversation is the backbone of our natural taken-for-granted
world. The natural units of speech are the utterance and the multi-utterance

sequence. Telephone speakers respond to each other both across and within turns at talk. These are some lessons we have learned on the telephone.

Conclusions

The telephone was invented in the USA late in the nineteenth century, and its use has spread faster and farther in this country than anywhere else. In 1880 there were thirty thousand telephones at use in the USA, but only five thousand in all of Europe (Crawley, 1931, p. 57). The contemporary disciplines of speech communication were born in the USA early in the twentieth century and have established their most secure pedagogical tradition in this country. Perhaps the North Americans' fascination with interpersonal communication (Katriel and Philipsen, 1981; Carbaugh, 1988) grows from telephone experiences. The people of the phone have spawned the students of speech communication.

Telephony undergirds our theories about communication. Telephone speech splits sound from the rest of the senses, splits the dyad from the rest of society, and splits communication from other activity. Telephone conversation is pure dialogic speech communication. Hence, descriptions of telephone conversation are central to theories of language, conversation, and interaction.

Telephone experience highlights the communicative. However, there are limits to its lessons. We may pass by the conduit metaphor quickly, as it has been discussed by others (Reddy, 1979; Lakoff and Johnson, 1980). Is everything about messages "in" a channel? Does the conduit notion bias our attention toward details of single messages and away from interactive issues?

There are also costs for focusing attention on the dyad. We must compare two-party speaking and multi-party speaking, especially in turn-taking achievements. In a two-party conversation, if a current speaker does not continue there is only one additional speaker; but in a multi-party conversation there is more than one candidate next speaker (Sacks, Schegloff, and Jefferson, 1974). Further, the existence of third parties leads to various possibilities of alignment and celebration. For instance, shared laughter shows a different shape in dyads than in multi-party conversation (Glenn, 1989).

Still, our telephonic experiences attune us to the importance of sounds and to the centrality of responsive turn taking. Tape recorded telephone calls capture a high percentage of textual detail without excessive intrusion. There is a methodic alliance between the telephone and the tape recorder.

The Telephone and the Tape Recorder

Current writing about telephones rarely gives the reader a sense of the sounds of speech. For example, in the retrospective assessment of the telephone by Pool et al. (1977) there appear no quotations from telephone conversations. In Hudson's (1984) account of telecommunications in rural development, there is little notice taken of how telephone speech sounds to its new users. Rather, these accounts focus on (presumably well-understood) functions of telephone communication and correlate these with economics and demography.

If a Martian, one thousand years from now, were to read those reports, could it understand the telephone as well as by listening to a single tape recording of a three-minute call? No; there is a principled relationship between the lessons of the telephone and what tape recorders capture. The evolution of tape recorders makes possible the detailed study of telephone speaking from a participant's-ear hearing. Consequently you may replicate any finding reported in this book by recording a few minutes of your own phone calls.

Saussure noted that language frequently escapes observation. A partial solution to this problem emerges when we tape record the telephone conversation. Recording of human speech was invented at about the same time as the telephone. Saussure knew about audio recordings of speech samples. He urged linguists to study recorded samples (echantillons phonographique) which were already being collected in Vienna and Paris (p. 44).

The importance of audio recording to studies of language is celebrated by Bernard Shaw's (1913) professorial anti-hero Henry Higgins. Higgins and his colleague Pickering are discussing language varieties and how to study them when Higgins' servant announces that a cockney flower girl wishes to speak to him. Higgins exclaims:

> This is rather a bit of luck. I'll shew you how I make records. We'll set her talking; and I'll take it down first in Bell's Visible Speech; then in broad Romic; and then we'll get her on the phonograph so that you can turn her on as often as you like with the written transcript before you.[21]

Higgins' utterance illustrates two principles of conversation analysis. First, a transcription of speech can often provide clarity to analysis, and special transcription systems (such as Bell's Visible Speech) are useful in these tasks. Second, we may gain analytic leverage by playing a recording many times, especially if a transcript is available during the replayings.

The machine Higgins used for his repeat listening exercises, which Edison dubbed the phonograph, was probably the same technology to which Saussure referred. It is the direct ancestor of today's cassette tape recorder. Sound recording achieved widespread utilization much more slowly than the telephone. High fidelity portable tape recorders were still rare in the 1960s. I borrowed my mother's fifty-pound reel-to-reel in 1964 to study oral interpretation of literature; and I lugged similar machines to class as a young teacher in the early seventies. It was these machines that Sacks, Jefferson, and others used to record telephone speaking in that era. The contemporary study of recorded speech began when Harvey Sacks handed Gail Jefferson a tape recording and asked her to write down just what she heard (Jefferson, personal communication). Jefferson has made this task into a lifework. Much of Jefferson's transcription corpus is telephone conversation.

Communication media may piggyback each other. Consider the telephone's relationships with the computer and with television. The present work rests upon the methodical combination of the telephone and the tape recorder. This alliance stimulates description of older and more basic communicative technologies—those of human speech.

OPENINGS

Technology is imagined by culture and in turn constructs culture.

Thomas Benson and Carolyn Anderson

(UTCL A24.9)

	OPR:	Afternoon 'ts Gwe:n
	JAN:	Yeah I'd like to charge this to two one fi:ve (.) one two ni:ne (.) one one zero two. (2.0) / ((caller files nails?))
5	OPR:	Thank you for using A T and T:.
	JAN:	Thank you rin:::::::::::::::::::::g (2.2)
	MIMI:	Hello.
	JAN:	·hh Mimi?
10	MIMI:	Yes honey:=
	JAN:	=Jan
	MIMI:	Hi darlin how're you.
	JAN:	Fine how are you (0.2)
15	MIMI:	Awright sweetie pie:: ⌈Paw-
	JAN:	⌊cu whun-
	MIMI:	Muh Pawpa's alri::ght I know that's why you're ca:llin (0.4)
20	JAN:	Are you *sure*
	MIMI:	Yea:h he's- he's lying do:wn no:w and he was- (0.3) first stopped and got a knee br:ace ·hhhh and he's *fee*ling all right now honey: (0.2) Well he'll go to the doctor in the morning again we'll see:
25		
	JAN:	*How* wa:s he on the way home,
	MIMI:	Wuh he's- alri:ght he u:h (0.4) had to go to the *bath*room: (.) *dad*dy helped him (.) you know he- he did ar*i*ght- Jan hh
30	JAN:	hhhh Did it just *fri*ghten him
	MIMI:	Ye-u:m (0.4) little bi:t you know ·hhh but he's aright no:w (0.4)
	JAN:	I didn't know wh*a*t it was all of a sudden I heard everyone screaming (0.4)
35		
	MIMI:	Well uhhh you know guess he f*e*ll I- colla- I

		hih- ·hhhhh I don't know what happened mys*elf*
		I don't think I was *loo*kin when it *h*appened
40		except I knew he'd fa:llen (0.7) and u:m
	JAN:	Well I didn't know if he'd *f*allen or *f*ainted
		or what.
	MIMI:	No no hi- hid- his kn*ee* gave way on him=
	JAN:	=Ye:ah I know but it=
45	MIMI:	=He turn he'd tried to re*a*ch somn- just a
		minute honey naw well he w*a*nts to t*a*lk to
		yo(h)u ⌈huh huh huh
	JAN:	⌊Unkay hh
	MIMI:	·hhh Hold on darlin
50		(2.0)
	PAW:	Uh*e*llo?
	JAN:	Hi Pawpa
	PAW:	Yeh how are you sweetie=
	JAN:	=How do you feel
55	PAW:	Nah- I I feel aright I- I was gonna tell you
		I think that what the y'know th thee: remote
		(0.4) to your mother's gara:ge. (0.7)
	JAN:	Yeah=
	PAW:	=was on the d*a*sh boa:rd.
60		(0.7)
	PAW:	And I went to re*a*ch for tha:t (0.8) and I
		think I'd raised my right le:g to get read'
		to get in the car and I reach for that and my
		*le*ft leg just gave out from you know
65		(0.5)
	JAN:	Ul it sc*a*red me I didn't ⌈know
	PAW:	⌊Yeah it scared
		*e*verybody and I- I was so:rry
	PAW:	Well that was a ʳwonderful weekend
70		uh J- uh ⌈Jan
	JAN:	⌊Goo:d I'm glad you en*joy*ed it
	PAW:	I en*joy*ed it You were be*au*tiful s*o* was your
		*s*ister
	JAN:	Thank you=
75	PAW:	=And it was just great we had a real nice
		time.
	JAN:	I'm ↑gla:d,
		(0.2)

```
          PAW:     uh ( . ) Wait a minute
  80               (1.6)
          MIMI:    Sweetie:
          JAN:     Yeah
          MIMI:    It was=
                   =# BEEP # ((call waiting))
  85      JAN:     Hold on=
          MIMI:    =Yes
          JAN:     Hold on
          MIMI:    Aright
                   #
  90      JAN:     Hello?
          JOE:     Jan
          JAN:     Yeah
          JOE:     Is my wallet there
                   (0.2)
  95      JAN:     ·hh heh (0.2) um I don't- know?
          JOE:     Can I come over and get it.
          JAN:     Yeah
          JOE:     Okay
          JAN:     Bye=
 100      JOE:     =Bah.
                   #
          JAN:     'Kay
          MIMI:    Jan?=
          JAN:     =Yeah
 105      MIMI:    Thank you for being so wonderful honey
          JAN:     Uh ⌈huhh
          MIMI:       ⌊You're really a do:ll.
          JAN:     Unka:y.
          MIMI:    And we jus- we're so prou:d of you
 110               ⌈and Beth
          JAN:     ⌊Okay
          MIMI:    ·hhh And you're just so sweet
          JAN:     uh ⌈hhhh
          MIMI:       ⌊But anyway you gon' be in Fri:day?
 115      JAN:     Yeah I'll be dere Friday
                   (0.4)
          MIMI:    Al:right bu you'll ca:ll ⌈come by
          JAN:                              ⌊Yeah
          JAN:     Yeah make sure- tell Pawpa hope he feels
```

120		better
	MIMI:	Well thank you darling and thank you for *ca*lling=
	JAN:	Okay
	MIMI:	Okay
125	JAN:	Bye bye
	MIMI:	Bye bye

3

TELEPHONE OPENINGS

How to Begin a Speech Event

The telephone encounter titled 'Sweetie' shows several telephone openings. Its flurry of scenes shows Jan talking to:

- a telephone operator (Gwen)
- her grandmother (Mimi)
- her grandfather (Pawpa)
- Mimi again
- a call waiting intruder (Joe)
- Mimi again.

Jan does not begin any two of these speech events in just the same way, but adapts to each new partner. A listener to this call, and even a reader of the transcription, follows the transitions without great difficulty, because all of us are experts in telephone opening.

A scene from Tom Wolfe's novel *The Bonfire of the Vanities* illustrates our acuity for detail in the telephone opening. Sherman, who intends to telephone his mistress, mistakenly (by habit) dials his own home number:

> Three rings, and a woman's voice: "Hello?"
> But it was not Maria's voice. He figured it must be her friend Germaine, the one she sublet the apartment from. So he said: "May I speak to Maria please?"
> The woman said: "Sherman? Is that you?"
> Christ! It's Judy! He's dialed his own apartment! He's aghast—paralyzed!
> "Sherman?"
> He hangs up. Oh Jesus. What can he do? He'll bluff it out. When she asks him, he'll say he doesn't know what she's talking about. After all, he said only five or six words. How can she be sure? (p. 17)

Every telephone user knows that Sherman is in trouble: We surely *can* identify a spouse's voice from just a few words. But how do we accomplish such quick identification?

The telephone opening packs a great deal of information and communicative accomplishment into just a few seconds. We may not notice the information-density in telephone openings. Because we often perform them habitually, we may even believe that openings are merely rituals, or small talk too simple to reward serious description. Yet Sacks warns us

> that detailed study of small phenomena may give an enormous understanding of the way humans do things and the kinds of objects they use to construct and order their affairs. (Fall 1966/1984; p. 24)

Much that happens later in a call grows out of its first few seconds. Consider these two utterances:

UTCL A24.9

OPR: **Afternoon 'ts Gwe:n**
JAN: **Yeah I'd like to charge this to . . .**

In this brief space, two strangers meet each other, define the scope of their relationship, and begin to work together.

In telephone openings two parties, blind to each other's identities at the outset, use speech to recognize each other, to greet each other, and to sketch the context within which they encounter each other. How do communicators constitute speech situations during the same moments when they begin them?

A Canonical Telephone Opening

Here is a transcription of an ordinary telephone opening:

Schegloff, 1986, 115

R   **Hello**
C   **Hello Ida?**
R   **Yeah**
C   **Hi,=This is Carla**
R   **Hi Carla.**
C   **How are you.**
R   **Okay:.**
C   **Good.=**
R   **=How about you.**
C   **Fine. Don wants to know . . .**

This telephone opening is so ordinary in the way that it trips off the speakers' tongues that Schegloff (1986) describes it as "canonical." We hear some echo of our own experiences in this encounter. The features of this opening appear in a fictional sketch published in 1897 (chapter 2). Presumably these routines were established in the early years of telephone use and have remained somewhat stable.

Just what makes this instance so ordinary? To gain perspective, we may compare the canonical opening of the phone call to another canonical opening from the Episcopal *Book of Common Prayer*.

Celebrant:	The Lord be with you.
People:	And also with you.
Celebrant:	Let us pray

Like the telephone opening, this canonical opening involves interaction by speakers taking turns. The opening turns focus speakers' attentions and set up business to follow. The first turn projects an expectation to say something further upon the return of a ritual response. The second and third utterances occupy definite slots. Both the church liturgy opening and the routine telephone opening display two critical components of most openings: greeting and getting started speaking.

But there are also important contrasts between the canonical opening of the telephone conversation and that in the prayer book. Speakers use the prayer book to aid them in choral reading. Speakers have few options about what may be said. Each utterance is specified in advance. The prayer book illustrates prespecified *rituals* that are performed very much the same on each occurrence.

The canonical telephone opening is not quite ritual, but *routine* to the extent that its appearance approaches ritual. But the canonical telephone opening is not prespecified. There is no officially sanctioned opening dialogue specified in the telephone book.[1] Rather, the locus of this canon is the liturgy of the natural attitude, mundane oral tradition. The participants in any telephone opening compose their talk on the scene as a sequential collage of clichés.

The details of each opening show adaptation to nuances of its particular moment of occurrence. In telephone openings speakers align identities, intimacies, problems, and agendas. This chapter and the next one describe how partners accomplish telephone openings. Schegloff's instance provides a framework for this discussion because its speakers run into almost no difficulties. Or rather, they encounter only the routine problems that occur in every phone call, and they solve each problem smoothly. To show this smoothness, compare the canonical instance to a problematic telephone opening:

UTCL A10.13

	ri::::::::::::::::::ng
MAC:	Hello?
RICK:	Violin,

	(0.3)
MAC:	Pardon me?
	(0.4)
RICK:	Cello?
	(0.5)
MAC:	Hello?
	(0.2)
RICK:	Is: Tony there
	(0.2)
MAC:	No h*u*h uh
	(0.3)
RICK:	MacNutt *h*h
	(0.2)
MAC:	Huh?
RICK:	MacNutt
MAC:	Yeah
	(0.3)
RICK:	Who's there
	(0.4)
MAC:	Nobody

This nonroutine opening sounds different from the canonical opening. The rhythm is odd. The canonical opening shows no transcribed pauses at all, but this transcription shows nine between-turn pauses within the space of thirteen speaking turns.

However, one similarity unites these two phone openings and distinguishes them from the prayer book: The answerer's first utterance is 'Hello.' Hello is just one first thing you can say at an encounter-beginning in North America. But on the telephone, hello is *the* canonical opening turn—although we rarely teach speakers to say it. Alexander Graham Bell disliked hello as the telephone answer. He wanted us to say "Hoy." My own parents didn't like the hello answer either, and they occasionally prompted me to say things like "Hopper residence." But my parents said hello themselves, and so do I. This first-turn 'hello' is shared by the canonical and problematic telephone openings.

However, at the second speaking turn of the problematic opening, the caller's first turn, he does something unusual:

	MAC:	Hello?
⇒	RICK:	Violin,

There are just a few things a caller usually says in a first turn—Schegloff (1979a) identifies nine categories of these. Some of them, like "This is Tom," or "Is Jane there?" are utterly routine. "This is Tom Tower from Church," or "Is this the Cancer Information Service?" might appear less often, but are easy to understand. Some other first utterances like "Who is this?" or "Is this the lady that washes?" are rarer and risky, but still comprehensible. 'Violin' is an odd second turn compared to any of these. The answerer treats it as such.

	RICK:	Violin,
		(0.3)
⇒	MAC:	Pardon me?
		(0.4)
	RICK:	Cello?
		(0.5)
	MAC:	Hello?

Answerer produces a repair token 'Pardon me?' that may indicate failure to understand caller's turn. Following Next Turn Repair Initiators the previous speaker often repeats something, or explains it (Schegloff et al., 1977, chapter 1). In *this* instance, however, caller produces 'Cello?' which suggests an associative link between his first two turns: violin → cello, and also coins a possible pun with "hello." This seems to be an attempt at humor, but answerer shows no sign of detecting this.

Another pause ensues, then answerer offers a stunningly simple gambit: 'Hello?' This may be heard to start the encounter over.[2] Caller chooses to reply to this hearing; at next turn he asks to speak to Tony. After this, although other problems occur, this telephone opening heads back on a routine track.

To summarize: there are relationships between the canonical call and the problematic call, and the problems in the problematic call use details of the canonical opening as reference points. The 'Violin' call, though unusual, resonates with the ordinary.

We have contrasted a canonical opening with two other sorts of opening— one from ritual, and a second from a problematic telephone opening. We may now specify what is canonical about the canonical opening. Here is its transcription again.

1		((RING))
	R	Hello
2	C	Hello Ida?
	R	Yeah
3	C	Hi,=This is Carla
	R	*Hi* Carla.
4	C	How are you.
	R	Okay:.

C   **Good.=**
R   **=How about you.**
C   **Fine. Don wants to know . . .**

This example shows four sequential entities indicated by the numbers at the left margin:

(1) A summons-answer sequence, consisting of the telephone ring and the first thing said by the answerer;
(2) Identification/recognition sequences, consisting of each party self-identifying and displaying recognition of the other;
(3) A greeting sequence, consisting of an exchange of greeting tokens ('Hi');
(4) Initial inquiries ('How are you?') and their answers.

Each of these entities occupies a position, or slot, relative to the others. That is, these tasks get done in the order listed.

Sacks (1972, p. 341) distinguishes between a sequential "slot" and the "items" that fill it. Activities are accomplished when a participant places an item in a slot. The canonical telephone opening uses routine (or unmarked) fillers for each slot and thereby provides a comparison point against which numerous communicative tasks may be accomplished. Each slot in any opening may be filled in various ways, and these differing items carry communicative weight. We describe each slot in this telephone opening, and some of its uses.

Summons-Answer

Telephone calls begin not with speech, nor with visual prebeginning, but with a summons-noise such as a ring. The telephone summons repeats every few seconds till somebody answers, or until the caller gives up. In the USA, most callers allow thirty seconds or more for answers to their calls. The repeating ring is, in a sense, the first utterance in a phone call. Schegloff (1968) characterizes the phone's ring as a *summons* which compares it to speech objects like calling someone's name (Sacks, 1972; Nofsinger, 1975). A summons invokes a sequence at least three turns long. The summons should be answered by a brief item like "Hello" that returns the floor turn to the summoner. By implicating a three-turn sequence, summons objects propel participants into the midst of a speech situation. And since the summoner gets the third turn, s/he is in the best position to suggest the encounter's directions.

If two parties meet in public where they can see one another, they need not summon each other. Consider the ways you might encounter your friend Tracy:

—You call across a crowded room: "Hey Tracy"
—You knock on the door where Tracy lives.
—You dial Tracy's telephone number.

These beginning gambits summon a partner. Summons-begun encounters entail special control to the summoner. After the summons and its answer, the summoner speaks next. A summoner often has a purpose for starting an encounter. Contrast summons-begun events with these three circumstances:
— You run into Tracy at the supermarket
— You pass Tracy in a public place and say hello
— You walk into the kitchen, where Tracy is chopping carrots, and say "Hi."
The beginnings of these encounters are more symmetrical than telephone openings. Many face-to-face encounters begin without a summons, but with mutual visual recognition. In public settings, the interactive decision to speak to another person may begin when the other is still some distance away. Kendon and Ferber (1973) distinguish between the "distance salutation" and activities that happen when the parties are close to one another. In distance salutations

> the head is tilted back rapidly and then brought forward again. It is usually combined with a call—such as 'hi' or 'hi' followed by a name. Typically, the head is first raised and then, as it is lowered again, the call is uttered. As the head is raised, the mouth is opened. (p. 619)

Kendon and Ferber also describe typical responses to the "head toss," labeling these "head dips" and "nods." Each of these movements co-occur with certain hand gestures (Schiffrin, 1977).

In face-to-face interaction the canonical event is a symmetrical meeting, and summons-openings provide a marked case. But the summons provides the only way into telephone conversation. There were surely summonses (e.g., calling someone by name, knocking on a door) before the advent of the telephone. But the telephone elevates the summons to the position of required first item in an encounter. Summons-answer sequences become absolutely commonplace as a consequence of the telephone medium. The privileging of the summons leads telephone callers toward a certain assertiveness about opening telephone encounters in order to accomplish an objective. A telephone user may discover a large number of persons to summon.

On the receiving end, the summons repeatedly interrupts life. Once a telephone is installed in your home or your office, you become vulnerable to its summons at any instant chosen by any caller, from family members to the sales representatives who call during supper. The telephone transforms speaking persons into callers and answerers. You may answer a summons only by ignoring anything else. Of course, any summoned individual may choose to ignore the summons—but this requires some rowing against the current. Most of us answer a ringing phone most of the time. The telephone summons has become a demand to truncate ongoing lines of activity in order to answer the phone.

The caller's summons entails an answer as surely as one telephone entails another telephone. And the answerer's role is a role at-disadvantage. Not only is an answerer summoned out of any other activities that were going on, but in the telephone encounter, the *answerer must speak first*—even though she or he is only responding to heaven-knows-what. Also, an answerer may be recognized from what s/he says to answer the summons—and this vulnerability to recognition increases the power differential in the caller's favor.

The procedures for summons-answer sequencing interact with the mechanics of electronic telephony. Summons-answer sequences are necessary to telephone openings because of the blind character of the medium. To deal with the new medium, speakers adapt speech objects already in existence—materials that speakers previously used to drop by each other's houses, or to yell to a distant friend—and meld these into the grammar of the telephone. This motivates millions of humans to increased mastery over arts of summoning and answering. We continue to experience ecological aftershocks of these adaptations to telephony.

The telephone summons renders us vulnerable to a form of spoken intrusion. To begin every telephone speech event with a summons is to swing speaking's ecology toward purpose and to make dialogue asymmetrical in favor of the caller. But the callers' purposes may not be revealed to just anyone; the answerer must first be identified.

Identification/Recognition

We speak mainly to those persons whom we recognize. Therefore, we mutually display recognition at the beginning of each encounter. Goffman (1963, 1971) notes that we speak primarily to those persons we recognize, and who recognize us in return. We sort potential encounter partners into two classes: those whom we recognize (and to whom we should speak) and those whom we do not recognize (and to whom we should not speak.)[3] If we fail to establish mutual recognition, we do not speak, but show civil inattention (Goffman, 1963, chapter 2).

Unlike urbanites, lone camel travellers in the desert may see an other's approach at a great distance, and they are obligated to greet each person they see. But before any verbal greeting the sighted parties have some time to observe one another's approach. Travellers attend to details of each other's clothing, camel, and gait to gain information, for "the identification of the other—as early as possible—is critically important" (Grimshaw et al., 1981, p. 135). Early identification is accomplished in every face-to-face encounter-opening. In desert greetings when does an interactive event begin: first sighting, first recognition, first speech? This question complicates the description of any face-to-face greetings.

In telephone openings recognition and identification work cannot precede the summons-answer, and parties must identify each other within speech. These tasks become relevant immediately upon the answer to a summons:

> Whatever a telephone conversation is going to be occupied with, however bureaucratic or intimate, routine or unusual, earthshaking or trivial, it and its parties will have to pass through the identification/recognition sieve as the first thing they do. (Schegloff, 1979a, p. 71)

In telephone calls, mutual identification must occur in-and-through speaking.

The identification/recognition problem in telephone speaking is addressed at the second speaking turn in the call—that is, the caller's first speaking turn (Schegloff, 1986; 1979a, p. 28):

	R	Hello
⇒	C	Hello Ida?
	R	Yeah
	C	Hi,=This is Carla
	R	*Hi* Carla.

The answerer, by saying 'hello,' anounces: "that I'm a possible called; ignore me at your peril and recognize me from my voice" (Sacks, Spring 1972, lecture 3, p. 12). When the caller *responds* with a second "hello," this proposes that the answerer is in fact the intended called party (p. 5). So each moment in the opening holds implications for mutual identification. Each party by deploying 'hello' indicates candidacy for a conversational encounter. Answerer's 'hello' announces candidacy to be called; and caller's answering hello ratifies this possibility.

Telephone talk institutionalizes a guessing game based on voice recognition. Before telephones people

> could not perhaps have played voice recognition games with any seriousness. . . . Now what they do with the phone is to employ this feature of the phone— that you only hear the voice, to build an institution in which they test out "Do you recognize me?" from voice; so that a great deal of phone beginnings are either specifically or in effect voice tests in which the other party is now supposed to show that they know who it is and you're not telling them. (Sacks, SS285, Winter 1970, lecture 1, pp. 9-10)

In the instance at the start of this chapter, Judy recognized Sherman as the caller using a brief voice sample—even though he did not wish to be recognized. Recognition functions do not wait upon the completion of a summons-answer sequence. *Anything* answerer says in the first turn provides a voice-sample useful for identification.

In the canonical instance the caller's first turn includes a guess at the answerer's name. This is one way of showing that the caller has recognized the answerer's voice. The name guess is accomplished by the rise in pitch that makes it a question ('Ida?'). A caller may display greater certainty in this first identification turn by using a declarative pitch-contour:

Schegloff, 1979a, p. 37

C: **Hello?**
Y: **Hello Charles.**

Not including a surname indicates some familiarity with the answerer. Callers may claim even greater intimacy with the answerer by initiating a greeting with no names.

TG

Ava: **H'llo:?**
Bee: **hHi:,**
Ava: **Hi:?**

Self-identifying and recognizing without using a name

> constitutes a claim by caller that he has recognized the answerer from the answerer's first turn. And it invites reciprocal recognition from the single, typically small turn it constitutes. (Schegloff, 1979a, p. 34)

In the TG instance, caller Bee proposes recognition of the answerer from the speech sample of 'hello,' and also proposes that this brief speech sample ('hi') should suffice for the answerer to recognize her. Ava's return 'hi' ratifies that expectation, and the encounter proceeds. 'Hi' is a greeting, which is the speech act by which we signal that we recognize an acquaintance.

Greetings

Greetings are usually the first utterances in face-to-face encounters; they "go right at the beginning of the beginning." (Sacks, Winter 1970, lecture 4, p. 1). No matter how well you know somebody, or whether you saw them yesterday, greetings remain "ahistorically relevant" (p. 10).[4]

A primary function of greetings is to open up spoken interaction. A greeting occurs at openings of talk as a sign of recognition of the other and as a sign that an encounter with the other is acceptable (Grimshaw et al., 1984; Schiffrin, 1977).

Sacks argues that greetings are "non repeatable." That is, given a greeting-greeting pair at the opening of an encounter, it would seem extraordinary to find another greeting pair later in the same event. Further, greetings often occur in pairs: "given a first Greeting, a second should be done" (Sacks, SS

158X, Spring 1972, lecture 3, p. 1). If somebody says "hello" to you, you return the greeting immediately with a similar (yet distinguishably-uttered) greeting.[5]

Whereas questions elicit answers as seconds, and invitations elicit acceptances or refusals, greetings take greetings as seconds. This makes greetings a simple case of adjacency relationship, which may explain why children learn greetings so early in development. Also, "when we learn another language, greetings and goodbyes are among the first things we learn" (Grimshaw et al., 1984, p. 131).

Telephone greetings, unlike face-to-face ones, are not first utterances. Summons-answer and identification/recognition speech pushes greetings back into the encounter. Perhaps this helps explain the durability of 'hello' as a telephone-answering turn. Since the greeting has been displaced backward in phone talk, speakers may use 'hello' to perform proto-greeting functions. First hellos do not complete the greeting functions, or else "Hi" would not appear later. Still, an initial hello may (a) retain some greeting function or (b) survive as a vestige of beginning an encounter with a greeting token.

In telephone talk as elsewhere, greetings are especially relevant to previously-acquainted parties. In chapter 4 we show that telephone calls between strangers ordinarily omit greetings; and telephone openings between intimates omit almost everything but greetings. Therefore greetings in telephone openings still perform their traditional function of indicating previous acquaintance.

An exchange of greetings makes further talk relevant. In face-to-face talk further talk may not be compulsory, but it is allowed. On the phone, further speech continues after a greeting pair. The most frequent next utterances are questions.

Initial Inquiry: How Are You?

After greetings, the canonical telephone opening provides a slot for exchanges of brief inquiries and responses: "How are you"/"Fine." These inquiry-response exchanges do not carry heavy literal content, but nevertheless they set the direction for a telephone call. Telephone speakers use the "How are you" slot to preview purposes and resolve problems.

Callers usually launch the first inquiry. In the canonical example a first 'How are you' gets a quick response: 'Okay.' Caller next proffers a sequence-closing assessment: 'Good,' and recipient returns a reciprocal 'How are you?'

C	How are you.
R	Okay:.
C	Good.=
R	=How about you.
C	Fine. Don wants to know . . .

The routine response to a second, or reciprocal, 'How are you?' brings participants to an anchor point to launch a first topic (Schegloff, 1986). In this canonical case, the exchange of 'How are you?' inquiries runs off almost as if scripted. Yet actors must enact these lines on the scene. And deviations from canonical values do interactive work. For instance, when a caller inquires: "How are you?" a variety of responses may occur. Some of these are utterly routine (e.g., "Fine"). Others (e.g., "Oh not too bad") are marked items in that slot. The term *marked* describes items that depart from routine values in these sequential positions.

An initial inquiry: "How are you?" makes relevant in next turn a *value state descriptor* such as "okay," "lousy," or "great" (Sacks, 1975, p. 70). Negative value state descriptors (e.g., "lousy") lead to a "diagnostic procedure" such as a follow-up question (pp. 70-71). "How are you" / "Fine" fills a routine slot leading toward the first topic of the call. By contrast, filling this response-to-inquiry slot with a marked negative response (e.g., "How are you" / "Lousy") is hearable as unusual, possibly problematic.

Jefferson (1980) describes some of these subtly marked responses to telephone initial inquiries:

Jefferson, 1980, 153

	Bob:	[How are you] feeling now.
⇒	Jayne:	Oh.::? pretty good I gue: ⌈s::
	Bob:	⌊not so hot?

This response differs from a routine response to initial inquiry (e.g., "Fine"). The respondent begins with a stretched version of 'Oh.' Next, she qualifies the answer: 'pretty good I guess,' with the last word being vocally stressed and stretched. Taken together, these markings premonitor problems. In this example Bob responds to this marked answer with a follow-up inquiry about respondent's troubled state, thereby showing how he heard the marked response. Furthermore, not only the response to inquiry, but the inquiry itself is marked. 'How are you feeling now' is more specific than the utterly routine "How are you?" It refers to a particular time, and specifies 'feeling' as the topic of the inquiry.

Neither of these two turns—marked inquiry nor marked answer—conclusively shows a problem. Rather the entire three-turn interaction shows something special happening in this telephone opening. Neither actor does the marking with a solo speech act. Perhaps Bob's marked inquiry: 'How are you feeling now?' invites more than the phatic "fine." But Jayne could have responded routinely. Even Jayne's marked response to inquiry does not explicitly notify Bob of a problem, but rather indicates that something may be up. Bob then asks for further information, which Jayne later gives him. These two speakers open this topic across a three-turn exchange. Small talk does important work.

Telephone partners use "How are you?" exchanges as state-checks preliminary to further talk. This discussion of marked items applies in principle to
all four slots in the telephone opening. Each slot houses distinctive activities:
summons-answer, identification-recognition, greetings, and initial inquiries.
Each telephone opening partakes of this canonical routine, and deviations
from routine (there are almost always some) are used by speakers to signal
special circumstances.

The first two slots in the telephone opening, those for summons and
identification, are quite different in telephone openings than in face-to-face
openings. These contrasts emerge from the telephone's restriction to sound
and push the greeting to later in the opening. The greeting, in both telephone
and face-to-face talk, enacts reacquaintance, or claims a speaking relationship. The greeting is the royal road to further interaction, which often
proceeds from there by means of initial inquiries. These inquiries often set
directions for interaction that follows.

The canonical instance provides a frame for our description of telephone
openings. We next report some comparisons of this framework's goodness-
of-fit with naturally occurring telephone openings. Though few calls sound
just like the canonical instance, its frame helps to describe all telephone
openings.

Emergence versus Routines in Telephone Openings

Most telephone openings do not occur just like the canonical instance. Actual
telephone openings display diverse formats and shades of detail. The diversity increases in openings' later stages. Figure 5 shows that variations are
slight for summons-answer, but gradually widen in each later sequential
slot.

The earliest of the four sequences goes off routinely, but each succeeding
stage shows greater variation in what may occur. Each succeeding slot
merges toward spontaneous interaction.

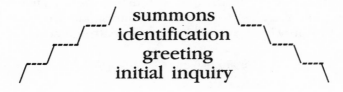

Figure 5: Variations from Canonical
Routines in Telephone Openings

Some of the variety in openings indicates that parties use deviations from the routine to claim intimacy with each other (Schegloff, 1986, p. 141; Horenstein, 1985). In our first test of the framework we minimize this diversity by focusing on openings between acquaintances, persons who are neither strangers nor intimates. We also limit this exercise to twenty-five telephone openings in North American English. (We expand the sample in chapter 4.)

Results show few departures from canonical form in summons-answer and identification. Three fourths of answerers said "Hello," and the others used job-related self-identifications. Sixty percent of callers attempted to identify the answerers at second turn. Six of the ten remaining callers asked for somebody else, judging they had not reached the party they wanted. This close fit to routines for summons-answer and for recognition/identification is represented in Figure 5 by the upper (narrow) end of the funnel-shape.

The picture grows more complicated with greetings. Setting aside call-initial 'Hellos' as not (by themselves) accomplishing greeting, only a third of the openings (8) displayed a pair of greetings. Eight calls showed no greeting tokens:

UTCL D8.3

	PAT:	Hello:?
		(0.3)
	JON:	Pat?
	PAT:	Yep
		(0.2)
⇒	JON:	Jon what are you *up* to
	PAT:	How you doin

This caller follows self-identification with an initial inquiry that turns out to be preliminary to a supper invitation. This move to inquiry apparently deletes the greeting slot. May either party, by deleting a slot, propose that it is unnecessary?

That description offers plausible fit with those nine openings with only one greeting: one party deletes part of the routine, and the other speaker ratifies this trajectory by carrying out an appropriate next action:

UTCL J10

	M:	MacKenzie
	K:	This is Ma:c?
	M:	Uh ha=
⇒	K:	=H::i this is Kate Shopper how are you=
	M:	=Yeah oka:y how are you Kate

In this instance, the caller greets with self-identification, then continues with 'How are you' before giving up the turn. Answerer's return 'How are you,' ratifies Kate's deletions, and the encounter proceeds. Schegloff (1986) describes various instances of slot-preemptions in openings.

This description of deletion also fits openings in which one or both initial inquiries do not appear. One fifth of openings show no initial inquiry but go straight to topic. Most of these calls are continuations of earlier events. In the following instance, Pat calls a friend he just visited to see whether he had left behind a notebook.

UTCL A10.6

	BRU:	Hell*o*?
	PAT:	Brumber.
		(0.4)
	BRU:	Ye:ah.
⇒	PAT:	Is there *a* um *red* astronomy folder (0.3) notebook (0.7) spiral notebook lyin around

This inquiry not only continues a prior event, but also shows the reason for calling.

How do we interpret divergences from the canonical opening? First, the canonical instance contains a full set of unmarked values for all the slot. Second, divergences from the canonical values become increasingly likely in the latter stages of the telephone opening. Third, most variations from the canon are deletions. Fourth, most of these deletions are initiated by a speaker rushing to take a second turn-unit (e.g., "Hi = how are you."). Finally, partners use marked turns to stimulate subsequent interactive alignments that occupy multiple speaking turns (Hopper, 1989b).

Telephone partners are not robots, nor ritual-users, but actors dancing around a semiotic maypole indicated by the canonical instance. In our twenty-five openings, there were none that sounded quite as routine as the canonical instance. Schegloff (1986) selected four canonical instances from a sample of over two hundred recordings. We must not read the canonical instance as a prediction that most openings sound just like it. Rather, we may hear the canonical instance in all openings, even though a fully canonical telephone opening may be almost as rare as a statement of a full theme in Bach's Goldberg Variations. Rather, the instance articulates tasks that must be done at telephone openings, orders these tasks, and indicates the relevance of adjacency pair organization in getting the tasks accomplished. The instance specifies tasks to which telephone partners orient as openings unfold.

In the next chapter we show how partners mark cultural identities, relationship states, and other aspects of situation using these slots of the telephone opening. The canonical instance provides a median case of telephone opening, and also displays the sequential resources we use in constructing actual openings. We may illustrate some of the instance's usefulness by using it to reconsider the nonroutine 'Violin' opening described at the start of the present chapter.

'Violin' Revisited: An Exercise

Let us return to the Violin opening to ask how the canonical opening helps us understand that unusual event.

```
                    r::::::::::::::::::ng
        MAC:        Hello?
⇒       RICK:       Violin,
                        (0.3)
        MAC:        Pardon me?
```

This opening becomes odd at the caller's first turn, just when we might expect orientation to identification/recognition. The identification stage allows little variation from canonical routine, yet this caller neither identifies himself nor specifies the identity of the other. This marks the caller's expectation to be identifiable to the answerer from his voice. Since Rick subsequently asks for Tony, he probably has mistaken the answerer's 'hello' for that of his friend. Instead, a distant acquaintance who does not belong with the phone happens to be alone in Tony's house. (It happens that we have recordings of over twenty of Rick's phone calls, including considerable play between Rick and Tony.) But in the Violin instance, Rick's play gambit flops due to a failure of identification. Mac immediately shows that he is having a problem: 'Pardon me?' This next-turn repair initiation functions to ask for a repeat or clarification (Schegloff et al., 1977), indicating that the answerer has difficulty with Rick's first turn. Rick nevertheless continues with his playful gambit, perhaps because the trick takes two utterances to unfold ('violin' → 'cello?').

```
        RICK:       Cello?
                        (0.5)
        MAC:        Hello?
                        (0.2)
        RICK:       Is: Tony there
```

The second utterance springs the joke, but it flops. After 'Cello?' and a pause, Mac starts again with 'Hello.' At this point, Rick asks for Tony, initiating a switchboard opening (Schegloff, 1979a, chapter 4). This virtual encounter restart puts the phone call back in the realm of the routine.

The Violin opening exits the canonical routine at the slot for mutual identification. This explains the call's odd features and thereby illustrates some of the usefulness of a framework based in the canonical instance. Violin turns odd just when it diverges from the canonical instance. The canonical instance helps us understand the details of any telephone opening.

Telephone Openings, Face-to-Face Openings and Communication Instruction

The telephone's channel constraints alter the tasks of opening somewhat, but face-to-face and telephone openings retain remarkable similarities in the tasks encountered and ways speakers accomplish them. As any partners set about the mundane tasks of opening, they perform the tasks of situation definition on the fly, or slightly off-center of attention. The canonical instance contains slotted locations at which situation definition may be addressed.

Deviations from routines perform emergent bits of situation definition: Parties may say "hi" as soon as the second speaking turn, or may answer a "How are you?" inquiry with a marked response like "lousy." Thus partners mark contrasts from canonical routines. Each turn's markings stimulate alignment in subsequent turns—or possibilities may be let pass. Therefore, much of what is accomplished at encounter openings cannot be described as the performance of any single speaker. Telephone openings are team efforts, mutual accomplishments.

This presents some puzzles to communication teachers and social engineers. How do we educate members of society to be effective communicators when communicative tasks are not best described as work done by individual speakers? How may an educator, whose habit is to evaluate individuals' achievements, teach skills in which accomplishment is achieved in dialogic team output that stretches across speakers' turns? Teachers conceive of their tasks as teaching individual communicators to encode messages that are clear, precise, vivid, or well-organized. Yet telephone partners frequently succeed by *not* being too clear, vivid, precise, or even too individual! Rather, effective partners adapt to each other and to the local occasion at the very moments that project its path. Partners muddle through openings, doing more than they say they are doing, using imprecise and elided speech objects across speaking turns to achieve allusive alignments. These difficult-to-specify *pas de deux* are the dances of good persons conversing well. We must seek ways to tailor speech instruction to students as community members—as dialogue partners. We also must learn the uses of dialogic muddling through as a complement to precise message encoding.

Meanwhile we each experience the telephone. Each communication medium massages its users in proportion to the frequency of its use and the extent to which the medium elicits interaction. By these standards the telephone is our most vital communication medium. Its influences include giving prominence to the telephone summons, which differentiates the roles of caller and answerer and makes the telephone opening more like knocking on somebody's door than like meeting by chance in a public place. The summons occurs in face-to-face talk. Telephony did not create this form. But its recurrent appearance in telephone openings elevates its importance. Like kudzu, the summons thrives in its new environment—and this leads to unanticipated consequences.

As citizens in the telephone age become increasingly summons-vulnerable, technical innovation transforms and constrains possibilities for speaking. In constructing summons and in answering them, we use resources already available in the speech community. But adaptation to this new medium alters communication patterns that are among our most priceless community resources. Ecological pollution may strike semiotic systems as well as air and water. We experiment on ourselves by using the telephone, which may be the electronic medium that transforms its users the most thoroughly.

Still, descriptions of telephone openings have implications beyond telephone use. Telephone openings provide a tell-tale on how we begin to speak to one another. How is it that we manage to define communicative situations at the very moment that we begin to enact them? An emerging answer: Interaction partners proceed through encounter openings, in person or on the phone, by addressing mundane tasks at hand: Tasks of summoning to attention, displaying mutual recognition, and greeting. In chapter 4, we show that the ways we do these mundane tasks are also the ways that we align about context.

		(UTCL A32.3)
	DAWN:	Hello?
		(0.2)
	GORDON:	Hello is Dawn there
		(0.2)
5	DAWN:	This is Dawn
		(0.6)
	GORDON:	Dawn this is Gordon Turner
		(1.6)
	DAWN:	⌈Yeah?
10	GORDON:	⌊u- Your old Hilton friend
		(1.0)
	DAWN:	My old who?
		(0.2)
	GORDON:	*Hil*ton
15		(0.2)
	DAWN:	↑O:h. (.) o:h this: a different Dawn.=
	GORDON:	Oh no.
	DAWN:	Oh » I was like « ·hhhhhh ⌈↑wo:.
		⌊Oh wait.
20	GORDON:	You're Dawn D*a*wn's friend.
	DAWN:	Ye(h)ah
	GORDON:	I'm the one that goes to U T that got
		you all that fun information=
	DAWN:	=Oh really?
25	GORDON:	Yeah *h*hhh
	DAWN:	↑O::h, I see:
	GORDON:	Huh,
		(0.3)
	DAWN:	U*m* (0.4) do you still- z- work at
30		Hilton though?
	GORDON:	No.
		(.)
	DAWN:	Oh you do*n't*=
	GORDON:	=I quit (.) forget that job.
35	DAWN:	Oh r*e*ally
	DAWN:	You got a better one?
	GORDON:	No.

```
                    ( . )
     GORDON:    I don't work,
40   GORDON:    I'm poor.
     DAWN:      O:h I was gonna say.
     GORDON:    huh huh huh ·hhh
     DAWN:      Gosh.
                    (0.4)
45   DAWN:      Cause- if you could find one I was like
                (0.2) tell me where you found it
                    ((encounter continues 12 minutes))
```

4

SITUATIONAL VARIATIONS IN TELEPHONE OPENINGS

Circumstances, Relationships, Cultures

MOM:	Hello?
ROSA:	Hi mo:m,
MOM:	Hi hello mija
ROSA:	How're you doing
MOM:	Muy bien

This telephone opening shows all four sequences of the canonical opening: summons-answer, identifications, a pair of greetings, and an initial inquiry. But one of the speakers uses both English and Spanish; in chapter 3 all examples were in English. Another difference is that these speakers address each other as 'mom' and 'mija,' which entails mother-daughter intimacy between them. How much of what happens in telephone openings may be attributed to such factors as *language* or *intimacy*?

The issue is complicated by the fact that few telephone openings, even among North American acquaintances, sound just like a canonical opening. This chapter's problem is how to separate variance due to culture from that due to relationship or momentary circumstance. How does a model based in a canonical opening between North American acquaintances help us understand the diversity of telephone openings all over the world?

In the present chapter, we sketch how partners use the details in telephone openings to adapt to situational variation, including:

(1) Special circumstances,
(2) Relational history,
(3) Culture and language.

The term *situation* encompasses the entire context of any speech event: background circumstances, relational history, culture, and so on (Goffman, 1964; Bitzer, 1968). Variations from canonical items in the four slots of telephone openings display adaptations to the local occasion.

We begin by contrasting two views of situation-definition: an *extrinsic-context view* and an *intrinsic-to-messages view* (Heritage, 1984b, chapter 8; Mandelbaum, 1991). We favor the latter view.

An extrinsic-context view treats situations as sets of independent variation that constrain messages. On this view, telephone partners' interpersonal relationships and their cultural backgrounds exist independent of messages and prior to them. These variations carry consequences for how interaction works. For instance a relational state such as *stranger* is extrinsic to communication; message variations occur as adaptive consequences of such extrinsic states. Figure 6 illustrates an extrinsic view of context. On an extrinsic view, we study communication by tracing the consequences of variables in the left-hand column of figure 6 onto message features (right column).

EXTRINSIC VARIATION ===> MESSAGE FEATURES

sex of speaker   **accent**
culture & language   **word choice**
personality   **speaking time**
relational history   **etc.**
etc.

Figure 6: An Extrinsic View of Context

Proponents of extrinsic views are able to describe only rough tendencies correlating contextual factors to message production: e.g., shy people tend to speak little; or natives of status-oriented cultures tend to protect the face of their conversational partners. These investigators find messages to be only loosely organized, with order springing from contextual variables.

No extrinsic view describes within-group differences, relational or contextual change, irony or dissimulation. These are accomplished in finely-organized details of speech communication, and much of this organization is intrinsic to messages.

Message-intrinsic theorists study situations by inspecting message details to see how partners mark adaptations to features of the local occasion. On this view, there are reflexive ties between message features and occasion: to be intimate is largely to speak as an intimate, and have an other respond in kind. To discern how message features index features of context is an ongoing problematic for telephone partners, as for researchers who study them. The goal is to study how partners adapt to context.

This shifts attention from variables to which partners adapt, like gender or culture, and to the interactive adaptations made to any of these categories, practices for showing an utterance's relevance to the local occasion. As ethnomethodologists, we search for *local occasioning practices*, or message details by which partners display situational relevancies to one another.

Over the short term (a telephone encounter), partners may orient to urgency, intimacy, and/or gender. How do partners reach alignment on which circumstances are relevant to what moments in discourse?

The present chapter extends our treatment of telephone openings to account for situational adaptations. We stress intrinsic accomplishments of situation definition in telephone openings to explore a reflexive mystery: How is it that we accomplish so much situation definition in the first few seconds of a phone call?

There are not specialized telephone-opening markings for each factor of a situation. For instance, there is not one sign for "I am worried you might be busy" and another for "We are very close friends." Marked turns in telephone openings are not specific in their uses, but generic indicators that something is up.

The canonical instance provides a framework for describing the interaction in telephone openings, *but it does not describe that interaction.* The interaction occurs as partners face problems and circumstances and work through lines of action. In this chapter, we examine how telephone partners adapt to circumstances, relationships, and culture.

Circumstances

Within the telephone opening, participants deviate from the four-stage routine to signal special circumstances. Schegloff (1986) describes "preemptions," or deletions of parts of the opening sequences. Preemptions mark greatest urgency when they occur early in the opening (e.g., deleting a greeting is more urgent than deleting a response to initial inquiry). We may illustrate this principle by describing two special circumstances in telephone openings:

(1) *Switchboard openings,* in which special markings appear in the slot for recognition/identification; and

(2) *Call waiting openings,* in which special markings appear in the initial inquiry (how are you) slot.

These circumstances show the mechanisms for deletion and marking that telephone partners use to adapt to problems—including problems involving culture and intimacy. Further, these two cases illustrate how markings are achieved in two different slots in the canonical model: identification and initial inquiry.

Switchboard Openings: Marked Identifications

Switchboard openings occur not only at institutions, but whenever an intended recipient of a call is not the answerer (Schegloff, 1979a). Switchboard openings are the most frequent divergence from the four-sequence routine in the sample of openings described in chapter 3. A switchboard opening exits the canonical routine during the recognition/identification stage—that is, as soon as the actual answerer proves not to be the party called.

UTCL J10.1

| | R: | Good morning Data Services |
| ⇒ | T: | Good morning. Is Mark Allan there ple:ase |

This opening becomes a switchboard encounter when the caller shows recognition that the answerer is not the party called. The answerer makes this easy by identifying her office location ('Data Services'). This institutional answer also provides a voice sample that displays the answerer to be, among other things, of a different sex than the intended-called party.[1] The caller short-circuits the opening routine at next turn and asks to speak to the desired party.

Asking for someone other than the answerer often happens so fast that we may not scrutinize how we accomplish it—unless something goes wrong. Then we notice that switchboard openings must be achieved (Schegloff, 1979a, p. 60):

UTCL A32.3

DAWN:	Hello?
	(0.2)
GORDON:	Hello is Dawn there
	(0.2)
DAWN:	This is Dawn
	(0.6)
GORDON:	Dawn this is Gordon Turner
	(1.4)
DAWN:	Yeah?
GORDON:	Your old Hilton friend
	(1.0)
DAWN:	My old who?
GORDON:	Hilton
	(0.2)
DAWN:	↑O:h (.) o:h this: a different Dawn.=
GORDON:	=Oh no.

In this instance, caller attempts a switchboard request, showing a guess that answerer is not the person called ('Is Dawn there?'). However, the called party and the answerer bear the same first name. This coincidence leads to answerer's mistaken self-identification ('This is Dawn.'). Subsequently, caller encounters difficulty in making himself recognizable. These problems grow from the identification failure.

Another kind of switchboard-identification failure shows up in the Violin opening (chapter 3). Whereas the failure in Different Dawn begins with answerer's problematic self-identification, the failures in Violin surface when caller incorrectly identifies answerer as his friend.

UTCL A10.13

	MAC:	Hello?
⇒	RICK:	Violin,
		(0.4)
	MAC:	Pardon me?
		(0.4)
	RICK:	Cello?
		(0.5)
	MAC:	Hello?
		(0.2)
⇒	RICK:	I:s Tony there

In this instance the switchboard question that would have been appropriate at the caller's first turn is not asked until the sixth turn in the encounter. Rick seems to have guessed, incorrectly, that Tony has answered the phone. Rick's playful initial turn, 'Violin,' errs in failing to enter a switchboard sequence. The answerer orients to Rick's failure by his Next Turn Repair Initiator ('Pardon me?').

These last two examples illustrate that participants may muff identification/recognition tasks essential to switchboard openings. Different Dawn begins with an answerer's error; problems in Violin begin with a caller's error.

To summarize: Switchboard openings, one common situational variation in a telephone opening, get accomplished as participants exit the canonical routine at the identification slot. We next describe some markings in the last stage of the opening, the How are you slot.

Call Waiting Openings: Marking Turns in the How Are You Slot

Initial inquiry turns serve as state-checks, or places for participants to preview agendas or signal problems. The initial inquiry slot is a critical site in telephone call waiting.

When the call waiting subscriber answers a call after putting a partner on hold, the new caller does not know about the call-waiting problem. Caller places an ordinary phone call. Before the eighties, this would have resulted in a busy signal. But now an ongoing call to a call-waiting subscriber may get interrupted while the subscriber answers a new one. Subscriber then must juggle two sets of obligations—those owed the old partner and those owed the new caller. These problems get addressed in the initial inquiry (How are you?) slot of the telephone opening.

UTCL A24.7

SUBSCR: Hell*o*?
            (0.3)
CALLER: Brian?
SUBSCR: Yeah
CALLER: Carol.
SUBSCR: H*e*llo.
⇒   CALLER: **What are you d*o*in.**
            (0.3)
⇒   SUBSCR: **I:m (.) on the other l*i*:ne**

Subscriber notifies caller of the call waiting problem in response to initial inquiry: 'What are you doin.' Subscriber says 'I'm on the other line.' In this case, and many like it:

(a) Subscriber notifies caller of the call waiting problem in a response to caller's initial inquiry.
(b) The notification does not occur in response to 'How are you?' but in response to 'What are you doin.'

The notification is a marked response to initial inquiry.

UTCL A24.7

CALLER: **What are you d*o*in.**
            (0.3)
⇒   SUBSCR: **I:m (.) on the other l*i*:ne**
            (0.5)
CALLER: Oh you a:re?

UTCL D8.3

CALLER: **What are you doin**
⇒   SUBSCR: **I: was (.) *ta*lking the other l*i*:ne**
            right no(h)ow-
            (.)
CALLER: Oh you ar:e?

These notifications explicitly specify the call waiting problem. By comparison, trouble-premonitory responses to initial inquiries (Jefferson, 1980, chapter 3) only hint that something is up without specifying the problem.

Callers' responses to 'I'm on the other line' signal that they hear marked notifications. The next turns are response cries (Goffman, 1978) that begin with the vocalized particle 'oh.' Heritage (1984a) notes that turn-initial "oh" displays a speaker's "change of state," or receipt of news. These callers mark 'I'm on the other line' as situation-transforming news.

Having shown these marked *responses* to inquiry, we may turn to the inquiries themselves: 'What are you doin' is a marked form in the How are you slot. 'What are you doin' occurs in other telephone openings besides call waiting openings, and the unmarked response to it seems to be 'nothin.' But in call waiting openings, 'What are you doin' elicits a notification of the call waiting problem.

The call waiting notification does not occur in response to 'How are you?,' which is the most common initial inquiry by callers to friends and business colleagues. A comparison of call waiting openings and other openings recorded on the same phones, (A10, A20, A24) and listing occurrences of 'How are you?' and 'What are you doin,' appears as Table 2. Table 2 shows that 'How are you?' is the most frequent initial inquiry in ordinary call openings, but that it does not occur in call waiting openings. 'What are you doin' is the most frequent initial inquiry in call waiting openings.

Table 2
Acquaintances' Initial Inquiries from Three Telephones

	ORDINARY	CALL WAITING
How are you?	8	0
What are you doin	0	4

To summarize: Participants in call-waiting openings use the marked initial inquiry, "what are you doin" to elicit a notification of the problem. This typifies how marked turns may be used to adapt to context.

The canonical instance provides an unmarked case against which participants may mark situational variation or problematic circumstances. We illustrate this thesis for switchboard answers and call waiting openings.

Variations according to relationship and to culture answer a similar description. This makes these sources of variation difficult to distinguish from one another in the unfolding of any particular telephone opening.

Relationships

Do strangers or intimates begin telephone calls in distinctive ways that mark their state of relationship? Horenstein (1985) recorded a number of telephone calls from one telephone, including calls to a variety of acquaintances. She then asked raters to evaluate the recognition/identification portions of these telephone openings on the criterion: "degree of explicitness." Horenstein's raters evaluated openings between strangers as most explicit and openings of intimates as comparatively implicit—with openings of casual acquaintances rated in between. Horenstein defines relational history as extrinsic to communication. Accordingly stranger-stranger interactions (characterized by high uncertainty) display predictable formats, while more intimate relationships are more spontaneous (see Berger and Bradac, 1982; Knapp, 1978).

Horenstein (1985) focuses on "how intimacy is conveyed by conversational style" (p. 671) and argues that acquaintances' openings are more implicit than those between strangers. Horenstein's results do not mesh with our observations. Rather than being relatively explicit, telephone openings of strangers are reduced in format compared to those of acquaintances.

Strangers' Telephone Openings

Whalen and Zimmerman (1987) and Frankel (1989) claim that calls to emergency service agencies display a distinctive "reduction" of canonical format, characterized by deletion of the greeting and "How are you?" sequences. These deletions affect the placement of first topic.

> [MCE/21-9/12] (Whalen and Zimmerman, 1987)
>
> D: **Mid-City Emergency**
> C: **Um yeah (.) somebody jus' vandalized my car,**
> D: **What's your address.**
> C: **Thirty three twenty two: Elm.**

The first topic, a vandalized car, is stated in the caller's first turn. Caller does not produce a greeting token, does not self-identify, does not ask "How are you?" Are these reductions consequences of an emergency situation? How could we evaluate that explanation against these?

(1) The speakers are strangers to one another.
(2) The speech events are institutional service encounters.

We collected thirty-four recordings of nonemergency strangers' openings.[2] Like emergency openings, these telephone openings between strangers usually omit greetings and initial inquiries.

> UTCL J16 ((doctor's office))
>
> A: **Central Allergy Associates this is Alice?**
>   **(0.9)**
> C: **Ye:s this is Ron Harrell (0.4) U::m (0.4) couple a**
>   **days ago I saw Doctor: uh (0.4) Hart on a uh (1.0)**
>   **I was having c*o*ughing**

This caller's first turn says: "yes," and then gets right to business. Caller does not greet the answerer.

> CIS 212
>
> A: **Cancer Information Service may I help you?**
>   **(0.2)**
> B: **Yes I was: uh (0.6) w*o*ndering if: there was a**
>   **p*o*ssibility of getting a list of thee: *f*oods that**
>   **ar:e available (0.9) to reduc:e risk of cancer?**

When the caller says 'yes,' then gets right to business, how do we choose between describing these openings as: stranger-stranger, institutional, or emergency? This terminological quibble visits the central issue of the present chapter: How do you specify the parameter(s) of context relevant to any specific message variation?

Also, not all stranger-stranger openings are reduced in format. In the most striking instances callers greet answerers in their first turn.

UTCL J16

	A:	Metro Allergy Associates this is Alice
⇒	C:	Hi there Alice this is Sandy Welch
	A:	Hi
	C:	·hh U::m I have a problem, My husband u::::h is Barry Welch

((3 lines deleted))

Do *you* think maybe Dr Hart might consider calling him in a prescription for emoxacillin instead of having to see him

Greetings are absent in most calls between strangers, yet this caller uses a greeting to claim special accessibility to the institutional answerer. With the return greeting, the answerer acknowledges this status, and may subsequently experience constraint to treat the caller much like an acquaintance: The caller then requests an exceptional medical favor. Caller acts like an acquaintance during the opening as a strategic gambit.

Another case of stranger-stranger greeting occurs on a radio talk show.[3] Talk-show callers may develop some sense of knowing the host vicariously. Still, this radio caller uses greetings to ask something extraordinary of the host.

UTCL M12a

	A:	Hall:o? you are on the a:ir.
⇒	C:	Good evening Doctor Ruth.
		(0.6)
	A:	Good evening
	C:	I just wanted to say my lady and I enjoy your show very much, and . . .

Thus begins an encounter in which the caller delivers a lengthy compliment on the host's show, then raises two separate and extended concerns. Most callers to this show raise only one question, but this caller greets the answerer as part of a gambit to exploit resources of air time. Answerer hesitates before returning this greeting, which indicates attention to the problematic caller's ploy.

One final example shows that telephone partners may self-consciously manipulate the details of the telephone opening to simulate acquaintance and turn that simulation to concrete benefit. In a story about calling to order pizza, the teller "quotes" her friend's telephone opening:

UTVL 8 ((face to face, video))

MOUSE: **She goes she calls up- HI HONEY? (0.2) HOW YA DOIN hih**

WHITE: **Calls up wh*o*.**

MOUSE: **The p*i*zza man so she can ge(h)=**

WHITE: **Hi ↑ho:ney?**
           (0.6)

MOUSE: **She c(h)alls an fl(h)irts with the pizza mah-**
           ·*h*hh- an *sure*, we could put two toppings for the price of one

This caller reportedly greets the pizza man as if they were intimates 'hi honey,' and forwards an initial inquiry ('how ya doin'). The recipient of this story (White) expresses surprise by repeating the quoted utterance ('Hi honey?'); and the storyteller explains that her friend 'calls and flirts with the pizza man' to get 'two toppings for the price of one.' This story's protagonist strategically manipulates details of the telephone opening to enact acquaintance, then she asks a special favor.

Relationship relevancies may be somewhat available for the creating. If a caller marks acquaintance with an answerer (a radio host, or a doctor's receptionist) this seems not entirely determined by some extrinsic degree of previous intimacy. Relationships are, to a degree, what we enact them to be. Greeting a stranger by name and eliciting a return greeting is also relationship development.

To summarize: In most openings between strangers, callers delete greetings and preliminary inquiries. We cannot separate *institutional* from *stranger* constraints in these openings. Some stranger openings are somewhat augmented from the reduced form. These variations are social gestures that display partners to be pursuing marked lines of action. Marked turns in telephone openings become self-explicating bits of context.

Intimates' Telephone Openings

For intimate telephone partners interpersonal relationship is an ongoing conversation. Their entry into ecounter is swift, and identification may be taken for granted. Intimate parties identify each other based upon as few resources as possible (Schegloff, 1979a). Intimates use greetings and delete much else. Intimate callers frequently greet in their first speaking turn.

	F:	Hello?
⇒	M:	Hey!
	F:	↑Hi

	MOM:	Hello?
⇒	ROSA:	Hi mo:m,
	MOM:	Hi hello mija

These callers' first turns display recognition of the answerer's voice from just 'hello' and propose that their greeting will suffice for mutual recognition. The answerer's return greeting confirms this expectation. These greeting pairs display intimate pretensions.

An intimate answerer may launch the first initial inquiry in response to a greeting. This shows that recognition has been achieved. So, adult sisters who talk to each other frequently may open like this:

NB:II:3:R

	Lottie:	LO:,
	Emma:	G'morning Letitia=
⇒	Lottie:	=U-hHow'r YOU:.=
	Emma:	=FI:NE HOW'R YOU:

In this opening, Emma, the caller, greets Lottie, using a special variant of her name. Lottie responds by providing a first initial inquiry. By this preemption, Lottie shows that identification of the caller has been so easy that neither a term of address nor a return greeting is necessary. Preemptions to first topic are also commonplace in intimate calls:

UTCL A32.6 ((son-mother))

MOM:	Hello?
SAM:	Mo:m
MOM:	Oh hi
SAM:	A:::h you're bein recorded on the phone do ya mind

In this instance, first topic is permission to record; in many instances it is weather, or some ongoing story. None of these matters is marked in a special-purpose way; nor is intimacy itself. All of these instances do include greetings, the most essential sign of previous relationship.

Having shown how streamlined intimates' openings may be, we must note that similar markings can show other things besides intimacy. For instance, here's an opening between intimates:

UTCL D10.3 ((steady dating partners))

F:	Hello?
M:	Hey!
F:	↑Hi
M:	Are you *ready ye*t?

This opening shows the callers establishing mutual recognition from greetings. Caller then states the reason for calling. These intimates presume a
continuing conversation, hence they simply greet and resume earlier business.

But nonintimate parties who have quite recently spoken to each other may
also produce a similar opening:

A24.6 ((female friends; return call))

M:	Hello
	(0.2)
C:	Hi
M:	Hi,
C:	Are you all ready?

These casual friends had earlier arranged to eat dinner together in a group.
M was to call when ready to pick up C by car. Recency may account for the
deletions in this opening. But who can be sure what context partners index
with the features for either of the last two instances? Much intimacy *is*
sustained recency; and any recency may sound much like intimacy. We
usually cannot tease out what is about intimacy and about recency. Often
both come into play, and the participants do not separate them. There
actually are interactional benefits for *not* separating them, such as building
intimacy from the naturally-occurring resources of recency.

To summarize: Intimates' telephone openings show streamlinings responsive to easy recognition, recency, and other factors. Relationship and circumstance bear reflexive relationships to each other, and partners may not
distinguish the two.

Table 3, presented with the caveat above, models variations in telephone
openings due to intimacy. To add flesh to this skeleton, conceptualize
stranger → intimate as a continuum constructed around the canonical middle point: acquaintance. In telephone openings, whatever *is* special, problematic, urgent, or strategic is marked by divergence from canonical format.
And something is marked in the vast majority of telephone openings: an
institutional answer, a switchboard request, a problem of identification,
premonitoring of troubles to tell, a presequential gambit, or other things may
come into play. The more frequent and subtle such markings, the more the
system allows expressions of free will.

Table 3
Telephone Openings and Relationship States

INTIMATES	ACQUAINTANCES [canonical]	STRANGERS
Summons-Answer	Summons-Answer	Summons-Answer
	Identification/Recognition	
Greetings	Greetings	Yes
Inquiries	How are you?	Get to business

The speaker at telephone opening is a "bricoleur" who uses a limited repertoire of tools to accomplish varied tasks-at-hand:

> The "bricoleur" is adept at performing a large number of diverse tasks.... His universe of instruments is closed and the rules of his game are always to make do with "whatever is at hand." (Lévi-Strauss, 1962, p. 17)

Telephone partners improvise openings on the scene using a fixed set of resources. Callers use a few options to perform a variety of tasks. The nature of these tasks emerges across multiple speaking turns. Callers must muddle through:

> to *muddle through* is to be not-over-exact, to let events shape themselves in part, to make up one's specific policies as one goes along, in accordance with the unforseen newnesses that occur in the course of events. (Burke, 1935, p. 108)

In telephone openings verbal semantics seems secondary to sequential collage. Systematic sequential ambiguity keeps options alive. Problem resolution is interactively constructed by partners upon a scaffolding of conversational routines. The procedures for problem resolution seem designed to stay as close as possible to those routines.

We now turn to issues of language and culture, which are as much embedded in situation as is relational history.

Telephone Openings across Cultures and Languages: Ethnography and Conversation Analysis

Some of the most perplexing sources of situational variation in telephone openings represent cultural and language diversity. Linguistic diversity, according to persistent legend, originated when humans tried to build a tower to heaven. Babel stymies us still: no theory of language satisfactorily explicates language diversity. We cannot speak to just any human, but only to co-members of language communities. Linguistic prisons limit our choices of conversation partners. Today, any of us could quickly telephone any of a hundred countries. But we rarely do so. Asked why, we might explain: it's a language problem. Or a problem of culture.

Our language and culture undoubtedly constrain encoding choices. Certain writers argue that the nature and structure of telephone openings differ across different language communities (Sifianou, 1989; Godard, 1977; Carroll, 1987). However, the different sounds of telephone openings in different languages may mask similarities to the canonical instance. Different cultures and languages also vary the format of openings in ways similar to marking of circumstance and relationship.

The canonical model reaches for cross-community generality. How can we amplify this model to mirror diversities as well as similarities?

The study of cultures is the province of ethnography, but conversation analysts bring unique challenges to comparative study of interaction practices in different languages and cultures. Gumperz (1982) argues that conversation analysis extends empirical linguistics because of its focus on the details of interaction. Goodwin (1991) shows children's stories and directive sequences in naturally-occurring richness. Thereby she illustrates some uses of conversation analysis in description of a culture's details.

Ethnographic studies and conversation analysis could profit by making common investigative cause. For the most part this promise remains elusive, perhaps because most ethnographic descriptions concentrate on intercultural diversities while most conversation analyses have forwarded universalistic descriptions. In this vein, Moerman (1988) expresses an ethnographer's impatience with conversation analysis:

> Its high-powered lens sacrifices range, breadth, and *mise-en-scène*. . . . This can make conversation analysis seem bloodless, impersonal and unimportant to anthropology's central concerns. (p. x)

Moerman sketches a fragile link between ethnography and conversation analysis: *culturally contexted conversation analysis*. He employs universalistic descriptions of conversational features to anchor ethnographic descriptions. From these beginnings he explicates what a culture's members take themselves to be doing.

For example, Moerman argues that various cultures use surprisingly similar conversational features for referring to persons (e.g., using as few descriptive terms as possible, then seeking the other's alignment). Speech objects used in many cultures for making and testing such references include try-marking—or saying a name with a questioning pitch contour (Sacks and Schegloff, 1979). Moerman uses such description in conjunction with ethnographic observations about how Lue-speaking Thai villagers distinguish varieties of rice or how they talk with government officials. By combining conversational detail with background sense, Moerman conveys certain textures of Lue discourse,[4] while emphasizing that similar discourse patterns exist in different languages. He argues that Thai and English use similar tokens for conversational repair, turn-taking, and reference to persons—even though these languages are unrelated linguistically.

Following Moerman, we argue that telephone openings in a variety of languages display some common patterns. Further, these may be explicated with reference to the canonical instance for English calls—as four sets of tasks more or less necessary at telephone openings. Cross-cultural testing is therefore vital to evaluating this claim.

A culture's telephone customs display tiny oft-repeated imprints of community ethos. Ask most any traveller, immigrant, or ethnographer about telephone conversations in countries outside the USA. You will hear about differences. For example, Carroll (1987), reflecting on twenty years' experience in France and twenty years in the USA, writes:

> The telephone plays a very complicated role in the lives of French people. . . . [W]e subject it to all sorts of unspoken rules as if it represented a threat . . . whose power must be contained, limited. (p. 89)
> . . . .
> As an American, I consider the telephone first and foremost as a tool, a practical and indispensable instrument. Even before moving, for example, I arrange to have the telephone installed at my new address, so that it functions from the day I move into my new residence. . . . My telephone number quickly becomes an integral part of my identity. When I give my name and address, the number follows automatically. It is printed on my checks, accompanies all my credit purchases, and is available to whoever wants to take a poll, perform a market survey, or conduct phone sales. (p. 95)

Godard (1977) agrees with Carroll and argues that French callers are obliged at openings to apologize for calling everybody except their closest intimates.

Other investigators claim interlanguage diversity in what telephone answerers from different languages/cultures say in their first speaking turns. Sifianou (1989) argues that Greek answerers say "*ne*" (yes) about a third of the time, and verbs translated as "speak" or "go ahead" almost as frequently. These openings, she argues, are distinct from "hello" in the USA or England, and from the practice of stating answerer's phone number in England. However, these three different openings reportedly used in Greece are as different *from each other* as from the English comparisons. Sifianou makes no comment on circumstantial diversities that might correlate with these different Greek usages. Further, Sifianou, like most analysts to date, does not separate effects of Greek language from Greek culture. This thorny issue is illustrated by a survey of different telephone openings encountered in different Spanish-speaking countries: *Bueno* (Northern Mexico); *Dígame* (Spain); *Hola* (Paraguay) (Hopper, Doany, Johnson and Drummond, 1991). Closer analysis would indicate diversity within each country. Sifianou indicates that Greek telephone openings are diverse. This seems the case in most languages, and in most cultures. Which of these differences are best traced to culture alone?

A related point can be made about another obvious possibility at answerer's first turn: to state one's name. Houtkoop-Steenstra (1991) documents that telephone answerers in Holland say their own name in their first turn.

Houtkoop-Steenstra, 1991

A:	**Met Reina de Wind?**	It's Reina de Wind?
C:	**Hal*lo:*, met Bren**	Hello, it's Bren

This instance illustrates that there are other useful ways to answer the telephone besides saying hello. Answering with self-identification explicitly gets on with the work of identification, which is the most immediate next task at hand.

Do these Dutch data contradict the canonical model? Houtkoop-Steenstra takes exception to the sequential ordering of an "identification" phase after "summons/answer," because the data show self-identification during the summons-answer. However, in every culture and context imaginable, answering turns forward recognition. Further, there are North American settings, mostly institutional ones, in which answerers state their name in first turn. How do we distinguish cultural variation from within-culture variation?

As a cultural norm the Dutch practice of self-identifying accepts an information deficit in the conversation, an answerer-vulnerability. It is tempting to speculate on the ethos of the Netherlands from this basis. In nearby France the scenario for identification has been described as less open from the answerer's end and more open from the caller's. That is, French answerers do not give their name first, but callers frequently do. On this basis Godard (1977) challenges the applicability of the canonical instance to French telephone openings, explaining that in France the caller assumes that the call will be a disturbance. Being a "virtual offender" the caller must show that there is a good reason for the call. Therefore telephone openings in France show: (1) the caller checking the number, (2) the caller naming himself or herself at first opportunity, and (3) the caller apologizing for the intrusion. (This last is optional if one calls an intimate.) Godard illustrates these claims with idealized reconstructed exemplars. Carroll, who like Godard has lived in both countries, corroborates these observations:

> If I call someone who occupies a position of the slightest importance, I must immediately identify myself by answering the insistent question "*de la part de qui?*" ("who's calling?"). . . . If I ask to whom I am speaking, the person will give me his or her first name, in a country where I do not often allow just anyone to call me by my first name. But then, it is not really a first name, but rather "Tell them Monsieur André," or "Ask for Madame Anna." (p. 90)

Carroll's description suggests institutional discourse, which makes cross-cultural comparisons challenging.

Based in such claims for cultural diversity in identification, we might construct cultural stereotypes about France, the Netherlands, or other specific speech communities. But actual openings in each culture mingle orientations to culture with those to other situational factors: degree of acquaintance, whether you reach the person called, the linguistic fluency of either party in the language community, race, gender, and so on.

Each difference between the norms of two communities can lead to difficulties. For instance, a call to a casual acquaintance may be more of an intrusion in France than in the USA. Still, summons-intrusiveness seems a basic feature of telephone openings everywhere. And the answering turn provides data relevant to recognition in any setting. These features of the canonical model seem confirmed in these diverse European cases.

Future investigations must record the actual words, sounds, and timing of telephone openings in as many locations and languages as possible. We take baby steps in that direction here. Data from non-European languages and cultures can be expected to provide sterner tests than those addressed to date.

Our studies of telephone openings in four languages (English, French, Spanish, and Arabic) find that summons-answer sequences are necessary first occurrences in telephone speaking, and mutual recognition displays are the first-next-business in-and-after summoning and answering. Further, greetings are relevant between previously acquainted persons immediately upon recognition. Finally, many calls move out of their opening by means of initial inquiry. A caller most commonly launches the first inquiry. Each of these statements describes a canonical value, and divergences from these values, which are commonplace, mark situational adaptations (Hopper and Doany, 1988; Hopper, Doany, Johnson, and Drummond, 1991).

The canonical instance illuminates telephone openings in that a variety of languages show cases that conform to its specifications. In these instances, A refers to answerer, C is caller:

French: (Kelly)

A: Allo
C: Allo Mali:ke
A: Oui?
C: Salut c'est Marie:
A: Salu:t Marie:

Mexican: (Gonzalez/Johnson)

A: Bueno hh
C: Louisa
A: Ah ja
C: Hola (.) habla Maria Mejia   Maria M. speaking
A: Ay hola

Translated Arabic: [Hopper and Doany show Arabic]

A: **Hello?**
C: **Hello Shiri::ne?**
A: **Yes**
C: **Nadia**

Finnish [Hakulinen/Jefferson (simplified transcript)]

A: *A:lli H—*
C: *Ee: Hannu V— Lah:desta.=Hei:h.=*   from Lahti=Hello
A: **Hei:h** *hhh*
      (0.3)
C: ↑*Kuu::'e* **(.) vehhh Kuule- kuule**   hey hey hey

Many details of these instances elude my detailed understanding. But as a group these transcriptions illustrate a canon for ordered tasks performed in telephone openings. The initial utterances of answerers are diverse, but all serve primarily to answer a summons and secondarily to contribute to identification and/or greeting functions. Mutual identification is prior to or simultaneous with greetings. Cultural variations from the model also may be seen to resemble somewhat the variations due to other aspects of situation—such as the nature of the partners' relationship.

Within any speech community, there develop standard ways for performing telephone openings. Schegloff's instance captures many particulars of these for North America. Other investigators claim canonical status for slot-items that are marked in North America (e.g., self-identification in Holland). Every speech community evolves formats for displaying situational facts such as intimacy, or the degree of rudeness represented by summons-intrusion.

There seems to be cross-cultural generality not only in the ordering of canonical opening sequences, but also in how participants mark exceptional circumstances: pauses, quantity of identifying tokens, deleting a slot, and insertion sequences.

In examining telephone openings in different languages, we also find numerous instances in which assignment to a particular language is problematic. A simple example is this telephone opening between native-speaking Chinese living in Texas.

Duan (Pingyin transcription)

A: **Hello?**
C: **Ei? Xaiofu ma?**   Hi? Is this Xaiofu?
A: **Ai Shi wo ya**   Yes it's me

The first turn is 'hello,' the rest is Chinese. I asked my informant-transcriber how this opening compares with those in his native Beijing. Well, he explained, since there is only one telephone for each apartment building, the first opening would be with a porter, a retired gentleman who would fetch the called person. Is reliance on a switchboard answerer a matter of culture? Of technology? Is this opening a North American or a Chinese one? Such reductive choices cannot help us describe the principled mutual embeddedness of culture and relationship with other aspects of situation.

Some telephone openings are even more thoroughly multilingual. What is their status in our approach?

> UTCL L17
>
> M: Hello,
> D: Hi mom,
> M: Hi hello mija,
> D: How are you doin,
> M: Muy bien (.) está viendo el boxeo

	Doany	
A:	'llo:?	
B:	Hi::	
A:	H:i	
B:	Sho:u. Qu'es tu *fais* h?=	what (Arabic)
		what are you doin
		(French)
A:	='Am bout↑boukh	I'm cooking (Arabic)

What languages are these openings in? Does the concept, *in a language* apply to such instances? What is the status of multilingual openings in a search for conversational universals? A complication: both these openings display intimacy, especially in the early greetings. How may one partition the effects of language, culture, intimacy in these openings? Is culture relevant to these participants in the same way that intimacy is?

We mention these complications to indicate possibilities for testing a universalist model of telephone openings. The opportunity is that, in addition to examining openings across several languages, one might systematically examine openings in which more than one language is used. If a model finds generality across several (linguistically unrelated) languages, and also in multilingual telephone conversation—then perhaps it describes tasks of wide occurrence. Any such model must begin with Schegloff's surprisingly robust canonical instance.

Conclusions

Telephone partners orient to four routine sequential tasks, within ordered slots, each of which may be filled by adjacency-pair constructions. The model shows close detailed fit with only a minority of telephone openings. Its picture of interaction is built upon divergences from routines. These marked openings unfold across turns, including issues of relationship and culture.

When all divergences are considered, we find far more non-routine openings than routine ones. Canonical cases provide a template for participants, a line-of-best-fit when nothing special is going on. There seems to be a fixed set of ways to mark divergences from routine, including pausing, failing to return a greeting, bypassing a slot by packing two items into one turn, or asking a marked initial inquiry such as "What's goin on later?"

These divergences are nonspecific in their uses. They generically mark that "something is up." Their sequential ambiguity (Sacks, Fall 1967, lecture 7; Schegloff, 1984) allows a small number of tokens to perform a variety of functions within a variety of scenes. Any first-occurring marking may be followed up in future turns, or participants may let the possibilities pass. The participants on the scene, in interaction, work out what, if anything, is special about any encounter.

Telephone openings around the world resemble nothing so much as each other. This position is universalist, though not dismissive of the diversity of sounds by which people open their telephone conversations. We must move to a new stage of testing these ideas, one that transcends simplistic argument: Are telephone openings across languages and/or cultures more alike or more different? This dialectic could settle into a comfortable rut in which each set of protagonists preaches to its own choir.

To get past stale dialectic, we must explicate the details of single instances in the widest variety of settings conceivable, and based upon evidence from tape recordings. Sifianou, who presents no tape recorded exemplars, argues against their relevance: "Since my concern was only with recording as many brief opening exchanges as possible, tape recording was not deemed necessary or desirable" (1989, p. 528). I disagree.

Further, we should explicate how telephone partners invoke any particular feature of situation: language, culture, relationship, institution, or urgency.

We articulate in the present chapter some beginnings toward a message-intrinsic approach to context. Like Heidegger's phenomenology, such an approach reveals only glimmers of discovery. A comprehensive hearing eludes us, perhaps due to the categories around which we organize this chapter: circumstance, relationship, and culture. Mundane understandings of these notions may obscure how participants enact telephone openings. So we articulate a message-intrinsic approach to intimacy but then chart the differences in openings by degree of intimacy. We describe not only message variations that are associated with well-researched contextual differences, but also how contextual indications get achieved across speakers' turns. On the slippery and elusive path that meanders toward description of the planet-wide human conversation, the telephone opening plays an important role.

```
                (UTCL L17.1)
        MOM:    Hell↑o,
        ROSA:   Hi mo:m,
        MOM:    Hi hello mija
        ROSA:   How're you doing
5       MOM:    Muy bien (.) está viendo el boxeo
        MOM:    ⌈ja ja
        ROSA:   ⌊Ah:::↑::      Como está de frío alla
        MOM:    No::? está: lloviendo
        ROSA:   Pero no está haciendo frío
10      MOM:    No: no (es- no que yo) poquito pero no
                it's not cold very very no
        ROSA:   ⌈Eh yeah
        MOM:    ⌊No-
        MOM:    Y alla cómo están ustedes
15      ROSA:   Sí:: it's getting co:ld,
                     (0.2)
        MOM:    S- how a ver que tal
        ROSA:   Pues- uh right now it's drizzling verdad
                pero I- I guess it's abouw h- h- how: uh
20              how cold do you think it is Doug
                     (0.4)
        DOUG:   Probly:  ⌈::::: fifty: six
        MOM:             ⌊About it's eh seventy
        ROSA:   About the e:( . ) upper or middle sixties
25      MOM:    Sí: pues yo creo que sí aquí a- aqí
                también
        ROSA:   Re:ally:
        ROSA:   Cómo están todos bien?
        MOM:    Muy bien gracias a ⌈dios
30      ROSA:                       ⌊Bichea cómo ⌈está
        MOM:                                     ⌊Pues
                aquí no más es que he wants to go to a
                sleep pero no porque de- le dimos de a
                cenar le di carlito esto no: no no puede
35              (esta la darite)
        ROSA:   ⌈Sí:
        MOM:    ⌊Nada más de esta hondadita así
```

	ROSA:	Na:h ⌈mi
	MOM:	⌊Pero está bien gracias a dios
40	ROSA:	Au- y cómo s- cómo sa siendo la señora bien?
	MOM:	Pues sí pues sí- you know he's eh (0.3) cooking and he fixes everything for me (.) of my (.) for my mother
45	ROSA:	Re:ally mom
	MOM:	Sí ⌈so-
	ROSA:	⌊Does she sleep there f- with her?
		(0.3)
	MOM:	She sits there
50	MOM:	⌈But she doesn't-
	ROSA:	⌊How does she do- Uh- during the night
	MOM:	Bueno si she (tusn't)- (0.3) and help me (0.2) (But I have no) (su- and help for lisa) feeds the face and cannot handle
55		(qui pasé) the carry her.
	ROSA:	Yeah=
	MOM:	=I have to ·hhhh give each (0.2) pero es eso que she helps me and Lotti she just started cooking
60		(0.4)
	MOM:	She made empanadas toda:y?
	ROSA:	My:↑:::
	MOM:	Oye- ·hhh How did you like my (0.3) c- uh corn bread
65	ROSA:	Estaba bien grasoso mother
	MOM:	Sí esto mucho mantequilla sí
	ROSA:	Le puso mucha mantequilla?
	MOM:	Sí (.) Yo creo que sí después es ⌈que-
	ROSA:	⌊A:h es
70		like manteca mom it's- it's ba:d don't- I mean d- that's- (.) that's too thick, I think too
	MOM:	Sí porque le puso ⌈four eggs
	ROSA:	⌊Too greasy mom
		((call continues 5 minutes))

TURNS

*. . . those little things which are more important
than big ones, because they make up life.*
Ivy Compton-Burnett,
A Family and a Fortune

(UTCL F14: A. L. Sims)

r:::ing

F: Okey dokey.

W: How are ya?

F: Okey dokey.

W: You all by yourself tonite.

F: Ye:s.

W: Am I spozed to be (looking) for something special.

F: No:.

W: No. Did ya have dinner tonite?

F: Yes.

W: Wadja have?

F: I dunno.

W: Pizza?

F: No.

W: Something Mary made?

F: Yes.

((call continues 3 minutes))

HOW DO I KNOW
WHEN IT'S MY TURN?

In the past two chapters we showed that telephone partners accomplish critical details of situation definition within the first few moments of each new call. In the present chapter, we describe a smaller and more frequent beginning: that of each speaking turn. In telephone conversation you cannot see your partner; how do you know when to speak?

In the duet preceding this chapter, speaker F uses very few words, yet manages to participate in a rather ordinary telephone opening. His major accomplishment is in timing just when to begin each next turn.

The maxim "well begun is half done" applies with particular force to speakers' turns in telephone conversation. Each time you say anything on the telephone, you must get the floor to do so. Much of the accomplishment of turn beginning is timing. Telephone partners calibrate the beginning of each new turn with reference to the progress of an ongoing turn. This chapter tests a model of turn beginning against evidence found in *gaps*, or inter-turn pauses in telephone conversation. We show that:

(1) Speakership rarely changes following nontransition-relevant pauses.
(2) Gaps (inter-turn pauses) in conversation are frequent.
(3) Most gaps do communicative work.

There is a joke in which a teacher asks three kids to name the greatest invention in modern life. None of them mentions telephones. One says TV, the second says rockets. The third child says "the thermos, because it keeps hot things hot and cold things cold." The child wonders: "How do it know?" This kid poses a problem from simple materials. How can a single technological device prevent two properties that are opposites? The child praises something so simple that nobody has asked how it works. Turn taking is obvious in ways a bit like the thermos, which uses a single set of principles to preserve two opposites: heat and cold.

The thermos serves as a first analogy for the *next speakers problem* in telephone conversation: How do you know when it's your turn? Any telephone speaker must accomplish the beginning of each turn precisely as the partner stops talking. This is complicated because there are lots of times when the current speaker might be finishing. At each of these *transition-relevance places* the current speaker might stop, or might continue. The next speaker's job is to speak as soon as the current speaker's turn is finished, but not to speak if the current speaker is continuing. Somehow we do this! This empirical fact is a cornerstone for the sequential analysis of conversation, that

> Overwhelmingly one party talks at a time, though speakers change, and though the size of turns and ordering of turns vary; that transitions are finely coordinated. (Sacks, Schegloff, and Jefferson, 1974, p. 699)

If any next speaker fails to speak precisely upon a current speaker's completion, there ensues a *gap*, or a pause between turns. These three possibilities in Sacks et al.'s description, overlap, gap, and smooth transition, appear in this instance:

UTCL F1.1:1 simplified

	MOTHER:	...when people withdraw from terminally ill people you know and- and ↑don't talk to em and don't- (0.8) you know just ignore em that's really hard.
1⇒	DAUGHTER:	Yeah,
2⇒		(2.2)
	MOTHER:	↓S:o do you wanna go to u::h (0.8) Llano with us tomorrow afternoo⌈:n
3⇒	DAUGHTER:	⌊No: Mother I *ca*:n't

This extract pictures three turn transitions. The first is smooth, but the second shows a gap. Sacks et al. claim that every long gap in a telephone encounter is a marked event, an event that needs explanation.

Most often, the fine coordination of turns produces smooth turn transitions like the first one above. At other times, there are *overlaps* between turns (3⇒) when the next speaker begins to speak while the current speaker also continues. If a turn begins in overlap, one's telephone partner might experience a hearing problem. In some circumstances, speech overlap may also lead to perceptions that one speaker interrupts another (chapter 6).

The next speaker's problem is that, to begin a turn, you should minimize both gap and overlap. But gap and overlap are opposites, like hot and cold.[1] If you prevent gap, do you thereby make overlap more likely? And vice versa? How does the next speaker know which problem to prevent? The next speaker's problem is like that of the thermos in that the goal is to minimize both gap and overlap: But how?

Speakers' turns, like beverages, require insulation from their surroundings. Speakers who begin a next speaking turn exploit principles of turn taking that minimize, yet do not entirely prevent, both gap and overlap. Speakers follow these principles on most speech occasions, although telephone conversation displays the purest instances of these principles. These principles, articulated by Sacks, Schegloff, and Jefferson (1974), carry myriad consequences to every corner of the ecology of speaking:

(1) One speaker talks at a time.

(2) Each speaker projects the length of any turn in progress.

(3) Next speaker should begin as soon as current speaker's turn is complete (minimizing both gap and overlap).

These principles of turn taking are among the first things that children learn about speaking (McTear, 1985; Naremore and Hopper, 1990). Also, turn taking may be among the last things that certain speech-handicapped individuals lose following accidents, strokes, and diseases. In the duet before this chapter a linguistically handicapped speaker shows no difficulty performing the timing of each turn beginning.

> UTCL F14 (Sims)
>
> r:::ing
> | F: | Okey dokey. |
> | W: | How are ya? |
> | F: | Okey dokey. |
> | W: | You all by yourself tonite. |
> | F: | Ye:s. |

This segment begins a telephone encounter between two people, one of whom, speaker F, suffers a verbal handicap. This gentleman says few things except yes, no, and okey dokey. Given these limitations, it is noteworthy that F should be answering the phone at all! To answer the phone he says 'Okey dokey,' which works due to its timing. Caller W responds with an early initial inquiry, 'How are you.' F responds with the identical token he used to answer: 'Okey dokey.' In this postinquiry slot, this item serves as response to 'How are you.' These speakers thereby execute a complete telephone opening episode: summons-answer, initial inquiry and response, then first topic. F's disabilities lead to problems a bit later:

> | W: | No. Did ya have dinner tonite? |
> | F: | Yes. |
> | W: | Wadja have? |
> | ⇒   F: | I dunno. |
> | W: | Pizza? |

F:	No.
W:	**Something Mary made?**
F:	**Yes.**

Here F seems, at first blush, to be denying knowledge of what he had for supper. But F's conversation partner does not interpret 'I dunno' in that way. She asks follow-up questions about supper, and F answers. This demonstrates that 'I dunno' has been neither intended nor heard as denying knowledge about dinner. Perhaps it is uttered in reference to not being able to respond to the question as asked. F does not allow this incapacity to interfere with turn taking, and this gives his partner a chance to continue the encounter. F applies limited resources to accomplish the tasks of answering the phone and conducting interactive conversation. The transcription shows neither gaps nor overlaps at moments of speaker change. Speaker F displays no difficulty with the next speaker's problem.[2] F's performance carries implications for therapy and for language instruction. How much of the accomplishment of normal speaking is sheer timing of turn beginnings? Is it more important to the course of an encounter that speakers say just the right thing, or that they say something at an appropriate time?

The Importance of Turn Beginnings

Turn beginning is basic to telephone conversation. With turn beginnings, we establish an encounter's rhythm. Speakers F and W interact using restricted verbal resources because they take turns smoothly. Much communicative work gets done in turn beginnings. First, a turn beginning is necessary to get the floor. Second, a turn beginning addresses relationships to immediate prior turns (Sacks, Schegloff, and Jefferson, 1974, p. 722). Third, the first syllables of a turn project the turn's ending, hence the moment when a next speaker may be expected to begin (Schegloff, 1987b, p. 71).

The role of timing in turn beginnings can scarcely be over-emphasized. Try this "Aggie Joke": An interviewer asks the Aggie comic "What's the secret of Aggie humor?" The Aggie comic answers with the single word, "Timing!" But this word is inserted very early in the question, say in overlap with the word 'secret'; thus showing bad timing.

	((simulation))
Interviewer:	What's the ⌈secret of Aggie humor?
Aggie:	⌊Timing!

The point is that it takes considerable effort to say this word 'timing' at a *wrong* place before transition relevance. Try it.[3] This demonstration highlights the taken-for-granted precision-timing of turn beginnings.

A smooth beginning is vital to any utterance. But how do telephone speakers accomplish the smooth beginning of each turn? How does any next speaker know just when to speak? In telephone conversation there is rarely a long pause between turns. As each current speaker stops, the next begins to speak. We actually anticipate in advance, or *project*, the ending of the previous speaker's turn. How do we do that?

Some investigators claim that face-to-face speakers utilize visual cues— eye contact, gesture, etc, to aid turn taking (Duncan and Fiske, 1977). But we take turns with at least as much dispatch in telephone conversation as face to face, and visual cues are notably absent from telephone speaking. If anything, telephone speakers' pauses are shorter than those in face-to-face conversation. Thomason (1990) compared pause lengths in telephone conversation and face-to-face encounters. Long pauses are more frequent in face-to-face conversation.[4] We may conclude that telephone speech carries sufficient resources to cue turn taking. How do we project the end of a prior speaker's turn and time our next turn to come immediately after it?

Unmarked next position

Telephone partners begin each speaking turn to occur upon completion of the prior turn. Jefferson labels this sequential accomplishment the beginning of a turn in "unmarked next position" because

> A recipient/next speaker produces his talk in such a way that it occurs with neither haste nor delay . . . but permits just a bit of space between the end of the prior and the start of the next. It is "simply next" . . . the most common, the usual, the standard relationship of one utterance to another. (1986, p. 162)

In our transcripts, as in a play script, the absence of special marking between speakers' turns indicates that the next speaker begins immediately upon completion of the prior turn.

A turn beginning in unmarked next position seems contiguous to the last turn. Using a sound digitalizer (MacIntosh Soundcap) for precise measurement, we have observed that many of these inter-turn moments display about five hundredths of a second of silence, a mini-beat of pause, between speaker turns. Speakers do not ordinarily perceive this as a pause (Walker and Trimboli, 1982), hence we do not mark it in our transcriptions.

If a perceptible pause occurs between complete speaker turns, it belongs to neither speaker's turn, as shown in the first pause below:

UTCL F1.1:2

D: Yeah,
            (2.2)
M: ↓S:o do you wanna go to u::h (0.8) Llano

The inter-turn pause occurs at a moment when transition is relevant. However, the second pause in this fragment occurs at a moment when speaker change would be inappropriate, so the transcription shows the pause within M's turn. She does not give up the floor during the pause. The current chapter turns upon the distinction between transition-relevant pauses and those projected to fall within a speaker's turn.

To summarize: A next speaker begins a turn in unmarked next position by minimizing both gap and overlap. Each next speaker must resolve this puzzle of timing and project possible completion points in advance of the end of the current turn.

How Telephone Speakers Project Transition Relevance

At most moments during conversation speaker change is not appropriate. There are, however, moments at which participants may project transition relevance. Speakers project only approximate transition points, so brief gaps and speech overlaps do occur between turn units. Sacks et al. (1974) argue that these gaps and overlaps, in their brevity and other details of their deployment, show second-order regularities in turn taking. That is precisely the point we investigate here. Telephone conversation is the best site for such investigation because its constraints simplify the next-speaker's problem: There are only two speakers in a vocal-only system. Figure 7 shows a schematic turn beginning.

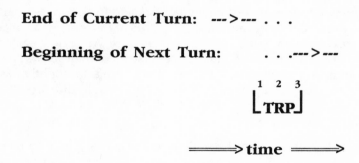

Figure 7: Pictorial Model of Transition Relevance
in Telephone Conversation (TRP signifies
Transition-Relevance Place)

This figure[5] pictures the speaker of a current turn approaching a point of possible completion, such as the end of a sentence. The model shows a transition-relevance place as an opportunity zone for a next turn beginning. The numbers 1, 2, 3 show a succession of moments within the transition-relevance place: from earliest opportunity (1) to latest opportunity (3) to begin at unmarked next position. Next speaker should begin a turn within this opportunity space to avoid disrupting the tempo of the encounter. (For North American English speakers the numbers represent a continuous transition space about two tenths of a second long.)

The term transition-relevance place indicates that during this span of time,[6] the floor is open for speakership bids. The current speaker seems to have the first opportunity to select the next speaker, say by asking a direct question (Sacks et al., 1974, pp. 704, 716-20). Although a current speaker projects possible completion points in advance of their occurrence, current speaker still maintains an information edge over a partner for projecting a moment of completion for a turn unit. This gives current speaker power in the economics of next-speaker selection.

Near transition-relevance places, Sacks et al. argue that speakers experience ordered opportunities to take the floor:

(a) current speaker selects next speaker.

(b) next speaker self-selects.

(c) current speaker may continue.

These opportunities are ordered in that the first one can operate before the second, and so on. A current speaker may select a next speaker at any time during a turn unit, say by asking a question or calling that speaker by name. If that does not occur, then at each transition-relevance place a speaker may take a turn. If nobody begins talking, then the turn-opportunity cycles back to the prior speaker, who may choose to say something. Wilson and Zimmerman (1986) argue that these rules apply recursively, in real time, resulting in the opportunity to speak next bouncing back and forth between partners.[7]

We may consider three candidate indicators of transition relevance: utterance syntax, terminal pitch contour, and pauses. We review each of these explanations below, favoring the first, because it not only allows speakers to identify transition relevance as it occurs, but to project it slightly in advance of its occurrence—as "up-coming" (Sacks, Fall 1967, lecture 3, p. 9).

Syntax-for-Conversation

Many turn units seem to be sentences. Some also prove to be phrases, words, or word-like noises such as "uh huh." Most turn-constructional units are units of grammar: sentences, phrases, clauses, or single items. Once begun, any of these units is ordinarily carried through to completion. Sacks, Schegloff, and Jefferson state that turn unit-types

> allow a projection of the unit-type under way, and what, roughly, it will take for an instance of the unit-type to be completed. (1974, p. 702)

These specifications allow speakers to improvise turn length, yet require listeners to project a turn unit's conclusion a bit in advance.

To summarize: speakers use syntactic and lexical features of their language to judge whether a turn is at (or nearing) a state of hearable completeness. As noted in chapter 2, these constraints subsume syntax into a syntax-for-conversation (Goodwin, 1980; Schegloff, 1982; Volosinov, 1930; Hakulinen, 1990; Auer, 1990). We presently lack a definitive framework in this area, but a dialogic theory of utterances promises to transform linguistics.

Pitch

The pitch contour of the final syllable of an utterance frequently seems to indicate turn ending. Punctuation in Jefferson's transcription system (see Appendix) indicates final pitch contour, rather than sentence grammar. For example the symbol "?" does not mark a grammatical question, but indicates rising terminal pitch. A period shows a falling terminal contour, and a comma is used to mark more subtle final intonations. Pitch contour is strictly local; its cuing of transition relevance requires no advance projection. Some evidence favors a two-stage model for transition relevance, in which approximate projection is achieved by surface syntax, then pin-point readjustment uses terminal pitch (Walker and Trimboli, 1984, p. 268).

Jefferson has tested some pitch-transition relations with unspectacular results. She examined a sample of 1600 final intonations, 800 clean transitions, and 800 overlaps.[8] She observed that roughly three-fourths of the instances showed pitch cues at turn junctures. But there were no differences in whether these transitions were clean or overlapped. In other words pitch may indicate turn completions, but this does not aid speakers in preventing overlap. Nor does completion intonation make it less likely that the current speaker will continue.

Terminal pitch may be a probable and redundant correlate of transition relevance. Speakers may find terminal pitch cues of some use, but they do not reliably distinguish transition relevance primarily on this cue alone.

This matter is by no means settled. Terminal pitch contours remain targets for future research. For instance, Selting (1990) argues that terminal pitch is important to tracking the intentions of speakers of questions—that is, whether the question asks for information, indicates failure to hear, etc. Perhaps pitch contour may be useful for projecting completions in certain subsets of questions (see also Local and Kelly, 1986).

Pauses

I have asked hundreds of people in recent years how they know when it is time to start each turn in telephone conversation. The question surprises people, indicating that they have not thought much about an action they have performed thousands of times. Upon reflection, many informants suggest a pause hypothesis: That speakers wait for a pause, then speak (see Cappella, 1979).

This answer contains one grain of truth: If speakers find themselves participating in a long pause during telephone conversation they notice that something is wrong, and this may lead them to speak. Telephone speakers do classify pauses for transition relevance. But the pause hypothesis fails to explain most turn transitions because almost half of pauses are not transition relevant, and because most turn exchanges are also "pauseless."

To illustrate these points, consider the two pauses marked in this example:

UTCL A21

⇒   **PAM:**   **And so um (0.4) Go:d dang it there are *so* many roaches in this *kit*chen it's making me *si*ck**

       GLORIA: **hhuh ↑huh uh- don't worry I have em too.**

⇒   **PAM:**   **Go::d. ·hhh anyway- u:m (1.2) so...**

Each of these pauses occurs *within* a single speaker's turn. These pauses are not transition relevant. If speakers waited for a pause before beginning a turn, we would have to predict speaker change at these moments. Second, Pam and Gloria *do* begin each new turn in the segment with smooth transitions. Speakers do not wait for pauses to begin a new turn, but manage to begin most turns without a pause.

To summarize: Syntax-for-conversation, more than pause or pitch contour, indicates transition relevance and makes it possible for listeners to project unit completion a bit in advance. Pauses, upon their occurrence, may be classified in terms of transition relevance—which may affect turn beginnings subsequent to pauses.

Still, there remains much that is unexplained about speakers' achievement of turn beginnings. It is doubtful that speakers experience themselves as doing syntax and prosody, but rather as speaking and acting. We must enlarge our account by characterizing how telephone speakers do the tasks of projecting transition relevance. The telephone pause gives us a vital window into these issues.

Pauses and Transition Relevance

Speakers, Sacks et al. argue, routinely minimize both gap and overlap. Do they guard equally well against both? For the balance of this chapter, we consider this question using evidence from pauses in telephone conversation. In the next chapter, we consider speech overlaps and the notion of interruption.

To introduce these concerns, we show a distributional analysis of gap and overlap. We selected one hundred turn beginnings by a randomizing procedure from six different telephone conversations in North American English.[9] These tabulations indicate that inter-turn pauses—even lengthy pauses—are frequent. Table 4 supports the Sacks et al. emphasis on smooth transitions between speaker's turns. Most turns come off quite smoothly. Sixty of these

100 beginnings occurred in unmarked next position. The twelve overlaps are easy to explain in terms of the Sacks et al. model: eleven of these overlaps were brief and occur near transition-relevance places (TRPs).[10] We defer further examination of overlap till the next chapter and describe here some ways that speakers use pauses in constructing turn beginnings.

Table 4
Timing of 100 Turn Beginnings

| | GAP AND / OR OVERLAP | | |
	Prevented	Brief	Lengthy
Unmarked	60		
Overlap		11	1
Gap		10	18

The most startling observation from Table 4 is that more than one turn in four begins after a pause, rather than smoothly. Eighteen of these twenty-eight gaps lasted half a second or longer.

A relay-race analogy for turn taking (Figure 7) suggests that conversational pausing is like a runner dropping the baton. It seems important to observe the precise moment at which this problem occurs. If the runners drop the baton while it is being passed to the next runner, that next runner should retrieve it. If the drop occurs away from such a transition place, the current runner must retrieve it. Similarly, some pauses in conversation occur at transition-relevant moments; others do not.

Sacks et al. (1974) argue, and others generally accept, a connection between transition relevance and speaker change. But no distributional confirmations of this connection have been attempted. Should we wish to calculate a distributional connection between transition relevance and speaker change, we encounter the technical difficulty that speakership often does *not* shift at TRPs. For example, consider these two segments in terms of the number of transition-relevance places they may include:

> UTCL F1.7
>
> M: Misty I *do* like him
>   he's a nice young ma:n,
>   but he's a baby.
> D: *He is* ↑not a ↑baby Mother.

> UTCL A10.4:4
>
> J: Well thank you.
>   B- Billy's at swim practice
>   I see:?
> S: Yeah

In each of these instances, the first utterance in the segment shows at least three points of hearable completion—marked here by line breaks on the transcriptions. In each case, however, the entire utterance is spoken without any pause, within a single speaking turn. Therefore, there is no evidence whether *these* speakers perceive transition relevance at the termination of each line.

These examples illustrate the concept's resistance to distributional description.[11] There seem to be indefinitely large numbers of TRPs in any conversation. It seems futile to try to locate all the possible completion points in an encounter. Therefore conversation analysts usually refer to *possible* turn completion in analyses of single instances.

If, however, we select a limited set of moments at which the question of transition relevance becomes especially relevant, the task becomes manageable. Pauses provide such an environment. Speakers frequently do stop speaking when they complete an action. If there ensues no immediate next turn by some other speaker, an inter-turn pause occurs, and a speaking opportunity remains open to both partners.

Telephone partners seem to classify any pause longer than two tenths of a second in terms of its transition relevance. If speakers perform such classification, may observers perform it for tape recorded and transcribed materials? We have, in fact, succeeded in reliably classifying pauses according to transition relevance. To illustrate our procedures for coding the transition relevance of pauses, consider this example, which includes two pauses of equal length just moments apart.

UTCL A21:12

GLORIA:	I just talked to my sister a few minutes ago?=
PAM:	=Yeah
	(0.4)
GLORIA:	pt and I promised her: ·hhh that I would u:m
	(0.4) you know- go over there

The first pause occurs after the acknowledgement token 'Yeah,' which comprises a free-standing turn. This pause occurs at a transition-relevance place. The second pause occurs in the middle of a clause whose content is, at that point, unspecified. This pause is not transition relevant.

In a sample of telephone conversation, we located every pause of two tenths of a second or more[12]—and classified each individual pause in terms of its transition relevance. We predicted that speaker change would not occur following the overwhelming majority of non-transition-relevant pauses.

This analysis forced us to distinguish two categories of transition-relevant pause moments: (1) those in which the prior speaker has selected his or her telephone partner to speak next, and (2) those in which the next turn seems to be up for grabs. The Sacks et al. (1974) model of turn taking provides that a current speaker gets the first opportunity to select a next speaker. If the current speaker has already selected a next speaker, then a pause following a TRP belongs to that selected speaker (Wilson and Zimmerman, 1986, p. 384).

UTCL A10.3:3

R: **Billy**
        (1.0)
B: **That's my na::me**

At this pause speaker R's turn is a complete unit in which B is summoned to attention. During this transition-relevant pause the turn is not "up for grabs" because it has already been assigned to B. In two-party telephone encounters, any clear first pair-part entails other-speaker selection. In these pause environments we predicted speaker change.

The remainder of pauses following transition-relevance places, those not preceded by speaker selection devices, leave speakership up for grabs. We predicted that speaker change would follow these pauses about half the time.

To summarize: we predicted that three combinations of transition relevance and speaker selection devices have differential consequences for speaker changes following pauses. Non-transition-relevant pauses belong to a current (or continuing) speaker; pauses following transition-relevance places do not belong to either speaker, except when current speaker has selected the telephone partner, in which case the pause belongs to that partner.

We classified 1105 telephone pauses according to their transition relevance and further classified transition-relevant pauses in terms of speaker-selection devices. Table 5 shows that sixty percent of these pauses follow transition-relevance places. About one sixth of these follow turn units in which current speaker has selected the other to speak next.[13]

Table 5
Distribution of Pauses by Transition Relevance

TYPE OF PAUSE	FREQUENCY	PER CENT
NTRP (pauses not occurring at transition-relevance places)	446	40
TRP (pauses following transition-relevance-places not preceded by next speaker selection devices)	561	51
TRP-SSD (pauses following TRPs preceded by next speaker selection devices)	98	9
TOTAL PAUSES IN SAMPLE	1105	

We cross-tabulated these three classes of transition-relevance with subsequent occurrences of actual speaker change.[14] Table 6 shows the predicted relationships between transition relevance and speaker change in the environment of telephone pauses. Non-transition-relevant pauses (right column) are rarely followed by speaker change. A non-transition-relevant pause still belongs to the current speaker's turn even though no speech sounds are being produced, because a turn unit remains in progress.

Table 6
Percentage of Pauses By Speaker Change and Transition Relevance

	TRP-SSD (n=98)	TRP (n=561)	NTRP (n=466)
Speaker Changes	12*	51	98+
Previous Speaker Continues	88	49	2-

*Figures represent column percentages.

Table 6 distinguishes two categories of transition-relevant pauses: those that belong to neither telephone speaker (center column), and those in which the previous speaker has selected the partner as next speaker (left column). In 88 percent of the latter instances speaker change follows; but in the former instances, the distribution is nearly fifty-fifty. These findings demonstrate a distributional relationship between transition relevance and speaker change—at least within pause environments (Thomason and Hopper, 1992).

These distributional results support predictions. However, analytic induction demands more than statistical corroboration. We must also ask whether, in exceptional instances, participants orient to the unusual occurrences.

Exceptional Cases: Speaker Change without Transition Relevance

The conclusion that speakers classify pauses' transition relevance is strengthened by analyses of the seven instances in which NTRP pauses ended with speaker change. In six of the seven instances, the pauses occur immediately subsequent to a transition-relevance place followed by a free-standing conjunction. That is, a current speaker reaches a transition-relevance place, then continues by uttering a conjunction such as "so," "and," or "but."

NB:I:6:R:2

EMMA: B*ud*'s goin on a trip here wihth'comp'ny in a
           c-(.) *coupla weeks: so,

⇒   (0.3)

LOTTIE: ·hhh Hey *I* gotta good trip if *he* wantstuh go

Emma's post-TRP conjunction 'so,' just before the marked pause, represents a continuing speaker's new turn unit. That is, at a point when her turn is hearable as complete, Emma begins an additional turn unit with a conjunction.[15]

Lottie, when she does take the next turn in this instance, overrides the non-transition relevance of the pause. She begins her own turn by expressing urgency with 'Hey,' an interjection showing that something has just occurred to her. The suddenness of this new thought explains her override of turn taking rules. Lottie indicates that she is doing something exceptional by beginning a turn at this moment, and she projects that the intrusion will be justified by what follows.[16]

Five of these six next-speakers' turns following a non-transition-relevant pause begin with a lexical item disjunctive from what went before (e.g., the word 'Hey'). Such marking seems useful when beginning a turn at a proscribed location.

Exceptional Cases: Current Speaker Continues after Selecting Other

A second kind of exceptional case is one in which speaker change is expected but does not occur. In most instances the current speaker apparently interprets a silence following a first pair-part as indicating probable disagreement and subsequently volunteers a revised version of the utterance to orient to the preference for agreement (Sacks, 1987, p. 64).

> NB:II:4:R:2
>
> N: **Ken yih wa↑:*lk*?hh**
> ⇒   **(0.3)**
> N: **W'd be too hard for yuh?**

N's turn unit, prior to the marked pause, contains a direct question that would typically be followed by speaker change. But in this instance, N's next turn after the pause reverses the polarity of the first question.[17]

To summarize: A pause may not, in itself, explain how speakers project transition relevance. However, the occurrence of pauses triggers coding options connected to transition relevance. Telephone partners perceive a non-transition-relevant pause as occurring within the turn of the current speaker. Rare exceptions to this principle (1) follow a TRP + conjunction, and (2) are marked as exceptional by the next speaker.

Pauses following transition-relevance places mark the turn as up for grabs. If there is no indication of next-speaker selection in the previous turn unit, speaker change occurs half the time. If, at a-post TRP pause, the previous turn unit has included speaker selection, then the partner does speak next in almost nine of ten cases. If current speaker selects next, pauses, then takes another turn, that next turn shows orientation to the partner's failure to speak. These instances display no violation of turn-taking rules, but rather show speakers pursuing interactive negotiations.

Turn Beginnings and Inter-Turn Pauses: An Exploration

Table 4 supports suspicion that the turn-systemics are more efficient with overlap than with inter-turn pausing. More than one turn in four begins after a gap, and most of these gaps are lengthy. How can we accommodate these facts to the Sacks et al. model? Two possibilities are:

(1) Inter-turn pauses are deployed in orderly ways within action trajectories such as disagreements (Pomerantz, 1984a; Sacks, 1987). On this view, inter-turn pauses mark turn transitions as problematic.

(2) Pauses may show little besides lapses in turn taking systematics. If these pauses are frequent, we may question the Sacks et al. model's predictive power.

We argue below that most inter-turn pauses do display marking of disagreement and other action trajectories. This can be shown in the details of the twenty-eight pauses in our random sample of one hundred turn beginnings. These pauses mark interaction trajectories such as disagreement or repair.

Disagreements. Twelve of the twenty-eight pauses in the sample (mean length 0.7 seconds; speaker change on seven) occur after first pair-parts in which either (a) the second part shows disagreement with the first, or (b) the current speaker continues after the gap, showing orientation to possible disagreement. The use of pauses with other delaying objects in such environments has been described in terms of preferences for agreement and contiguity (Sacks, 1987; Pomerantz, 1984a). Agreements are preferred/unmarked in these sequential environments, so these inter-turn pauses mark disagreement:[18]

UTCL F1.5:50

	D:	*Dee* **has it hh**
⇒		**(0.3)**
	M:	**We:ll I think Dee gave it to Da:ddy.**

UTCL A32.3:64

	GORDON:	**Oh that's good.**
⇒		**(0.2)**
	DAWN:	**Yeah. It's kind of- expensive**

Repairs and Newsmarks. Another five of our twenty-eight inter-turn pauses occur just before NTRIs and newsmarks (mean duration 0.3 seconds; speaker change in all cases). Schegloff et al. (1977) argue that a speaker of a "repairable" is entitled to the first two repair opportunity slots: during the turn unit of the repairable, and just afterward. Next-turn repair initiation occurs only after these two opportunities have expired. Therefore, these instances also mark special speakers' trajectories and do not disconfirm the Sacks et al. model:

UTCL A21:52 [ntri]

GLORIA: ...anyway so what's been going on did you have
           today and tomorrow off
⇒   (0.4)
PAM: Have I done anything what?
GLORIA: I said do you have toda:y and tomorrow off

Two instances precede newsmarks that behaved something like NTRIs.[19]

UTCL A10.2:57 [newsmark]

JES: I didn't even see him
⇒   (0.8)
SKE: Oh really
JES: Yeah

To summarize: Seventeen of the twenty-eight inter-turn pauses in our sample of one hundred turn beginnings marked a speaker's disagreeing, repair-
ing, or marking news. In other words, two thirds of our sample of pauses can
be explained in terms of sequential phenomena consonant with the Sacks et
al. model.

The remaining one third of the pauses (one tenth of total number of turn
beginnings) are *not* accounted for by these means. What are speakers doing
in these instances? These pauses seem to occur after the end of some action
or episode unit and before the beginning of something else: Informally, we
label these post episode-completion pauses.

Post Episode-Completion Pauses. (n = 11; mean length 0.5 seconds, 7 of the 11
show current speaker continuing after the pause). These cases may have in
common that some interactive trajectory or business has run its course. The
next speaker begins a new line of activity.

UTCL A21:52

GLORIA: I'm back
PAM: Okay
⇒   (0.2)
GLORIA: Anyway...

This instance occurs just after a break in the phone call. Gloria has put Pam
on hold to answer a call waiting summons. Gloria announces her return with
'I'm back.' Pam's 'Okay' ratifies the resumption. A brief re-beginning sequence has then been completed. After a pause Gloria begins another turn
with 'Anyway,' a token announcing that what follows is not coherent with
what has gone before. The pause divides a completed action from the start

of a new action. In the next instance, the pause is followed by the last speaker making a gesture to continue:

UTCL A24.9

	MIMI:	I don't know what happened myself I don't think I was lookin when it happened except I knew he'd fa:llen
⇒		(0.7)
	MIMI:	And u:m
	JAN:	Well I didn't know if he'd fallen or fainted

Mimi begins her second turn with a conjunction. Then she says 'And u:m' and Jan takes the next turn. Our present focus, however, is the pause marked by the arrow. Mimi says something that may be worthy of response, but which neither selects the partner to speak nor compels a particular response. No response occurs, so Mimi shows readiness to resume her turn. Jan takes this resumption as a prompt that if she is to respond to the last utterance before the pause, the present moment is her last opportunity. Perhaps the fact that this override of turn-taking procedures, and the fact that it produces no further turn contention or aftershock, may show that the pause marked by the arrow represents an interactional problem for the encounter.[20]

To summarize: most inter-turn pauses show speakers *doing* something. These pauses are therefore not lapses in turn taking, but uses of turn-taking rules to make silence accomplish interactive work. These results combine with the statistical associations between transition relevance and speaker change to support the principle that speakers minimize gaps.

Conclusions

How do telephone partners figure out when it is appropriate to begin a turn? First, each current speaker projects the completion of each turn unit's syntax-for-conversation. It seems that telephone partners periodically analyze each utterance-in-progress for hearable completeness as an action. Pauses make relevant such analyses, the fruits of which show in patterns of speakership. We find these relationships between transition relevance and speaker change:

(1) Participants usually limit speaker changes to pauses following transition-relevance places.

(2) Half of the pauses following transition-relevance places in telephone conversation are ended when the current speaker continues—unless the prior turn unit includes speaker-selection.

(3) Speaker change following non-transition-relevant pauses is rare, and speakers treat this event as exceptional when it occurs. Most

exceptional occurrences occur after a TRP and a free-standing conjunction by a continuing speaker.

(4) Gaps in conversation occur frequently. About two thirds of gaps
mark actions such as disagreements and repairs. Most others follow
an action's completion.

Both these crosstabulations and the analyses of exceptional instances confirm the Sacks et al. (1974) model of transition relevance. Future research
may extend the generality of these results.

Our data do not include all possible phenomena related to pauses and
transition relevance. For example, the following instance shows a second
speaker completing the utterance of a first speaker following a pause.

UTCL A10.14

	JESS:	Did you guys go *out* or wh*a*t.
	RICK:	Yeah
	JESS:	U:h
⇒	RICK:	We um (0.6)
	JESS:	Cruised six street so you could get att*a*cked by gi:rls

Jessie takes the floor after a pause that clearly belongs to Rick and she does
so to complete his turn. Lerner (1989) has demonstrated some details of the
structuring of such instances. Is it mere chance that no such instance fell
within our sample, or are most sentence completions pauseless?

The fact that pauses following transition relevance places (and *not* preceded by speaker selection devices) are followed by speaker change just half
the time suggests these questions: Are there variables associated with the
difference between these two outcomes? Are there speech objects that distinguish post-TRP pauses eventuating in speaker change from those in which
current speaker resumes? And are telephone pauses different from face-to-
face pauses in these respects?

Acoustic properties of pauses and of immediate preceding speech also
merit further investigation. Local and Kelly (1986, p. 195) argue that speakers
use glottal closures or stops, maintained through a "holding" pause, to
indicate that the speaker wants to continue the turn after the pause. Speakers
use "trail-off" pauses (with hearable out-breathing, lower stress, and sound
stretching prior to the pause), to indicate transition relevance.

Finally, the present research suggests macro considerations that may affect
speaker change. All our instances of non-transition-relevance place violations occurred in conversations between comembers of nuclear families.[21] It
may be that such violations are more likely to occur between intimates. Such
an argument would be congruent with Zahn's (1984) claim that next-turn
repair initiation is more frequent among persons with relational history than

it is during initial encounters. However, research on this issue is subject to cautions expressed in the next chapter.

How does the Sacks et al. model fare in accounting for the facts of inter-turn pausing as revealed in these data? As the model specifies, speakers orient to transition relevance of pauses, and most exceptions may be described in terms of known features of adjacency pair organization.

The number of pauses between turns raises questions about projectability of turn-completions. The Sacks et al. model explains most pauses in a parsimonious manner that allows us to hold to the thermos analogy. However, the model's stunning account of overlap may be stronger than its reasonably satisfying account of inter-turn gap.

In the next chapter we consider instances of speech overlap. These provide further support for the Sacks et al. model's account of overlap. However there remain bitter debates about what participants are doing with speech overlap, and how instances of speech overlap may show competition and power.

(UTCL F1.7:2)
((MOTHER-DAUGHTER ENCOUNTER, IN
PROGRESS))

	D:	We have nothing to talk about that's
		(1.0) ⌈int
	M:	⌊relevant ·hh Sa⌈:y.
	D:	⌊intellectual.
5	M:	What are you goin be doing March twenty
		fi:rst.
		(0.9)
	D:	·hhhh Well ↑I ↑don:t ↑kno:w Mother lemme
		check my calendar ↑I don't know what I'm
10		gonna ⌈be doing
	M:	⌊*I* need: *t*wo more people to do: *pho*ning
		for Phil Gramm.
		(0.3)
	D:	I: am not v*o*ting for Phil Gramm. I'm not
15		working for the ma:n I don't- (0.2) like him.
	M:	Why not
	D:	Because ↑I ↑just ↑don'*t* no:w you find
		somebody else, I'm not v*o*ting- I am- ·hh
		twenty-thr*ee* years old and I can v*o*te- for
20		who I *w*ant to now.
		(0.5)
	D:	You can't *ma*ke me you can't make me you
		can't make ⌈me.
	M:	⌊There's a little orange marmalade
25		in there- okay I just thought maybe you might
		li:ke to. He's v*e*ry intelligent and he's been
		in Congress for a long ⌈ti:me
	D:	⌊Mother:- *you* like him
		because he's a D*e*mocrat and he turned
30		R*e*publican you'd vote for- (0.7)
	M:	Well *l*isten (.) if- (0.2) if *he* win:s the:-
		n- u::h (0.3) *nom*ination for the:
		·hhhhhhhhh to run for Senator on the
		Republican ticket then will you vote for him?
35	D:	·hhhh I don't know?

		(0.5)
	M:	·hh Well see it's between he and Mossbacher.
		⌈And if he-
	D:	⌊I *like* Mossbacher.
40	M:	Well I know but if Mossbacher doesn't
		get the nomination ⌈if-
	D:	⌊I kno:w what you're
		sayin- I don't know if I'll vote for him or
		not.
45		(0.2)
	D:	I don't *particu'*rly like the man.
	M:	·hhhhh Well what do you kn*ow* about him.
	D:	We:ll? (0.3) I've just s*een* him and I
		don't know if I ↑like him or not.
50		(1.4)
	M:	pt ·hhhhhh We:ll=
	D:	=I may vote- (0.2) s- a str*ai*ght Democratic
		tick*et* hh
		(1.0)
55	M:	Well
	D:	*h*hh
	M:	Whatever turns you o:n.
	D:	*H*uh huh ·*h*hhhhhh You are s*u*ch a d-
		·hhhhhhhhhh hh ⌈You'd vote for- (1.7)
60	M:	⌊I-
	M:	What.
	D:	You'd vote for- (0.4) *hh*h the *de*vil if he was
		Republican.
	M:	·h No I wouldn't *I-* I did get a real nice
65		letter from u:h- M*o*ssbacher h*e* was the
		sp*ea*ker at the Republican L*a*dies Club last
		week ⌈I didn
	D:	⌊*Why* don't you like Mossbacher
	M:	·hhhh- Misty I *do* like him he's a n*i*ce
70		young man but he's a b*a*by.
	D:	*He* is not a ↑ba:by ⌈Mother:?
	M:	⌊He *is* a baby thi- he's
		just runnin th*i*s time to get his *na*me out He-
		he doesn't have- (0.4) have any idea that
75		⌈he's gonna win this
	D:	⌊W e :: l l I agree:: I- I agree, but you

```
                        gotta start somewhe:re.
        M:              Well that's fi:ne. (0.2) ⌈but-
        D:                                      ⌊That's what they
 80                     were sayin about Mark White a- (0.2) few
                        years ago now look where he ⌈is.
        M:                                          ⌊Hey did you see
                        his pla::ne?
                            (0.4)
 85     D:              Who
        M:              Mark White.
        D:              Oh Mark White makes me s: ⌈i c k .
        M:                                        ⌊Did you see his
                        three and a half million dollar jet?
 90     D:              ⌈N : o : .
        M:              ⌊that's outfitted like a cadilla:c?
        D:              Oh yeah, yeah ·hhhh u:h- hh he makes me ill.
                            (1.2)
        M:              We:ll- maybe we better not talk about
 95                     politics (1.3) while we're ⌈being recorded
        D:                                         ⌊Well I-
                            (1.4)
        M:              We:ll. hh anyway I need somebody
        D:              ·hh W- We:ll I need to go:.
                            ((Call continues for five minutes))
```

TURN BEGINNINGS, SPEECH OVERLAP, AND INTERRUPTION

Floor Access as Power

In the duet, "Vote for the devil," a mother and daughter argue about politics. These telephone partners compete in a number of ways during this scene— including competition for the floor. One way that this competition shows is in fifteen instances of speech overlap in the segment's forty-five speaker changes. The present chapter sketches relationships between speech overlap and competition for telephone speaking time.

The Sacks et al. model of turn taking specifies that one party speaks at a time, which of course is an idealization. Speakers frequently speak in over- lap—every time you see a transcript bracket, two people speak at the same time. Most overlaps are brief and occur near transition-relevance places. This argument has received stunning empirical support (Jefferson, 1986).

One extension of the finding that speakers avoid overlap is to argue that certain speakers repeatedly take power from other speakers by overlapping into turn units in progress. Particularly, it has been argued that men interrupt women by means of intrusive speech overlap. This is a serious charge, and one that touches the place of speaking in sexual politics. Telephone dyads provide a prime location to test these notions—uncomplicated by visual context or third parties.

We have studied telephone conversation in search of interruptive overlap. We found numerous competitive speech events like 'You'd vote for the devil,' but we have not been able to replicate previous findings about inter- ruptive overlap. We detail these (largely negative) results in the present chapter because contrary findings have received widespread attention in both scholarly and popular writings about language and power. We also provide a cautionary anecdote on when researchers may count speech ob- jects. The last chapter includes successful quantitative analyses, but in this chapter similar methods are shown to produce little insight and to lead to important misconceptions. To show these findings and issues, we must review previous studies of speech overlap.

Speech Overlap and Transition Relevance

Speech overlap can be interpreted as a clash, or as contention for finite floor time. Some investigators relate speech overlap to speaker power. The relay race analogy associated with Figure 7 (chapter 5) calls attention to the possibility of brief overlap at turn exchange. In sprint relays, the norm for excellent performance specifies a brief period of overlap when both racers hold the baton. Speaking turns, by contrast, are built to avoid overlap. Still, it is not unusual for speakers to experience brief inter-turn overlap:

> UTCL A24.9
>
> MIMI: Al:right but you'll ca:ll and ⌈come by:?
> JAN: ⌊Yea:h-
> ↑Yea:h make sure- *t*ell Pawpa I hope he feels better.

Mimi's turn completion overlaps the next speaker's utterance. But Jan does not argue with Mimi, nor does she interrupt her. Rather, she agrees with Mimi, and their turn exchange overlaps a bit. Such instances show that overlaps cluster at moments of possible completion. In the above instance, Jan could easily hear Mimi's utterances as coming to an end at the word 'call.' Jan answers at an appropriately projected moment, but her turn happens to begin in overlap with Mimi's continuing speech.

Overlaps like this one, occurring within a syllable or two of a transition-relevance place, are commonplace in telephone conversation. Our study of one hundred turn beginnings located twelve overlaps,[1] all beginning within two syllables of a transition-relevance place. Most overlaps are brief (eleven of our twelve last a single syllable) and cause little communicative difficulty. These routine overlaps reveal the normal processes of turn taking that produce them. The performance details of these instances also show how speakers deal with overlap's vulnerabilities.

A speaker may maximize chances of getting the floor by beginning as soon as a current turn may be projected to end. Such an early beginning will overlap any current turn whose speaker does not end quite as soon as expected. If a current speaker stretches a sound to minimize gap, the next speaker may overlap the stretched final word.

> UTCL F1.7 139
>
> D: Oh Mark White makes me s: ⌈i c k.
> M: ⌊Did you see his three
> and a half million dollar je:t?

UTCL A21 573

PAM: Wuh how quee⌈r::.
GLORIA: ⌊Yes. Tell me queer.

These next speakers begin at a projected point of completion that happens to
overlap the stretched ending. Speakers seem little inconvenienced by these
brief overlaps, which usually pass by unremarked.

Overlap also occurs when a current speaker tags additional material onto
the end of an already complete utterance as next speaker self-selects at a
transition-relevance place.

UTCL A24.9

PAW: Well that was a rwonderful weekend
            uh J- ⌈Jan
JAN: ⌊Goo:d I'm glad you enjoyed it.

This current speaker, Pawpa, delivers a compliment. After slight hesitation,
he appends the name of his recipient. Meanwhile, that recipient, Jan, projecting transition relevance at the end of the word 'weekend,' becomes next
speaker with the word 'Good.' This first word overlaps the prior speaker's
added term of address. Here is a similar instance:

UTCL D8

CAROL: Should be around nine⌈or so
⇒   RICK: ⌊Well do you have an extra
            bed in your- in your uh (.) place?

Carol's turn is hearable as complete at the word 'nine.' Rick chooses that
moment to begin a turn. However, Jan continues by tagging on 'or so,' and
overlap results.

A related phenomenon occurs when current speaker self-selects for an
additional turn unit, while next speaker begins a turn (Jefferson, 1986, pp.
154-57).

UTCL F1.7

M: Well see it's between he and Mossbacher.
M: ⌈And if he-
D: ⌊I like Mossbacher.

In this instance, M comes to a point of possible completion at the end of the
first line. D responds at the transition-relevance place, but at the same instant
M begins an additional turn unit. At this point, speech overlap occurs. The

continuing speaker drops out, cutting off the drop-out clause before bringing it to a completion to show that she drops out due to the overlap. Such unilateral dropping out is the most common way for overlapping speakers to adapt to overlap. But speakers may also "go competitive" by increasing volume, or restarting (Schegloff, 1990). The continuing speaker does not always drop out in such cases. Jefferson (1986) argues there is no consistent pattern of who drops out, or who "wins" an overlap.

Turn beginners are vulnerable to beginning in near overlap with another turn beginner.

> UTCL A21: 413
> ((GLORIA ACCOUNTS FOR REFUSING
> PAM'S INVITATION.))

GLORIA:	... we're gun take the little *girl* to get her something to *eat* and some *ice* cream or summ' (.)
PAM:	O:: [:h how cu::::*te*]
GLORIA:	[So plus I have t-]
	(0.2)
GLORIA:	Plus I have to *type* this *s*tupid...

This fragment opens with Gloria as current speaker. Upon her apparent completion, Pam attempts a turn beginning. Since Pam starts first, shouldn't she have turn rights? Perhaps, but the frequency of near-simultaneous starts at transition suggests that a speaker about to begin a turn "is in a 'blind spot.' He no longer is in recipient orientation but initiating speakership" (Jefferson, 1986, p. 164). Given the normal overlap-vulnerabilities sketched above, speakers have evolved devices to minimize overlap-related problems.

Guarding against Overlap Vulnerabilities

Two ways that next speakers build the beginnings of turns so as to minimize negative consequences of overlap are the *pre-placed appositional* and the *recycled turn beginning*. The first of these begins a turn with an unnecessary filler (e.g., like, well, maybe), a word that does not carry much meaning. Such an item secures the turn, but if it gets lost in overlap the turn suffers little loss:

> UTCL D8

| CAROL: | Should be around *nine* [or so] |
| ⇒ RICK: | [Well] do you have an extra *bed* in your- in your uh (.) place? |

In this instance little information is lost due to overlap. Rick's first word, 'well,' takes the floor but commits to very little. And if the first word 'well' cannot be heard due to overlap, almost no information is lost. Here is a similar instance:

UTCL A21 857

PAM: O my Go: ⌈:d
GLORIA: ⌊Like I won't even know the address...

Here, Gloria begins her next turn at a reasonable moment, a moment at which Pam's current turn (an exclamation with an expletive) can be expected to end. Pam stretches the expletive and it occurs in overlap with Gloria's first word. However, as if in anticipation of just such a problem, Gloria begins her turn with a semantically empty first word, 'like.' So the overlap does little harm. Schegloff (1987b, p. 88) refers to initial items like "well," "but," "so," or "you know" as pre-placed appositionals or prefatory "overlap absorbers." These beginnings minimize gap and prevent some possible negative consequences of overlap. They provide an overlappable beginning to a turn, and also allow the earliest possible beginning for the turn. The pre-placed appositional begins a turn without committing to a particular course for the turn-in-progress.[2]

Turn beginners also guard against overlap using the recycled turn beginning:

Schegloff, 1987b, p. 75 ((face-to-face))

R: ...he's been in the hospital for a few days, right?
          Takes a ⌈bout a week to grow a culture⌉
K: ⌊I don' think they grow a ⌋
          I don't think they grow a culture to do a biopsy.

Speaker K begins a turn to answer R's question; K has a right to the turn-space. Yet as it happens, R restarts just before K's turn beginning.[3] K begins in overlap with the added unit of the previous speaker. Several words get spoken in overlap, as speaker R does not drop out, but instead concludes a turn unit. As soon as R stops speaking, K recycles the turn beginning uttered so far—thus showing orientation to both R's overlap and to the moment that it stopped. Recycled turn beginnings display a

> remarkably precise relationship between the end of a prior turn and the emergence of the new turn from the overlap and the beginning of the recycle. (Schegloff, 1987b, p. 75)

Many brief recycles occur when the second speaker makes a reasonable projection of the prior's turn completion.

UTCL A24.7

MIMI: Al:right but you'll ca:ll and ⌈come by:?
JAN: ⌊Yea:h-
JAN: Yea:h make sure- *t*ell Pawpa I hope he feels
           better.

In this instance, Mimi's turn is hearable as complete at the word 'call,' and
Jan answers affirmatively. As it happens, however, Mimi continues her turn
in overlap with the answer. Jan copes by recycling 'yeah.'

A recycle begins at the actual end of the prior speaker's turn—hence at the
end of the speech overlap. This demonstrates that the speaker has attended
to the fact that the prior speaker has continued to talk, projects the end of that
talk, and begins the recycle at that moment. Schegloff argues that this shows
a "second order relevance of the orientation to the minimization of gap and
overlap" (1987b, p. 75). That is, when speakers fail to achieve no overlap they
do not have to declare a communication breakdown, but may carry on to
achieve a subsequent restart without gap or overlap.

To summarize: Overlaps are, as Sacks et al. claim, relatively common, quite
brief, and utterly routine. Many overlaps do not indicate communicative
difficulties; in fact speakers seem to deal with them habitually, often collaboratively, and almost below consciousness. These overlaps are normal
troubles for which the human conversational ecology routinely compensates
in objects like recycled turn beginnings and pre-placed appositionals. It is
against this background that we must consider claims that certain speakers
routinely interrupt each other using speech overlap.

Not all speech overlap represents competition for the floor—though some
of it undoubtedly does. Consider the overlaps in the "Vote for the devil"
episode, in which overlaps are plentiful. Are M and D interrupting each
other, or competing for turn time as well as arguing politics?

Competing at Turn Beginnings

Sacks et al. (1974) conceptualize speaking turns as scarce resources. Because
only one person speaks at a time, there is potential for one telephone partner
to hog the floor time. Speakers may be collaborative in their overlap management but sometimes display competition for the floor.

The recycled turn beginning appears to bid for the listener's attention,[4]
revealing a next speaker's weapon in such competition. Schegloff claims that
recycles are used almost entirely by speakers who overlap current speakers,
not by continuing speakers. In a battle for floor time, the arsenal of the
current speaker includes rushing through to an added turn unit, or adding
additional tag-elements (Schegloff, 1987b, p. 77). There is a natural balance
among these devices.

Schegloff (1990) proposes that when turn-initial overlap occurs, its resolution must be worked through by participants on the scene. We cannot predict the basis upon which any overlap gets resolved; rather these details must be worked out on the local scene. Schegloff proposes that participants process feedback about an ongoing overlap, bit by bit, or beat by beat. At each beat speakers may drop out, continue as before, or go competitive.

There is delicate mix of competition and collaboration in speakers' interactive floor management. Because the floor seems to be a scarce resource, turn distribution carries micro-political consequences. Contention for the floor may be an environment for accomplishing power. One may take power at another's expense by beginning a turn without waiting for a transition-relevance place. This results in *interruptive speech overlap*. West and Zimmerman (1983) argue that powerful persons repeatedly interrupt the turns of other speakers: especially, men interrupt women more than vice versa. Let us unpack this claim, which grows from Sacks' lectures, and from Sacks et al. (1974).

Sacks (Fall 1967, lecture 3, pp. 9-11) notes that a next speaker may correctly project an utterance completion but subsequently appear to have made a mistake, because the previous speaker can add to the prior utterance.

> A guy asks a question. The next speaker doesn't answer the question but starts
> something else. It's obvious from the first two words that he's starting up
> something else. . . . The first speaker then 'continues' by adding a second part to
> the question; making, then, the person who talks after him, not merely not an
> answerer of his question but an interrupter of his utterance . . .
>
>   A: Is she coming?
>   B: I went ⌈ to-
>   A: ⌊ or should we start without her.

In Sacks' instance, competition begins when B's turn beginning does not respond to A's question. Speaker A's question anticipates a response. However, B's next utterance shows in its first syllable or two that it will not provide an answer, but may instead do something else. A forestalls this move by B, and re-asserts his question-agenda by "adding" an additional clause to the "original" question. Thus A makes it appear that B's turn beginning had been interruptive of A's continuing turn.

Following Sacks, researchers have attempted to find instances of interruptive overlap and to relate such instances to extrinsic indicators of power or status—such as maleness or organizational position. Abandoning the complexities of Sacks' instance, most investigators define interrupting as speech overlap in which a next speaker usurps a current speaker's turn-in-progress (West, 1979; Kennedy and Camden, 1983; West and Zimmerman, 1983; Zimmerman and West, 1975; Dindia, 1987; Roger, 1989). Taken together, these studies argue that there is a countable phenomenon, *interruptive overlap*. In the UTCL collection we have not been able to replicate the existence of interruptive overlap using such a definition. Because we cannot corroborate this definition, we cannot confirm or deny claims that certain parties (e.g., males) repeatedly interrupt others (females). This position puzzles me, for power and interruption must be related in some way, and it seems likely that men do interrupt women. Yet this has not yet been shown, and perhaps it cannot be shown, in studies that tabulate interruptive overlaps.

We discuss this problem in terms of studies by Zimmerman and West, which have most explicitly specified their empirical procedures for identifying instances of interruption. Their notion of interruptive overlap is depicted in Figure 8. This model resembles the one used to depict normal turn exchange in chapter 5. According to this model, speaker A is producing an utterance (time 1) when B begins to speak in overlap (time 2). Speaker A subsequently relinquishes the floor (time 3) and B completes the turn alone (time 4). Speaker B has interrupted speaker A. On this analysis, the interrupting party is powerful.

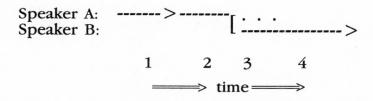

Figure 8: Interruption as a Subclass of Overlap

West and Zimmerman argue that men interrupt women more than vice versa. They support this claim in two studies: A first study (1975) examined instances from diverse social settings, and a second study (1983) utilized tape recordings of initial meetings of pairs of students. In both studies, men performed more interruptions than women.[5] West and Zimmerman's claim entails their successful isolation of a representative sample of all interruptions. It is certainly plausible that certain speech overlaps (those not explained as normal brief overlap earlier in this chapter) may be taken provisionally as interruptive.[6]

West and Zimmerman argue that an interruption is a speech overlap displaying next speaker's deep intrusion into an current speaker's turn (1975, p. 523). Operationally, a "deep interruption" must satisfy two criteria:

(1) The overlap must begin at least two syllables from any transition-relevance place in the current turn unit.

(2) The overlapping utterance must not support or facilitate the current speaker's utterance (1983, p. 104).

West and Zimmerman choose the two syllable criterion to eliminate from consideration normal overlaps near TRPs. Sacks' example (above, p. 126) qualifies as interruptive to West and Zimmerman's criteria *if* you begin with B's turn, and hence consider A as interrupting B.

B:	I went ⌈to-
A:	⌊or should we start without her.

This seems a clear case given just these two turns. B speaks two syllables before the overlap, and A is not being facilitative. Therefore, according to West and Zimmerman's criteria, A has interrupted B. However, Sacks appears to read his example the other way around. Here is the entire instance again:

A:	Is she coming?
B:	I went ⌈to-
A:	⌊or should we start without her.

Given all three utterances, Sacks describes A's pretense to pursue one consistent question, and this pretense depicts B's (competitive) attempt to change directions as having interrupted A's single turn unit.

A lesson from this instance: most competition has at least two active parties, each of whom is likely to make more than one competitive move. Therefore, to code any instance as simply "A interrupts B" is to ignore all moves by the noninterrupting party. West and Zimmerman's definition of interruption only considers the actor who begins to speak in overlap. It does not capture any of the interactive tug-of-war that makes competition competitive. Perhaps West and Zimmerman's results show power asymmetries in part because their definition of interruption regards only one speaker at one moment in time.

The West and Zimmerman definition does quite rigorously exclude a number of instances of normal overlap from the category of deep interruption because they occur too close to a transition-relevance place:

UTCL A21.573

PAM:	Wuh how quee⌈r::.
GLORIA:	⌊Yes. Tell me queer.

This instance fails on the two-syllable criterion, and it should. Unfortunately, the two-syllable criterion might exclude some turn transitions that actually are competitive:

UTCL F1.7

M:	He's very intelligent and he's been in Congress for a long ⌈ti:me
D:	⌊Mother:- you like him because he's a Democrat and he turned Republican

These two speakers are competing head-to-head, in turn-space and in content. D's rejoinder competes with M's assertion, dismissing its contentions and accusing M of crass partisan politics. However, West and Zimmerman cannot consider this instance as an interruption because they have, for excellent if arbitrary reasons, excluded overlaps near TRPs.

To summarize: the two-syllable criterion makes a good guess about the location of interruptive turn beginnings. It excludes, however, certain events we might study further. West and Zimmerman's problems deepen when we consider their second criterion, that an interruption must not be facilitative.

In the following instances (which do satisfy the two-syllable criterion) the overlaps are not competitive, but facilitative. Hence West and Zimmerman would not code these instances as interruptive, and I agree.

> UTCL J10.1
>
> A: You can wr ⌈ite requis ⌈itions
> K: ⌊Yeah   ⌊Right

> UTCL J10.1
> K: ...the vendor can always invoice for less you
>   don't ⌈ ha:ve ⌉ to pay for everything you=
> A: ⌊ Right ⌋

West and Zimmerman exclude facilitative overlaps mainly to exclude brief acknowledgements, which are often spoken in overlap. Drummond (1989) notes that some earlier studies (Meltzer et al., 1971; Wiens et al., 1965) have failed to exclude facilitative overlaps. To illustrate the distributional importance of this exclusion, Drummond examined a recording and transcript of a thirty-minute (face-to-face) business conversation and found that 82 of 102 overlaps were brief supportive statements.

However, West and Zimmerman also exclude as facilitative those cases when the overlapping next speaker says virtually the same thing as the continuing speaker. This corollary raises problems in instances that provide more than acknowledgement tokens. Drummond considers this instance that meets both of West and Zimmerman's criteria.

> UTCL A21
> GLORIA REPORTS AN ENCOUNTER WITH A FORMER BOYFRIEND WHO HAS A PAIR OF HER EARRINGS.
>
> GLORIA: ·hhhh »that's what I s(h)aid I said well
>   ⌈you can send em to me now« huh ⌉
> ⇒ PAM: ⌊You probably wouldn't just say⌋ bring em in
>   person or something

Drummond observes that this utterance qualifies as interruptive according to West and Zimmerman's criteria. The overlap occurs more than two syllables from a transition-relevance place and does not say the same thing as the prior. However, Pam clearly agrees with Gloria's assessment of the situation, and so her utterance seems more an enthusiastic expression of support than a one-up power move.

To summarize: the "facilitative" category proves problematic for classifying candidate interruptions. If we adopt a definition of "facilitative" broad enough to include the last instance above, then many instances fail to qualify as interruptive. If weaker criteria are used, the concept of interruption seems watered down, less related to speaker power and competition.

Gloria manages to complete her utterance in overlap, so she is not driven from the floor by Pam's talk. Are some overlaps more successful than others? Roger (1989) argues that it is important to distinguish between *successful* and *unsuccessful* interruptions. Here is an apparently successful interruption:

> UTCL F1.7
>
> M: Well I ⌈hope
> D: ⌊O:h- I want you to ca::ll- Chester Farrell
>   for me

Here D overlaps M, who then stops her turn in mid-unit. Unsuccessful interruption occurs when the current speaker continues and thwarts the overlapper's attempt to begin a turn:

> UTCL F1.7
>
> M: Well- maybe we better not talk about poli*tics*
>   (1.3) while we're ⌈being recorded
> D: ⌊Well I-

M continues speaking after D's overlap attempt, which D abandons. Roger is certainly correct to note that these two events have different consequences. However, it probably is too simple to merely distinguish success from failure in overlap-attempts; and it is certainly too simple to confine the success judgment to the two turns in which overlap occurs. What if a recently-overlapped speaker later repeats an utterance, seemingly ignoring overlap? Was the interruption still a success?

Is a success/failure dichotomy sufficient to represent the various paths that competitive overlap events may take? Here are some overlap-elicited trajectories that occur in the same encounter as the last two instances, which is the duet before the current chapter. In the next instance the current (interrupted) speaker finishes the current turn and thus avoids any appearance of being driven from the floor.

UTCL F1.7

M: He doesn't have- (0.4) have any idea that
⌈he's gonna win this ⌉
D: ⌊W e : l l   I a ⌋gree:: I- I agree: but you
gotta start somewhe:re.

This appears at first blush to be a successful overlapping interruption. D begins in the middle of M's turn unit and continues talking longer than M does. However M does manage to continue speaking for five more syllables and to bring her turn to an orderly conclusion. D orients to M's completion by recycling her turn beginning after M's completion. Hence D's interruption attempt neither succeeds nor fails, but ends in sort of a stand-off.

In the same encounter, here is an instance in which the current speaker seems to get interrupted successfully if you just consider the current and next turn. However, the interrupted speaker retaliates in next turn to re-assert what had been cut off.

UTCL F1.7

D: We have nothing to talk about that's
(1.0) ⌈int
M: ⌊relevant ·hh Sa⌈:y.
D: ⌊intellectual.
M: What are you goin be doing March twenty fi:rst.

M attempts to complete D's utterance, and her suggested completer, 'relevant,' overlaps D's own attempt to continue, and drives her from the floor. M therefore interrupts D (according to West and Zimmerman's criteria), and does so successfully (according to Roger). M then begins a new turn unit with 'say,' but D cuts her off to recycle her own former completion: 'intellectual.' Does this recycling of D's turn completion vitiate M's interruptive success? While this recycle ('intellectual') overlaps M's 'Say,' it cannot be considered a deep interruption due the two-syllable criterion.

Ignoring D's recompletion, M counters at next turn by continuing the abrupt topic-shift prefigured by 'Say.' This is perhaps the most competitive turn in the exchange, but it displays no speech overlap. Surely this exchange shows power struggle, but if we carve up the event looking only for instances of interruptive overlap we find only a crude tally: Mother 1, Daughter 0, which obscures most our current description. The description of competitive speech events may be seriously unspecified by counting interruptive overlaps.

Any focused tabulation of interruption events misses precisely the character of competition unfolding-in-time. At the point where we left M and D, the competition is just heating up. M continues by asking D to help campaign for her favored Senate candidate. D refuses heatedly:

	M:	**What are you goin be doing March twenty fi:rst.**
		(0.9)
1⇒	D:	·hhhh Well ↑I ↑don:t ↑kno:w Mother lemme
		check my calendar ↑I don't know what I'm gonna
		⌈be doing
2⇒	M:	⌊*I need: two* more people to do: *pho*ning for
		Phil Gramm.
		(0.3)
3⇒	D:	I: am not voting for Phil Gramm. I'm not working
		for the ma:n I don't- (0.2) like him.
	M:	Why not
	D:	Because ↑I ↑just ↑don'*t* no:w you find somebody
		else, I'm not voting- I am (.) pt ·hh twenty-
		thr*ee* years old and I can vo*te*- for who I w*a*nt
		to now. (0.5) You can't *m*ake me you can't make me
		you can't make ⌈me
4⇒	M:	⌊There's a little orange marmalade
		in there- Okay I just thought maybe you might
		li:ke to. He's *ve*ry intelligent and he's been in
		Congress for a long ⌈ti:me
5⇒	D:	⌊Mother:- (0.2) you
		like him because he's a D*e*mocrat and he turned
		Re*pu*blican

There is plenty of empowered competition in this instance, competition for the floor, and also competition for persuasive control. Each speaker forwards a project. M wants D to help her Senate candidate. D asserts her political autonomy. In the last two turns (the arrows marked 4 and 5), M and D each play very strong cards. M responds to a D's asserted autonomy not by replying to her at all, but instead speaking *to someone else* about orange marmalade (4⇒)—thus flouting that she is ignoring D. Then M extends her turn to reiterate her prior argument without even addressing D's autonomy issue. D responds (5⇒) by accusing M of blindly partisan politics. Neither of these last two utterances qualify for West and Zimmerman's definition as interruptive, for both fail on the two-syllable criterion! West and Zimmerman could not treat any of this instance's power-battles, except the turn contention:

	D:	↑I ↑don:t ↑kno:w mother lemme check my calendar ↑I
		don't know what I'm gonna ⌈be doing
2⇒	M:	⌊*I need: two* more people
		to do: *pho*ning for Phil Gramm.

Perhaps M's utterance here qualifies as a deep interruption. But is the timing of this utterance the main feature by which it is competitive? Or should we also note that D has just lampooned M's obvious pre-request by saying 'lemme check my calendar' in an ironic tone of voice, and then she begins a second turn unit before M's overlap. Recall that the pre-request had been itself produced as an abrupt, competitive topic shift: tit for tat.

The competition continues as M, in the face of D's resistance, presses her manipulative request. At 3⟹, D strongly refuses: at 4⟹, D finishes an impassioned declaration of her autonomy, and M ignores it completely while she speaks to a copresent person about food. This encounter is rife with power issues. But since there is no overlap at 3⟹ and only one syllable near a TRP at 4⟹, a perspective concentrating on deep overlap has no observations to make about this classic enactment of intergenerational conflict.

M and D fight as dramatically as characters in any poem or movie. If we study language and power by tabulating interruptive overlap, we miss the exquisite competing across many turns that makes their encounter fascinating. That is precisely the sort of simplification required if one insists on counting interruptions to test whether parents (vis-à-vis children) or men (vis-à-vis women) interrupt more. If we follow these dangerous simplifications, we impose arbitrary boundaries for reasons of extrinsic theory, which is like studying wildflowers with a lawnmower (Moerman, 1988, p. 72).

We consider West and Zimmerman in such detail because they provide the most thorough work in this tradition. West and Zimmerman agonize considerably about their operational definition for deep interruption (see 1983, note 4) and go much further than others in specifying details of their procedures. However, they do not question the usefulness of a single operational definition for the concept: interruption.

Drummond (1989) concludes (and I agree) that there may be no stable phenomenon of interruption that is best identified as a subclass of speech overlap. Rather, interruption is a folk-interpretive category that refers to a variety of experiences—some instances of which do not utilize speech overlap. Bennett (1981) notes that certain interruptive experiences may not display speech overlap at all. Perhaps, for instance, to speak to somebody else when your daughter has just passionately asserted her autonomy (3⟹ above) is interruptive whether done in overlap or not.

To focus on a narrow definition of interruption obscures the vital issues of gender and politics that sparked much of the current debate. Here is an educational instance relevant to this point:

> [W]omen found it difficult to deal with the way in which men in their classes acknowledged and built on each other's statements and ignored the women's: a woman student who made a number of critical points in her class analysis only too often found that the man who followed her picked up the discussion where the last man left and what she had worked painfully hard to achieve was made to seem irrelevant and worthless. (Henning and Jardim, 1977, p. 23)

This account describes something that any classroom teacher has observed: a speaker addresses someone other than the immediate prior speaker, thereby ignoring the most recent contribution. This is an important interactional issue, and probably men do such acts to women frequently enough to merit our concern. However, it seems unlikely, given classroom formality, that most of these degrading interruptions utilize speech overlap.

We should not assume that speech overlap is the main tool for accomplishing interruption. The vast majority of speech overlaps actually show the efficiency of the turn-taking system, and not dominance or bad manners on the part of the next speaker. Jefferson (1984) notes that

> at the point of overlap onset the recipient/now-starting next speaker is doing something perfectly proper, perfectly within his rights and obligations as a recipient/next speaker. He is not doing what we commonly understand to be 'interrupting'—roughly, starting up 'in the midst of' another's turn at talk, not letting the other finish. On the other hand, the current speaker is also doing something perfectly proper. He is producing a single turn at talk which happens to have multiple components in it. (p. 6)

Next speakers must project moments of transition relevance somewhat in advance of their occurrence. Telephone partners may only approximately predict timing of transition-relevance places and must mutually adapt to brief gaps and overlaps at turn transitions. The vast majority (perhaps ninety percent) of speech overlaps occur in these ways, which illustrates the robustness of the turn-taking model.

Research on competitive speech overlap does show that:
(1) Some speech overlap far from transition-relevance places is competitive.
(2) Speakers' floor-contention plays a role in power struggles.

We must study these issues one competitive episode at a time, following each struggle's trajectory from first warning of trouble until the issue is resolved or both parties move on to other matters. We have provided an instance of such description in the political dispute between M and D. This approach does not yield a definitive specification of interruption, but it does allow us to consider turn taking infractions in the context of other devices that speakers employ when they struggle with their telephone partners.

Conclusions: Power in Discourse

Feminist and Marxist analyses correctly claim that power enactments show in the small details of communicative interaction (Thompson, 1984). Analyses may eventually lay bare how speakers enact hegemony within details of interaction—against women, minority-group members, poor people, and the like. Conversation analysts have contributions to make in such projects. In the absence of data, it remains tempting to speculate on these issues.

Although the current chapter details a critique of current research on interruptions, our examination of the argument between M and D exemplifies possible paths for analyses about language and power. Such studies can illuminate specific instances of power struggles and specify speech objects by which power is accomplished. Deep overlap is one such device, though much deep overlap is not interruptive, and much interruptive communication does not exhibit deep overlap. We can specify some other conversational objects relevant to language and power.

We have described the **recycled turn beginning** as a next-speaker's weapon against a continuing speaker's turn piracy. The major device for abuse of current speakership is the **rush-through** (Schegloff, 1982), which occurs when a speaker arrives at a transition-relevance place but hurries up the rhythm of discourse just at that point in order to take another turn unit. A current speaker has a tactical advantage at such moments of having the most information about when the turn unit is to end.

UTCL A21:8

GLORIA: **I can't type to start with=**
    =you know how bad I type

UTCL F1.7

D: **I'm not working for the ma:n=**
    =I don't- (0.2) like him.

In these transcriptions latching [=] indicates a TRP that gets rushed through. In the second instance, a hitch slightly after the rush-through may offer a late opportunity for repair or taking back the turn. Rushing-through is commonplace and not always entirely competitive, but if it happens repeatedly, its user may hog the floor. Such extreme cases stand in need of detailed study.

Rush-throughs can be expected to resist quantification for the same reason that transition-relevance places do (see chapter 5): they happen at possible transition-relevance places. Instances of rush-throughs can, however, be described for work done in combination with such features as competitive overlap.

Competition at simultaneous starts. Drummond (1989) recommends studying simultaneous starts. If one speaker finishes a turn, then there is a pause, and then both speakers bid for turns at the same moment, it might be a good measure of power to see who wins these relatively equal contests.

A21:8

GLORIA: **I can't type to start with you know how bad I**
    type
PAM: **Yeah**

GLORIA: You know?
            (0.7)
⇒   GLORIA: ⌈hA:nd-
⇒   PAM: ⌊Well Gloria if I can ever help you *out* on those
            things ⌈you know ⌈you can (c'mon)⌉
GLORIA: ⌊·hhh   ⌊Pam *you* would be⌋ pulling your
            hair out on this oka:y

The two arrows in this instance point to such a location. There has been an apparent running down of a topic, and a pause. Then each party self-selects. Gloria drops out rather quickly in this instance.[7] Supposing that these simultaneous starts often have clear winners, and that such items could be counted, Drummond tabulated them across four encounters and found that they were unevenly distributed in each encounter. He wondered whether this asymmetry might correlate with other measures of dominance, so he counted the number of lines of transcribed speech uttered by each speaker. In each encounter, this total was asymmetrical in the *opposite* direction![8] One moral of this story is to be suspicious of any single indicators of power in discourse. If hegemonic discourse is overdetermined, one would expect power enactments to utilize varieties of speech objects.

Gross measures of the quantity of talk have some promise, if taken with the caveat that no single feature makes up dominance (See O'Barr et al., 1980). Quantitative indices include number of syllables spoken in a given length of time, and syllables per turn. Total speaking time is also of possible interest, since not everybody speaks at the same rate.

Laugh tokens. There are grounds for arguing that getting others to laugh at things you say may have relevance to power. The laughter described in analyses of play (chapter 8) could also be examined in terms of power. For instance, in courtship flirtations, do women laugh more than men? Who speaks the laughable lines? Are there ways to contrast whether you "laugh with" or "laugh at" your telephone partner?

This is a laundry list of some features that could be implicated in analyses of power in telephone conversation. In each case, there are pitfalls proscribing early tabulation of these variables, but some of these problems may eventually submit to quantitative investigation. But even then, the richest paths to analysis of power in discourse are those that make fullest use of the greatest number of details of single episodes in which partners struggle over time. Competitive speech occurs within turn units; but only in rare cases are power struggles primarily *about* turn units.

And still more rarely are power struggles resolved within single turn units, but rather extend across many turn units. We have begun to illustrate analysis of longer episodes, and only such analysis can reveal the micro-politics of power relations. Power struggles continue over time. If we limit inquiry to devices used within single turns, we cannot describe continuing struggles. To further elaborate an approach to longer segments of discourse, we must leave the study of individual speaking turns and move to a larger level of analysis: the trajectory of a communicative episode. That is the goal of the final section of this book.

TRAJECTORIES

*Frame within frame the evolving conversation
is dancelike, as though two could play
at improvising . . .*

Amy Clampitt
"Dancers Exercising"
The Kingfisher

```
                   ((UTCL F1.1: in progress))
       D:          I don't know what to do: because I'm afraid
                   I'll start cryin or somethin
                        (0.2)
       M:          We:ll just try not to: honey she thinks a lot
5                  of you and she would love to see you I'm
                   s u:re.
                        (0.5)
       M:          ·hhhhhhhhhh it's gun be hard to do: I kno:w.
                        (0.6)
10     D:          ↑We:ll (0.3) ·hhhhhhhh hhhh I just don't know
                   what to do:: I get choked up over things like
                   this.
                        (0.3)
       M:          Yeah.
15     D:          I: get choked up over » things like this « I
                   can't- anybody that di:es that I barely even
                   kno:w and ·hhhh I me:an especially fts
                   somebody who I'm gonna be looking at and I
                   know they're gonna be dead in a few months
20                 it's just ·hhhh I don't know what to do: its
                   just horrible.
                        (0.3)
       M:          pt We:ll just go and try to be as cheerful as
                   possible because that seems to be the
25                 attitude that June's taking
                        (0.4)
       D:          ·hhh I know Mother but- maybe I'm jus.(1.1)
       M:          And if you feel yourself- choking up why
                   just- you know kind of excuse yourself an-
30                 (0.7) an just- (0.2) squeeze her ha:nd and
                   tell her how much y- you enjoyed workin u-
                   with her up there that summer and ·hhhhh hhhh
                   you know (1.3) ·hhhh just like tha:t is all
                   ↑I know to tell you to do:,
35                      (1.5)
       M:          It's har:d but they say the worst thing:-
                   (0.2) u:h- (0.6) is when people withdra-aw
```

		from terminally ill (0.2)
	D:	Yeah,
40	M:	people like that you know and- and *don't* talk to em and don't- (0.8) you know just ign*o*re em that's *r*eally ha*rd.
	D:	Yeah,
		(2.2)
45	M:	↓S:o do y*o*u wanna go to u::h (0.8) Llano with us tomorrow afternoo⌈:n
	D:	⌊No: Mother I ca:n't (.)
		I've got- u:h I'm *m*eeting a gir:l at two: and we've got to um (1.2) *stu*dy
50	M:	Yeah. (.) Okay.
	D:	So: there's no way I can go::
	M:	We:ll Timmy ca:lled you know Barry's uncle?
	D:	Uh huh=
	M:	=And he has a *r*anch for us to look a:t so
55		we're gonna go just l*oo*k at it ⌈just
	D:	⌊How much
		(0.4)
	M:	·hhhh We:ll I- I don't know I don' know h- don't wanta dis- dis*cu*ss it on the
60		*te*lepho:ne=
	D:	=O:h.
		(0.3)
	M:	Bu:*t* u:h (0.2) W*e*'re gonna go over there and l*oo*k at it (.) just kinda get the l*a*y of the
65		la:nd Misha said sh*e* didn't wanna invest in anything that wasn't- on the- on the *wa*ter you know either a ·hhhhh *la*:ke or s*o*mething: recreational.
	D:	I: don't kno:w I don't a* y*o*u just go:- ↓and
70		(0.8) pt cause John and I are planning on bu*y*in some land (.) and we're gonna l*i*ve on about ten acres.
		(0.8)
	M:	At Ll*a*no:=
75		D: =*No*::. not at Lla⌈no: Wher*e*ver we end u:p
	M:	⌊hih hih hih
	D:	we're g*o*ing to cause I'm gonna have a- all kinds of animals.

	M:	I:: ↓see:
80	D:	*I* think it's im*po*rtant for children to grow
		up around *a*nimals.
	M:	I:: ↓see: ⌈well
	D:	⌊And they can get m*a*rried to each
		other you know like- (0.3) Sally and Ike did.
85	M:	Uh: hu:h.=
	D:	=But *a*nyway (0.2) ·hhhh u:m (.) what.tu:h-
		h:ow long are you gonna d- be down the:re.
		(1.0)
	M:	Well? wi:hhh u:h we won't be gone- (0.4) if-
90		Daddy doesn't get away from the office till-
		(0.3) eleven thirty or so and it'll take us
		an hour and a half to ⌈get *o*ver there
	D:	⌊↑*N O* : : : :
		I'm talkin about how long are you gu- are *you*
95		going down to visit June?
		(0.8)
	M:	I don't kno:w.
		(1.1)
	M:	I don't- know whether I was in*vi*ted or no:t.
100	D:	Well- u*h*hh *Mo*ther if I:m invited you are
		*ce*rtainly invited=
	M:	=W*e*ll maybe I wou:ld. Maybe I would just go
		by the *o*ffice and pick Daddy u:p, and that
		way we could just leave from there. som'in
105		like ⌈that-
	D:	⌊Well you're not gun be dressed up then
		(1.2)
	M:	Well I don't kno:w. I'll ↑pro ji- de↑pends on
		what the weather's li:ke tomorrow.
110		(0.3)
	D:	·hhh We:ll- I tell you what- you think about
		it and you call me back and tell me if you're
		gonna go visit June cause if you're no:t I
		wanna go to Jazzercise in the morning (.)
115		cause I'll be wastin a time. ·hhhh But- (0.7)
		I *fee*l like I should go visit June because I
		feel like that's what God wants me to do.
		(0.8)
	M:	·hh We:ll do you m*e*an you're not gonna go if

120		I don't go:?
		(0.2)
	D:	·hhh I don't kno:w. uh- I- uh no: I don't
		think I will. Cause I don't know how to-
		·hhh I feel real haw- uh awful about this but
125		I don't know how to ha*n*dle- (0.2) I don't
		know how to handle it
		(1.5)
	M:	We:ll=
	D:	=I'd h*a*te to get in there and just- (0.3)
130		ba:wl in front of everybody
		(0.7)
	D:	Things like that- (0.4) I guess maybe it just
		shows that I'm insecure within my*self* because
		·hhh it *make-* it- (0.2) it o*ffen*ds me real- a
135		wh*o*le lo*t*
		(0.7)
	D:	I ⌈know
	M:	⌊It offends you:.
	D:	*Death* o*ffen*ds me It really (0.3) b*o*thers me
140	M:	Yeah.
		(0.8)
	D:	And I guess it's afraid of- ·hhhh hhh I'm
		afraid of you *k*icking off some day or
		something I don know.
145	M:	O:h. (0.2) we::ll (0.8) ·hhhh *Well* did jou
		know Barry's si:ck?
	D:	Yeah I know I just talked to him.
	M:	What'd he sa:y.
		(0.4)
150	D:	pt He just said that he threw up this morning
		when he got to wor:k
		((encounter continues 10 minutes))

BEGINNING DISCOURSE EPISODES

The duet "It's gun be hard to do" depicts a mother and daughter struggling with a moral dilemma: how we should act toward a dying friend.[1] The speakers' orientations toward death pervade this segment. The topic of the sick friend is the main and recurrent point of discussion, although other topics also appear—studying, buying land, and fixing food. There are moments when these partners leave the topic of the sick friend. When they return to this issue, they do so as a continuation of an earlier path. How can we describe telephone partners' interactive construction of such a continuing episode?

In the last few chapters we have described telephone openings and the beginnings of speakers' turns. We skipped from large units of discourse (phone calls) to very small ones (turns) because we can specify these units' beginnings. To move between these extremes, and to consider such units as topics and stories, is to lose clarity about when units begin.

Take *topics* for instance. Telephone partners sometimes stick to one topic for a time, then clearly change to another topic. M and D discuss a ranch at Llano in this way. May we suppose that most topics show such clear boundaries? Or do a great many topics (like that of the sick friend) appear, go away, then return? May not telephone partners also discuss more than one topic at a time? Given these complexities, how can we describe the beginings of each "topic" as a discourse unit?

The current chapter sketches how telephone partners interact to begin episode units such as topics and stories. The beginnings of such episode units ordinarily occur across multiple turns by multiple speakers in pursuit of multiple purposes. At the beginning of these episodes, partners interact to define a path, or trajectory, for the episode. How do telephone partners select, and begin to enact, pathways through interaction episodes? We begin with stories.

Story Prefaces

One problem any storyteller faces is that stories may last longer than a single utterance unit. The turn-taking system for conversation allows telephone speakers one turn unit at a time. Schegloff likens this property of the turn-taking system to a door attached to a spring. The door opens with a little effort, but must be held open to prevent its closing. Similarly, beginning a turn gains an allocation of speaking time that soon expires unless a speaker holds it open.[2]

At the beginning of a story the incipient teller must project to the other speaker that the floor is to be taken for an extended telling. Sacks (Spring 1970, lecture 2, p. 11) notes that certain stories may just be announced

> e.g., just "I have a story to tell," "You wanna hear a story?" "You wanna hear a joke?" etc., and others are designed more or less with the particular story in mind, i.e., "I have something terrible to tell you"...

These utterances begin a story preface, the function of which is to secure for the teller an extended turn in which to tell the story.

UTCL A21:10

GLORIA:	**I've to tell you something**
PAM:	**What**

In this instance Gloria announces that she has something to tell. She does not say what it is. Pam, in saying 'What,' puts herself into a recipient role for Gloria's story.

It is not always the storyteller who starts discourse rolling toward a story. A telephone partner may request a story, thereby assigning tellership to the other party:

UTCL A20

E:	**↑So- how- how's the guy situation**
M:	**O:h it s:lips in an ou::t.**

Here, E asks her friend about the 'guy situation' and M responds with a suggestive idiom that foreshadows both the content and form of the erratic-romance story that is to follow.

Sometimes, a first indication of a forthcoming story leads to lengthy prefatory interaction before a telling actually begins:

UTCL A21:10
((GLORIA HAS JUST REFUSED PAM'S INVITA-
TION TO HAPPY HOUR, AND PAM HEADS TO-
WARD CLOSING THE CALL))

PAM:	**Okay well just thought ⌈I'd call**
GLORIA:	**⌊·hh ↑O::w.**
	I've to tell you something.

In this instance, Pam, whose invitation has just been refused, offers Gloria a chance to mention anything that might have a higher priority than closing the call (Schegloff and Sacks, 1973). Gloria overlaps this pre-closing with a marked (almost screamed) 'Ow,' signalling that something has just touched off her subsequent pre-announcement. A dialogic story preface ensues:

	GLORIA:	I've to tell you something
	PAM:	What
	GLORIA:	O:h. You would not believe who called me
		(0.4)
	GLORIA:	Saturday night.
	PAM:	John.
	GLORIA:	Yes
		(0.4)
	PAM:	No way.
	GLORIA:	Yes
		(0.6)
⇒	PAM:	I can't believe you

⇒   PAM: I can't believe you
⌈waited this long to tell me that⌉
GLORIA: ⌊« T w o : o'c l o : c k i n t h e ⌋ m:orning »
        (0.2)
⇒   PAM: What did he ↑say.
        GLORIA: ·hhh He- he just wanted to talk.
                (0.4)
        GLORIA: Oh he said a who:le bunch of stuff
                (0.2)
        GLORIA: ·hhh And he just wanted to talk
⌈and I was like go-⌉
⇒   PAM: ⌊Was he dru:nk?⌋
                (0.5)
        GLORIA: ·hhh Uh- he was- he was- on somethin I don't
                know wha(h)t it wa(h)(h)(h)s: huh
        PAM: Ri::ght
        GLORIA: He was on something you got me but it was
                like ·hhhh I mean Pam it was wi:ld I'm
                serious I ⌈was like
⇒   PAM: ⌊What did he ↑say tell me what he
                ↑sai:d=
        GLORIA: =Okay » okay okay okay- « ·hhh u::m. (0.4)
                pt pt he said (1.0) oka:y I just a- answer
                the pho:ne and he goes ·hhh um (0.2)
                » Hi Gloria do you know who this « is and I

said (0.2) yeah hi John wait a second
((story continues))

Only in the final turn of this lengthy extract does Gloria finally begin recounting the tale of the newsworthy phone call. When she starts the story, she recreates certain details of a telephone opening in her reported speech (Volosinov, 1930). Between the announcement of 'something to tell you,' and this actual beginning of the tale there are twenty-one speaking turns. During these turns Pam displays repeated interest in hearing the tale (see ⇒). Pam shows familiarity with the characters in the story ('was he drunk?'), requests a story ('tell me what he said'), and assesses the interest value of the story ('I can't believe you waited so long to tell me'). By the time Gloria begins to tell the story, Pam's expressed interest merits a lengthy telling.

This example illustrates how telephone partners may use numerous prefatory turns to set up a story. During this interaction parties align on their roles as teller and recipient and establish the story's fit in the current occasion. Jefferson (1978) describes two means that tellers use to ground a story in the local occasion: *disjunct markers* and *embedded repetitions*. Disjunct markers (p. 221) such as Gloria's 'Ow!' show the story to have been "touched off" by prior talk, though not topically coherent with it. Embedded repetitions locate the words in the prior talk that touched off the story. Both these devices fit the story to the local occasion. Jefferson exemplifies disjunct markers and embedded repetitions:

GTS:II:64
((FACE-TO-FACE THERAPY GROUP))

KEN:	There's a place up in *Mul*holland where they've- where they're building those hous⌈ing projects?
ROGER:	⌊*Oh* have you ever
⇒	taken the Mulhollan' time trials? You go up there wid a girl ((story follows))

The prospective teller overlaps a turn unit in progress, using the particle 'Oh' to show that something has been touched off by current talk. Roger follows with embedded repetition of the word 'Mulholland,' showing that this place name is what touched off the present telling. This renders the new telling relevant to current talk, even if it disrupts the prior speaker's activity. Our telephone instance (Gloria's story preface) shows similar features:

PAM:	Okay well just thought ⌈I'd call
GLORIA:	⌊·hh ↑O::w.
GLORIA:	I've to tell you something.

> PAM: What
> GLORIA: O:h. You would not beli*e*ve who called me

Gloria begins, in overlap, with a disjunct marker, "Ow," then describes who 'called me,' a wording built upon Pam's possible pre-closing utterance: 'just thought I'd call.'

To summarize: stories do not just drop into conversational encounters. Nor do most stories display clear beginnings. Rather, partners' story prefaces lead into each story, establish an extended turn-space for a telling, relate the story to prior talk, and foreshadow the story's themes.

Story prefaces may be both lengthy and indeterminate in their beginnings, allowing the pretense that the teller's role has been interactively developed (Goodwin, 1991). Sometimes telephone partners' back-and-forth interaction merges into a storytelling in ways that retrospectively reframe previous talk as having been prefatory. In the next example M asks what D and her husband had eaten the previous evening. This leads to a story about the daughter's alcohol abuse, as follows:

> UTCL F1.7:1
> ((MOTHER-DAUGHTER, SOON AFTER CALL
> OPENING))
>
> D: We ate at- at Jorges
> M: Was it goo:d?
> D: Um:: it was all ri:ght
> M: pt ·hhhh you know, I don't *th*ink that's as
>   good as a l*o*t of people think it i:*s*
> D: We:ll- no I don't either- and nuh- we ate
>   over there- there's a new one- across from
>   Aquarius?
> M: Uh ⌈huh?
> D: ⌊and it's *k*ind of a di:ve.
> D: I- I really didn't ⌈enjoy it
> M: ⌊O:h yeah
> M: We've been over the:re. (0.2) befo:re.
>   (0.6)
> PREFACE⇒ D: Bu:t um- (0.3) I had two margaritas and I:
>   (0.4) felt like a truck hit me °this
>   morning°.
> M: *Two:* margaritas well th*e*ir margaritas are
>   strong ⌈Risty no wonder you don't feel so hot
> D: ⌊I know it feel-
> D: They wer- I- I h*ea*r:d (.) that they were made
>   from *e*verclear instead of te*q*uila or maybe

```
                     they're made with both I don't know but don't
                     ever ┌do it h
           M:              └They're killer margaritas I hea:rd.
STORY⇒     D:        Well I ↑had ↑o:ne and I didn't- feel
                     anything. I didn't feel dru:nk or anything
                     so I- ·hh we- .see we had a thirty minute wait
                     before dinner ·hhh and I had another one
                     (0.2) with dinner and I- walked out of that
                     place and I felt like I was a- (0.6) zombie
                     ·hhhh and I got up this morning and f- felt
                     horrible and I thought well if I go and ru:n.
                     ·hhhh I'll feel better and I went and ru:n
                     and (0.2) and uh I came home and I felt fine
                     and I was gonna pick up the house and then it
                     hit me.
```

At the first arrow D projects that she has a story to tell, and foreshadows its theme. Until then, the talk about the previous evening has not projected a forthcoming story. But in that turn D reframes earlier material into a story preface (PREFACE⇒). This transforms the previous talk about a restaurant into a scenic resource for a story. D outlines the story using a distinctive idiom: 'felt like a truck hit me.' This phrase not only dramatizes the topic of the forthcoming narrative, but also prefigures the eventual punch line: 'and then it hit me.'

If analysts were concerned to locate a precise moment at which this story begins, various moments could be candidates: the first premonitoring that a story may be told (the first line above), or when a theme or moral is first stated (first arrow), or the first extended telling turn (second arrow). The beginning of a story unfolds in interaction. There may be interactive benefits to obscuring a storytelling's precise moment of beginning.

Once stories begin, recipients as well as tellers continue to speak and to steer the tellings (Mandelbaum, 1989). Much of this detail may go unnoticed in later reports about a storytelling. Recipients might later report, for instance: "She told me a story about drinking too much and getting a hangover," or "She told me about an erratic romance." Such a view pictures stories as literary monologues, which is a problem with much of the scholarly literature about stories (Mandelbaum, 1987b; see also Goodwin, 1984). Telephone stories, although they are units longer than a single turn, begin and unfold in dialogue.

Beginning a Topic

Topics, like stories, often begin interactively, but the notion of topic beginning is even more problematic than that of story-beginning. The telephone story frequently shows role definitions for teller and recipient, whereas a topic may belong to both parties. While stories most often occur one-story-at-a-time, and each proceeds to its conclusion, topics may be raised and dropped repeatedly without speakers coming to conclusions. And several topics may be treated at once. Therefore topics are even harder to count than stories, and more problematic to assign discourse ownership by one party.

You might report a recent phone call by saying: "We talked about two topics, his surgery and our vacation plans." Or: "We talked about his surgery, then I changed the topic to our vacation plans." Such reports encourage us to picture telephone conversation's topics as discretely bounded. A telephone call, on this view, might be diagrammed as:

Opening + Topic 1 + Topic 2 . . . + Topic N + Closing

Some phone calls may actually unfold this way: with one topic on the floor at a time, and each topic ending as the next topic begins. In such cases transitions between topics seem abrupt and clear:

> UTCL J10.8:2
> ((K, A BUYER, DISCUSSES CONTRACTS WITH A
> LAWYER))

	K:	Okay let me read this and call you ba:ck
	T:	Alright
⇒	K:	·hh U:m and what about the Houston Instrument contract

Speaker K makes a statement, beginning with 'Okay,' that seems to be the last word on one topic. T responds with 'Alright,' which aligns with the move to end that topic. K immediately follows with an inquiry that raises a second topic. In this case, K manages the transition crisply, and the new topic clearly belongs to her.

Sometimes a partner raises a new topic quite abruptly after the previous topic dies with a whimper:

> UTCL F1.1:1
> ((MOTHER HAS BEEN ADVISING DAUGHTER ON
> VISITING A TERMINALLY-ILL FRIEND, WHICH IS
> 'HARD TO DO'))

M:	It's har:d but they say the worst thing (0.2) u:h- (0.6) is when people withdra-aw from terminally ill (0.2)
D:	Yeah,
M:	people like that you know and- and don't talk to

> em and don't- (0.8) you know just ignore em that's
> really ha*rd.

D: Yeah,

(2.2)

⇒   M: ↓S:o do you wanna go to u::h (0.8) Llano with us
> tomorrow afterno⌈o:n

D: ⌊No mother I can't

This topic gets strangled at M's twist on the word 'hard.' Daughter has been
asking for advice and support about visiting a terminally ill friend, because
it is 'hard.' M's response that not visiting such people is 'really hard,' twists
her commentary toward manipulation. D responds with a minimal 'yeah'
and lets the line fall silent. This topic lapses into a coma. Mother ends the
lengthy silence by saying 'So' in a way that suggests a marked change of
topic. In her next turn, D orients to the new topic by responding to M's
invitation. The new topic comes onto the floor officially when D follows M's
lead into it.

These last two instances illustrate that even abrupt topic shifts must be
ratified in interaction. But most topic beginnings are more interactive than
the last two examples. In certain instances speakers interact across three
turns to suggest, adopt, and ratify a next topic (Button and Casey, 1984). The
first turn is an inquiry, the second turn introduces a candidate topic, and the
third turn marks the newsworthiness of the topic, leading toward its further
development:

NB:II::1

A: Whaddiyuh kno:w.

B: ·hh Jis' got down last night.

A: Oh you di:d,?

F:TC:I:1:12

S: What's new

B: We::ll? 't *lemme see* las'ni:ght, I had
> the girls ove⌈r?

S: ⌊Yea:h?

These instances illustrate how a topic may be interactively opened up across
three speaking turns: requesting a topic, suggesting a topic, and aligning to
a topic.

Both of these instances occur as part of telephone openings. Further, these
instances partake of pre-sequence organization, which is discussed later in
this chapter. A great many topic transitions are not articulated this definitely
or simply. Rather, partners manage *stepwise transition* between topics, which
involves waffling on two topics.

[T]he best way to move from topic to topic is not by a topic close followed by a topic beginning, but by what we call a Stepwise move, which involves connecting what we've just been talking about to what we're now talking about, though they are different. (Sacks, Spring 1972, lecture 5, p. 16)

A stepwise transition between topics occurs when speakers' utterances show relevance to the old topic, yet also provide resources to begin a new topic.

		UTCL A24.1:2
		((L AND J HAVE JUST AGREED TO MEET AT A PARTY))
T1-Party	L:	That's cool five o'clock?
	J:	·hhh U::m yeah ↑who's all goin ↑I ↑want like a lot a people to ↑g⌈o : :.
	L:	⌊I have no idea.
		(.)
	L:	I mean Leslie dund even know if she can go: and Julia's leaving town (0.2) I just saw
Resource⇒		Julia she says she's called ub- every day this week (.) y'all hou- y'alls place and Mary won't call her back=
	J:	=I've called her ten *fuck*in times she ain't called b*a*ck
		(1.6)
T2-Mary	L:	Anyway where's Mary
	J:	·hhhhhh She getting u:m bikini wax
		(0.4)
	L:	Oh *is* she
	J:	Yeah=
	L:	=Ugh (0.2) I wouldn't do that if you p*a*id me
		((talk about Mary continues))

This segment opens with the partners discussing a party they both will attend. J asks who is going to the gathering. L responds (Resource) by listing some people who will not come, including Julia. Julia's usefulness as a contextual resource is highlighted when L mentions in passing that Julia has been trying to call Mary (who lives with J). This also introduces Mary into the talk.

Either of these persons, Julia or Mary, could become the basis for a new topic. In this instance there is some negotiation over which resource to topicalize. First, J extends the topic of Julia's calls, responding heatedly that she had repeatedly called Julia. A lapse occurs, which may show L not being sympathetic to J's argument. Then, instead of responding to J, L uses the previous mention of Mary as a resource to ask where Mary is. The answer: 'She's getting um bikini wax,' leads to a new topic, Mary's cosmetic excursion.

In this instance talk on the topic of the party moves into talk about Mary. Resources for this transition include mentions of both Julia and Mary in talk about the party. This could lead to further talk about either Julia or Mary. One partner tries to talk about Julia, but this topic is not ratified by the partner, whose subsequent bid to talk about Mary does attain ratification. Topic elicitations, like prefaces to stories, are designed to acquire both partners' alignment.

Topic-elicitation interaction indicates relevance to the local occasion. Let us reconsider the topic of the terminally ill friend in the mother-daughter telephone call duet preceding this chapter. The partners leave the topic after about a minute and a half of talk, and there ensues a discussion of a trip to Llano. Then talk returns, as if by accident, to visiting the sick friend. Many topics in telephone conversation appear, get dropped, and bubble up again during an encounter. M and D spend more than five minutes meandering to and away from the topic of a visit to the sick friend. Finally, D summarizes her viewpoint in a way that provides resources for topics to follow:

UTCL F1.1:5-7

D: *Death.* (.) *offe*nds me: It really (0.4)
bothers me.

M: Yeah.
(0.9)

D: And I guess it's afraid of- ·hhhh hhh I'm
afraid of *you* kicking *o*ff some day or
something I don know.

Topic 1⇒ M: O:h. (0.2) we::ll (0.8) Well did you know
Barry's si:ck?

D: Yeah I know I just talked to him.

M: What'd he sa:y.
(0.4)

D: pt He just said that he threw up this morning
when he got to wor:k.

.

. ((three turns deleted))

.

Resource⇒ M: You don't suppose it was your hamburgers ↓do
you=

D: =I don't kno- we:ll everybody else would be
si:ck. ⌈if it wa:s

M: ⌊Yea:h.

                              (0.3)
              M: Yeah well that's tru:e.
Topic 2⇒   D: pt ·hhhh Well I'm gonna make *John* some *jello*
                      because of his *te*(h)st
                      ((Talk about jello continues.))

Where are the topic boundaries in this segment? Is the discussion of death
still part of the discussion of visiting the friend, or is it a "new" topic? It is
both. Is the next illness-related discussion ('Barry's sick') part of it, or a new
topic? Certainly the segment above includes two new topics.
    Topic 1:   Barry's illness and the possibility that other people may have
               the same illness; and
    Topic 2:   Fixing some jello.
In a stepwise-resource utterance M asks her daughter whether the
daughter's hamburgers might be responsible for Barry's illness. This utterance still orients to the illness topic, but it also raises the issue of D's
preparing food.[3] Subsequently D mines the resource of food preparation by
stating her intention to make jello for her husband. The preparation of jello
then becomes a topic—and provides resources for subsequent topics. How
many topics appear in this segment? How do partners accomplish the transition points between topics? Cannot multiple topics be considered at once?
At the end of the segment what topic is on the floor? If the sick friend comes
up again, is it a new topic?[4] These questions illustrate the futility of counting
topics, or treating them as displaying clear boundaries between them.
    Certain investigators (e.g., Fishman, 1983) make frequency-counts of top-
ics only at the cost of simplifying how topics get raised and extended in
conversation. Many topics may emerge and re-emerge across a telephone
call. Speakers must show any utterance's relevance to current interaction,
but whether a turn raises new topics may be of little consequence to telephone partners. In fact partners may profit from not dividing up an encounter into discrete topic units. For example, in the last instance, who introduces
the topic of food preparation? If a first mention is a topic initiation, M does.
But D's is the first utterance to focus on preparation. Whose topic is it? The
beginnings of topics, like the beginnings of stories, often emerge as evolving
trajectories across multiple turns at talk.[5]
    The interactional issue is *topic management* much more than topic owner-
ship (Jefferson, 1981; West and Garcia, 1988; Maynard, 1980). As we examine
telephone conversation's details, the notion that people own topics recedes
before the workings of interactive emergence. The issue is not "whose topic
is it?" but how do partners manage and negotiate topics?
    So far, however, we have only shown some ways that partners build topic
beginnings. To reach deeper understandings of topic management we must
also ask what people are doing with topics. Telephone partners do not just
meander along, applying resources of topic management. Rather, speakers

introduce topics in the course of motivated actions. We can discern some shapes of these sustained action trajectories in the organization of pre-sequence objects. Let us now turn to the role of pre-sequence organization in the emergence of episode trajectories.

Pre-Sequence Organization

Telephone partners may begin (or project) lines of activity using a pre-sequence: an adjacency pair introduced in service to anticipated activity. Levinson (1983, p. 346) exemplifies pre-sequencing with this instance, labeled as pre-invitation:

> A: **Whatcha doin?**
> B: **Nothin'**
> A: **Wanna drink?**

'Watcha doin?' is the first turn not only of a question-answer adjacency pair, but also of a longer episode. Telephone partners do not hear the question 'Whatcha doin?' as if it were an item on a questionnaire, but rather as preliminary to subsequent action: as leading-up-to-something. Such an opening-gambit turn is a *pre*, and the longer sequential entity is a *pre-sequence* (Sacks, Fall 1967, lectures 8, 9; Schegloff, 1972, p. 109; Levinson, 1983, p. 345).

The following telephone opening, reported to me by a student, highlights uses and abuses of pre-sequencing:

> FN
> Alice: **Hello?**
> Fred: **Hello, Alice?**
> Alice: **Hi Fred.**
> Fred: **Hi what are you doin.**
> Alice: **Nothin what's up.**
> Fred: **How about if I come over in a while.**
> Alice: **Great, I'd love to see you.**
> Fred: **Okay, I have a paper that needs typing.**

The final line of this fragment reveals Fred to be a cad. Fred leads Alice to expect an episode trajectory toward a social occasion—then he asks for secretarial help. Fred initiates this false impression with his marked initial inquiry: 'What are you doin.' Alice aligns to an expectation that Fred may be leading up to something, possibly an invitation. Alice shows openness to an invitation by stating that she is not otherwise engaged and then inquiring as to Fred's agenda: 'Nothin, what's up?' Fred's answer is to ask whether he may 'come over,' which further indicates a social invitation.

Pre-sequential interactions often include an initiator's second indications-along-the-way, and these may be answered by a recipient's second encouragement of the projected line of action. Much of courtship culture is based upon these deviation-amplifying systemics. In this instance Alice responds enthusiastically to the second indication: 'Great, I'd love to see you.' Then Fred reveals a disagreeable task with which he desires assistance. Fred thereby exploits pre-invitation organization to suggest a social agenda, but then he switches to a request for a favor. This exploitation is possible because of the orderly ways that telephone callers pre-indicate trajectory—or display where they are probably heading.

Drew (1984) shows that a pre-invitation like "What are you doin" does its work by eliciting from its recipient a report of activities. This report provides resources that allow the subsequent invitation to be "interactionally generated" (p. 132).[6] Drew uses this telephone example:

> NB:II:14 ((simplified)) (Drew, p. 130)
> E: Whadiyih *doi*n.
>   (0.9)
> N: What am *I* ⌈doin?
> E: ⌊Cleanin?
> N: I'm ironing, wouldju believe that?
> E: Oh bless its ⌈heart
> N: ⌊In fact *i:* ir- I started ar'ning and
> ⇒   I'd I. Somehow or another ironing dis kind of
>   leaves me co:ld=
> E: Yea:h
> E: Wanna come down'n have a bite a lu:nch with me?

In this instance, 'What are you doin' leads the partner to report an activity, ironing. She reports that the ironing activity 'leaves me cold.' N's lack of enthusiasm for ironing provides an opening for the subsequent lunch invitation. Pre-sequence turns set directions for future turns and provide resources out of which to do those actions.[7]

> UTCL D8.3
> ⇒   J: Have you *e*aten yet?
> S: No: I h*a*ven't,
> J: You hav(h)?
> S: No:.
>   (0.2)
> ⇒   J: U:m dyou have Billy's ca:r?
> S: Yeah I do,

The two turns marked by arrows in this instance pre-indicate that J has placed this phone call to invite S to share a meal. Examination of the rest of the call shows this to be correct. You can tell that this is where these speakers are heading, even though there is no speech act in this fragment that invites. We describe these turns as pres to show their functions in dialogic trajectory construction. A pre carries first pair-part relevance that compels a second turn and some further activity—but a pre does not make compulsory, nor specify, any entire line of action. Rather, each pre-sequential trajectory emerges turn by turn, as the parties work it through.

Pre-invitations may last as long as story prefaces or topic transitions. The conversation between Pam and Gloria (A21) apparently begins with pre-inviting, and Pam pursues this gambit for six minutes. In the telephone opening, Pam says:

> A21:1
>
> PAM: **So what are you doin**
> GLORIA: **U:m. ·hhhh nothin I was just- » I been tryin to call you « for about the last five thousand da:ys what happened**
>   **(0.2)**
> PAM: **I fell off the ear:th**

Pam's initial inquiry 'What are you doin,' may proffer pre-invitation. Gloria responds with an unmarked value for this slot: 'nothin,' which might indicate openness to an invitation; however, Gloria immediately bids for an additional turn unit: 'I was just-' In this turn start, Gloria projects a report of her actual activity: e.g., "I was just typing my paper," or "I was just thinking about you." But Gloria cuts off this action and rapidly states that she has been trying to call Pam. She asks Pam for an explanation of why she has been hard to reach. In launching this first pair-part Gloria deflects the encounter's trajectory away from the possible pre-sequential agenda previewed by 'what are you doin,' and toward a discussion of Pam's recent activity. On one view, Gloria is simply returning an initial inquiry; but is it possible that Gloria is also, among other things, evading a possible invitation?

These friends next discuss Pam's recent activities, then Pam introduces a more specific pre-invitation:

> A21:7
>
> PAM: **U:m (1.0) What are you doin tonight**
> GLORIA: **·hhhh U:h I have to finish typing this stupid-***pa***per thing.**
> PAM: **Oh you do**

Pam's second pre-invitation is more particular than the first. She asks about a specific time, and thereby provides a second indication of a probable social invitation. This elicits a report of Gloria's actual activity, which is not an activity of casual importance (like 'ironing') but something with priority: 'I have to finish typing.' Pam receipts this activity-report utterance with 'Oh you do,' which indicates this is new information to her (Heritage, 1984a). Once again, the encounter's trajectory slides away from the possible invitation, as the friends discuss Gloria's typing. Gloria mixes this reporting, most of which is a complaint, with news about her allergies. Only after two more minutes does Pam take a third, and most explicit move toward inviting Gloria to a social event.

> A21:11
>
> PAM: ...sinus headache or somethin
> GLORIA: Yeah,
>   (0.3)
> PAM: U:m well Marie and I are gonna: go- well she just
>   called me about- (0.4) five minutes ago (.) and
>   ask me if I want to go to happy hour at Rumors?
>   ·hhhh So if you want to go with us you are welcome
>   to co:me.

Choosing a seam after a topic runs down, Pam says that she and Marie are 'gonna go-.' But Pam stops and restarts the utterance just before saying where. Pam next reports that Marie 'just' called her—presumably just before Pam's call to Gloria—marking the reason for calling now. Then, finally, comes the carefully-hedged invitation. Whew! Why is this so complex, and why is the invitation hedged? Perhaps because Gloria has resisted the pre-inviting throughout its course.

Pam and Gloria's lengthy dance toward an invitation resembles the shorter dance of Emma and Nancy (described by Drew, 1984; page 157 above) in that a possible pre-invitation 'what are you doin' leads to reports of activities. In the case of Emma and Nancy the report's resources ('ironing leaves me cold') are put to the service of offering the invitation. The case of Pam and Gloria provides such resources (e.g., complaints about a school assignment's dumb details), but Pam and Gloria do not construct an invitation out of these resources. Rather, Pam waits till the reporting ends, then performs a more explicit invitation. We may summarize the call as: Pam calls to invite Gloria to happy hour, but it takes a lot of preliminary activity to get the invitation stated. Gloria subsequently declines the invitation, which also requires interaction:

> A21:11 ((simplified))
>
> PAM: I'd love for you to come if you want to come.
>   (0.4)

GLORIA: pt Well I would but I just talked to my sister a
             few minutes ago?=
PAM: =Yeah
             (0.4)
GLORIA: And I promised her: ·hhh that I would u:m (0.4)
             you know- go over there cause I have the car cause
             I had to go take the ca:r- (0.2) over this morning
             we had to have some junk fixed on it had to take
             it over this mornin (.) and- she couldn't do it
             cause she works all day so
PAM: O::h.=
GLORIA: =You know- I gotta go return the car and then
             she's babysittin so we're am: we're gun take the
             little girl to go get her something to eat and
             some ice cream or sum'm
             (0.2)
PAM: ⌈O : : : h h o w cu::te.
             ⌊pt ·hh So plus I have t-
             (0.2)
GLORIA: Plus I have to type this stupid thing hh
PAM: uhhh hih hih
             (0.4)
PAM: Okay well just thought ⌈I'd (call)⌉
GLORIA: ⌊· h h ↑O: ⌋:w.
GLORIA: I've to tell you something.

This refusal episode displays a trajectory of its own. Gloria first affiliates
with the invitation 'Well I would but' and then constructs a compound
excuse: I have to get this car back to my sister, and we have to go get ice
cream with a kid; plus this typing I already mentioned. The story about the
car and the kid shows a preface structure like those described earlier in this
chapter. Gloria then begins to tag on the excuse about typing ('plus I have
t-'). Pam overlaps this continuation by assessing the car and kid story ('how
cute'). Gloria recycles the turn beginning for the typing excuse. Her re-men-
tion of typing in the compound excuse shows another contrast with the
invitation sequence analyzed by Drew ('ironing . . . leaves me cold'). In
Drew's instance, the reporting of ironing becomes a resource to *offer* the
invitation. In Gloria's case, the reporting of typing becomes a resource to
decline the invitation.

The present treatment of pre-sequencing emphasizes pre-invitations because these are so common in telephone calls, and because they can be
described with reference to the structure of telephone openings. There are

many other kinds of pre-sequences, and each kind shows its own distinctive ordering principles.

One pre-sequencing organization that is frequent in telephone conversation is the *pre-announcement*. Terasaki (1976) argues that pre-announcements occur when one speaker has information to relay to another. In a monologue view, an efficient way to accomplish such business is to state the information. However, actual announcers often elicit a recipient's guess, or series of guesses, which announce the news:

> HS ST:1 (Terasaki, 1976, p. 23)
>
> D: **Didju hear the terrible news?**
> R: **No. What.**
> D: **Y'know your Grandpa Bill's brother Dan?**
> R: **He died.**
> D: **Yeah.**

Who makes the announcement? In this case, the recipient of the news actually constructs its announcement to himself. When does this announcement begin? As so often in the study of beginnings, the trajectory is interactive and emergent.

Even in the most news-laden encounters, such as the announcement of a death or a medical diagnosis, there may be interactive advantages to the use of pre-sequencing. Maynard (1989, 1990), for example, reports that medical professionals' communication of bad news to clients follows a "perspective-display series." Therapists first inquire to elicit a client's guess about the situation, then formulate their diagnostic announcements to agree with the recipient guess. Maynard speculates that failure to deliver bad news in these ways may be perceived as blunt or insensitive (1990).

Conclusions: On Trajectory Management

We have described how telephone partners interact to begin actions such as topics, stories, and invitations. Partners often share responsibility for the activity paths that emerge. Telephone partners edge interactively into emergent trajectory building. For instance, to ask "What are you doin" commits the speaker to little, but may forward an opportunity (if the other assents, also committing to little) to pursue a line of action. Partners then work through the nature of any trajectory-in-progress while already beginning to travel upon its path. We use pre-sequence organization to break bad news by making the task collaborative; we edge through pre-invitation rather than abruptly asking another to commit. Individual accomplishment and verbal clarity fall aside together in effective interactive trajectory construction.

We conclude this treatment by raising three themes: sequential ambiguity, preference structuring, and the planning of motivated activity. In each of these areas, conversation analysis recommends unique solutions to classic problems of communication theory.

Sequential Ambiguity

Pres begin varied action trajectories. For instance, to ask "What are you doin" implicates a possible line of action but commits the actor to no specific action. This utterance is ambiguous at the time it is spoken, and this ambiguity is specifically useful. This raises the possibility that good language is not always the most precise possible statement of a clear intention (Wittgenstein, 1953). There are interactive benefits to sequential ambiguities (Schegloff, 1984).

Schegloff (1980) describes interactional uses of sequential ambiguities in *preliminaries to preliminaries*. When a speaker asks the (paradoxical) question: "Can I ask you a question?" it is rare for this to be immediately followed by that speaker asking a question. Rather, the speaker takes the floor for some other preliminary activity. The question then occurs after these preliminaries:

Schegloff, 1980, p. 109 ((radio talk show))

pre-pre   B: Now *listen*, Mister Crandall, Let me ask you
                  this. A *cab*. You're standing onna corner

                  .

                  . ((forty lines of preliminary dialogue))

                  .

           B: ...But I had come out-of where I
                  was, right there on the corner.
           A: Right?
           B: Now is he not suppose tuh stop fuh me?

This caller to a radio talk show states that he would like to ask a question, and then he specifically does not ask a question, but instead introduces preliminary material to frame a question that has not yet been made evident. Finally, the question is asked in the last utterance of this segment. In this instance the direction that the event is to take is by no means clear during its early utterances. The initial action projection may be heard as either "prepre" or as "pre-delicate," or both.

> It does not appear that these several uses (some of which can be co-operative in a segment of talk) are discriminated and differentially prefigured in the form or placement of the action projection. Which use is being made of an action projection on a given occasion is something worked through by the parties in the ensuing talk. A recipient may have to entertain the full range of possibilities momentarily, using the immediately following talk to find out what sort of sequence is in progress. (p. 135)

Action projections prefigure something, but whether it is delicate content or further preliminary material must be worked through in interaction. This necessity of working-through also applies to other pre-sequential beginnings and to prefatory interaction introducing stories and topics. There is interactive benefit to telephone partners in the very ambiguities that meaning-centered descriptions of speech acts may be at pains to dissolve. Ordinary talk "is replete with alternate interpretations" that do not come from sloppy language use but are "inherent to the language in ways that only situated interaction can resolve" (Suchman and Jordan, 1990, p. 238).

For example, let us review our earlier discussion of the utterance "What are you doin" in call waiting telephone openings. In chapter 4 we describe this utterance as a marked initial inquiry. In the present chapter, we show such an inquiry serving as pre-invitation. Any initial inquiry "What are you doin" is sequentially ambiguous, which provides resources for conversation partners to probe whether something is up while guarding against consequences of blatant action. Subsequent action may then show its natural emergence from the local occasion. Pre-sequencing begins trajectories, rather than committing partners to fully figured actions.

The beginning of an action is not limited to its very start. It must be worked through, in telephone dialogue. Pre-sequence organization, like the organization of telephone openings, provides a template for the organization of action trajectories. The similarity shows family resemblances among structures for episode-beginning.

Sequential Preference

We may now tie action trajectories to the conversation analytic notion of *preference* that is briefly mentioned in chapter 1. That earlier treatment emphasizes a preferred contiguous rhythm between agreeing adjacency pairparts:

UTCL L17.24

D: Is that what you're using?=
L: =Uh huh?

Contrastively, a break in the rhythm occurs when a second pair-part is posed in disagreement to the first.

UTCL F1.1:4

D: Are *you* going down to visit June?
       (0.8)
M: I don't kno:w.

That view is correct, so far as it goes, but it does not picture what participants are doing as they produce these conversation-structures. Partners manage action trajectories to position themselves in relation to the telephone partner (sociality) and to projected end points (purposes). Preference structures allow us to manage individual projects while minimizing disturbances to social order. For instance: parties may express disagreement, yet still orient to a preference for displaying agreement, by performing the agreeing response first and then disagreeing. This agree-disagree response trajectory allows interactants to balance orientations to sociality and purpose (Sacks, 1987; Pomerantz, 1984a; Heritage, 1984b).

NB:II:2:R:18

EMMA:	No one has heard a wo:rd hah,
NANCY:	» Not a word, «
	(0.2)
NANCY:	Hah ha, (0.2) n:not (.) not a word,h
	(.)
NANCY:	Not et all, except Roul's mother gotta call

The first two turn units in this exchange show the pattern in which a question designed to get a "no" answer gets such an answer immediately. Nancy then reiterates that original answer, that nobody has heard anything. Finally she notes that somebody has heard. Nancy thereby depicts a call that someone actually did receive as an aberration to the general pattern Emma has suggested—with which she agrees. Although her full response adds up to disagreeing, Nancy first agrees, then qualifies that agreement afterward.

If you conceptualize telephone partners as autotoma that do adjacency pairs, the above instance seems inefficient. But telephone partners' action trajectories provide ways to resolve recurrent social problems that occur as lines of action get collaboratively constructed. The ecological wisdom behind preference organization constrains and structures interaction

> in ways reminiscent of Mead's "conversation of gestures": like a gesture, a 'preface' is the initial part of an act; like a gesture, it 'anticipates' or 'projects' the act; and like a gesture, it makes social action transparent and enables the other to adjust and respond to the act before the fact. (Streeck, in press, a)

Mead's term "conversation of gestures" indicates preliminary activities' open-textured relationship to subsequent activities that emerge in interaction, preserving both purpose and sociality.

Speakers' Purposes in Interactive Trajectories

Suppose you observe, when you look from an upstairs window, a person walking across a park and entering a store on the other side of the park. You might describe the walker's action as relatively *purposeful* (she went to the store) or as relatively *emergent* (she crossed the park and entered the store).

The first description entails that the walker engaged in planned or strategic activity. The second account is comparatively agnostic about the walker's purposes. Notice that either account may describe the same observed activity, and that the second accounting may be as patterned as the first. A walker's trajectory through a park, like telephone partners' interactive paths through an encounter, may be described as more or less laden with actors' purposes.

Drew (in press) argues a distinction between trajectories undertaken in goal pursuit and those that emerge as found art. His argument uses an instance of pre-invitation cited earlier in this chapter:

NB:II:14 ((simplified, see page 157))

PRE-INV	E:	Whadiyih *doi*n.
		...
REPORT	N:	I'm ironing... [it] leaves me cold
INVITE	E:	Yeah Wanna come down'n have a bite a lunch with me?

These partners pursue a three-part path. There is evidence of E's purposeful pursuit of an invitation, and of interactive compliance with that pattern in N's report of activity.

Drew argues that, in a second kind of trajectory, the sequential relevance does not unfold in response to speakers' plans, but as something that just comes up. Drew's example of such a trajectory is a kind of teasing episode that occurs across three turns: (1) a speaker complains or brags to an "over-built" degree, (2) a second speaker teases the first, and (3) the teased party then responds as though the tease had been serious.

Campbell 4:5 (Drew, 1987, pp. 224;236-7)

OVER-	B:	I'm still gettin:g you know,hh ·hh *s*tomach pains I
BUILT		sp*ewed* last ni:ght, ... *ch*ronic diar
TURN		we-e-ll, just before I went to *b*ed and.... I've
		been getting *f*unny things in front of my *eye:*s
		actually. ·hh A *b*i:t, just slightly, *Li:*ght
		flashes. *B*ut uh, (0.3) .tsk (st*i:*ll.)
TEASE	A:	Well you *p*robably got a *l*east a week.
		(0.4)
PO-FACED	B: ·	What of *thi:*s:.
RESPONSE		(0.3)
	A:	*N*o a week before you di*e:*,
	B:	Ohh y*hh*h heh heh

By the end of this segment, a three-stage trajectory becomes evident: overbuilt turn, tease, po-faced response. Looking at this transcription, we observe a pattern among these three turns. Drew argues that the pattern is an interactive phenomenon relevant to the participants (Drew, 1987). However, no participant anticipates or plans this pattern. Rather, the speakers generate it out of the normal turn-by-turn course of interaction; the pattern exists as found art.

Drew's clear cases may be useful, but the present chapter's instances blur his distinction. Many interaction paths are neither clearly purposeful, nor only found art. Rather, it is a principle of the preliminary parts of trajectory organization that speaker's purposes remain emergent, indeterminate—sequentially ambiguous. Analysts' descriptions should be no more definite than what participants do; therefore we may wish to remain agnostic about speakers' purposes or conscious strategy during trajectory preliminaries (Heritage, 1991). This stance does not limit description of goal-pursuit across turns, for the primary task of such analysis is to show the ties between preliminary and later actions.

The "pre" prefix on the terms "preface" "preference" and "pre-sequence" indicates first-or-preliminary-position-in-trajectories. In normal sequencing of interactive speaking some things go before others. Preliminary actions are useful whenever self-assertion may run afoul of sociality. Preliminaries open possible interactive paths and thereby invite telephone partners to shape each trajectory as it is enacted:

> The way in which preference organizations operate is precisely captured in the Latin root of the term—*prae-ferre*, 'to forestall', 'to anticipate'—as well as by the literal reading of its German translation—*vor-ziehen*, 'to pull something in front of some other thing'. I.e. they operate by delaying an action and placing something before it, something which anticipates the action. (Streeck, in press, b)

Speakers interact to create lines of action. As telephone partners perform their way through the undirected play of an ordinary phone call, they construct plots, they walk paths, their interactive course assumes trajectories.

In this chapter we describe some ways to begin: story prefaces, topic elicitations and transitions, pre-sequence organization, and preference. In each case certain actions are constructed as preliminaries, actions that are not enacted in fullness but continue to evolve functions during enactment. Preliminary activities exhibit the property ethnomethodologists label reflexivity (Garfinkel and Sacks, 1970). Mehan and Wood (1975) illustrate reflexivity using Escher's etching, *drawing hands* (see Fig. 9). This etching shows two hands holding pencils and drawing each other. Escher enjoys one of his artistic jokes here, for an external artist did make this picture. Yet this joke indicates a profound truth for telephone conversation: telephone partners, like the drawing hands, sketch lines of action with the very utterances that become the enactment of those actions.

Conventional approaches to language may assume that conversational interaction, like Escher's drawing, has some omniscient maker, perhaps culture or other extrinsic variation. But could these theories, and the myths of clarity that they promote, be a hindrance to speakers—the hindrance of clarity that diplomats evade when they do not state clear goals at the beginning of talks. Rather, diplomats begin with sequentially ambiguous utterances that indicate paths along which to negotiate. Preliminary utterances must leave options open and allow interactants to muddle through problems as they arise. Like diplomats, telephone partners indicate possible trajectories with early utterances; they gesture toward anticipated paths to discover whether they can entice another actor to answer in kind.

Though we describe the emergence of preliminary activity in telephone conversation, face-to-face interaction exhibits every regularity of prelimi-

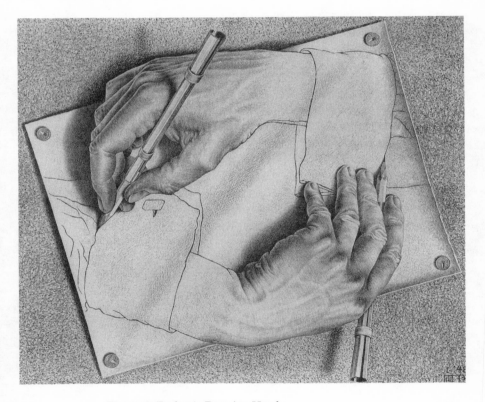

Figure 9: Escher's *Drawing Hands*
A Picture of Reflexivity
(© 1948 M. C. Escher/Cordon Art–Baarn–Holland.
Collection Haags Gemeentemuseum, The Hague.)

nary action that is described in the current chapter—and many others. Face-to-face speakers also use bodily activity, especially gesture, as preliminary activity. The term "conversation of gestures" applies to preliminary activity of all sorts, including that in telephone conversation.

Conversational interaction is intrinsically dramatic and interactive. It unfolds toward fullnesses of time, turning points of plots. Telephone partners' individual utterances align into episodes as gestures in sonic dance. Telephone talk's trajectories are constituted in artful interplay.

```
                    (UTCL D8.2)
                    = SETTING: RICK AND CAROL'S PALS HAVE
                    BEEN TALKING, WHEN CAROL'S FRIEND SAYS
                    "CAROL WANTS TO TALK TO RICK." THIS
                    BEGINS THE ENSUING ENCOUNTER.
        RICK:       Ye::ss? heh
        CAROL:      Rick?
        RICK:       ·hhh Ye(h)es?
        CAROL:      You quee:r w(h)at're you doin
5                       (0.4)
        RICK:       U:h I dunno what're you doin you queer bait
                    eh ⌈heh
        CAROL:         ⌊Nothing?
        RICK:       Eh ih
10      CAROL:      What's go'n on.
        RICK:       ·hhhhh O:h u:::h just sittin arou:nd jammin
                    some tunes
        CAROL:      Are ya=
        RICK:       =Mm hm?
15                      (0.3)
        CAROL:      ↑Hm:. (0.2) how fun
        RICK:       What're you guys doin
                        (0.3)
        CAROL:      Well- um we've been looking for: apartments
20                  all ↑da:y and no:w ( . ) we're (cooking)
        RICK:       you're- you're (punting)
        CAROL:      Cooking
                        (0.2)
        RICK:       Kicking
25      CAROL:      ↑Cooking.
        RICK:       Cooking hh hh
        CAROL:      Ye::s.
        RICK:       Oh ho ho ⌈ho
        CAROL:             ⌊Pumping we're pumping. hh ↑huh huh
30                  huh
        RICK:       ·hhh=
        CAROL:      =·hhh huh, what could that mean
        RICK:       U:h I don't kno:w u:h*
```

```
                        (0.3)
35    CAROL:    Huh?
      RICK:     U- You got me heh heh heh
      CAROL:    hhh You're the one that said the word.
                        (0.2)
      RICK:     ·hhhh
40    CAROL:    Right
                        (0.3)
      RICK:     Well 'at's what th- I thought that's what you
                said though
                        (0.2)
45    CAROL:    °Oh really°
      RICK:     Mm mm?
      CAROL:    What does that word mean
                        (0.4)
      RICK:     Pumping?
50    CAROL:    Pumping
                        (1.2)
      RICK:     Puppy? or pumping.
      CAROL:    ↑Pumping.
                        (0.2)
55    CAROL:    Isn't that what you said?
                        (0.2)
      RICK:     Pumping?
                        (0.2)
      CAROL:    Yeah
60    RICK:     Sexually heh heh heh
      CAROL:    Is that what you mea(h)nt
      RICK:     ·hhh no(h) not at a(h)ll.
      CAROL:    O(h)h,
      RICK:     ·hhh Is that what you meant?
65    CAROL:    ↑No. not at ↑all.  ⌈huh ↑heh heh heh.
      RICK:                        ⌊hehheh
      CAROL:    ·hhh⌈hh
      RICK:         ⌊·hhhhh.
      CAROL:    So how was your da:y
70                       .
                         . ((8 minutes deleted))
                         .
300   RICK:     Have you had dinner yet
                        (0.4)
```

	CAROL:	No I haven't
	CAROL:	[Have you.
	RICK:	[I- I'm so h(h)ungr(h)y,
305	CAROL:	Are you starving?
	RICK:	Ye:s
		(0.3)
	CAROL:	Have you *ate* today?
		(0.4)
310	CAROL:	*Eat*en
	RICK:	heh heh [heh huh
	CAROL:	[heh hueh I said *eated* ·*h*hh=
	RICK:	=No I- I- I already *eated* [*h*hhih
	CAROL:	[You already *eated*?
315	RICK:	Yes
	CAROL:	What did you eat at *h*h [↑hih=
	RICK:	[But I'm going to go-
		I'm gonna go- ran now ·*h*h *h*h *h*h
	CAROL:	You gonna go r*a*n
320	RICK:	I'm gonna go ran
	CAROL:	nh *h*ah *h*ah *h*ah hah
	RICK:	·*h*h
	CAROL:	Fuck you. ·hhh *h*ah hah hah hah °He's gonna go
		ran now° eyahuh huh hih *h*uh *h*uh huh huh huh
325		·*h*h [↑Leave me al↑o:ne.
	RICK:	[And the- and then- and then I'm gonna-
		and then I'm gonna *go*:n to a movie *h*hh *h*h
	CAROL:	Gonna g*o*ne to a movie?
	RICK:	Gonna g*o*ne to a mov[(h)ie.
330	CAROL:	[ehhih hih hnh hnh hnh
	CAROL:	·hhh *A*re you gonna gone to a movie?
	RICK:	Yeah,
		(0.2)
	RICK:	You wanna c*o*med? *h*no(h)o,
335	CAROL:	I wanna c*a*me.
	RICK:	·*h*h Wanna c(h)ome,
	CAROL:	hnh huh You wanna came ↑hnh hnh hhn ↑hnh
		hnh hnh (0.4) ·*h*hhh heh Leave me al↑o:ne.
	RICK:	·*h*h
340		(0.5)
	CAROL:	*uh*h (.) *h*eh I'm gonna went h*o*me Lee Anne
		says huh huh huh (0.3) ·k*h*hhh

                              (0.2)
          CAROL: *Rick laugh.*
345   RICK: I *mi*ssed it I di(h)dn't hear ⌈you*h*h huh
          CAROL: ⌊She said she's
                      gonna went home.
          RICK: ·e*h*hhhhh Why do I have to *la*ugh.
                              ((encounter continues))

8

BEGINNING TO PLAY

Play cannot be denied. You can deny, if you
like, nearly all abstractions: justice, beauty,
truth, goodness, mind, God. You can deny
seriousness, but not play.

Johann Huizinga
Homo Ludens

Play may be the most universal genre of communicative interaction. Children play, otters and dogs play, members of every culture play. Play activities
occur "as an intermezzo, an *interlude* in our daily lives" (Huizinga, 1944, p.
9). At one moment actors are not playing, then suddenly they are. But how
do we commence each intermezzo? How do we begin to play? In the present
chapter we describe play episodes in telephone conversation.[1]

As we evoke play, we evoke the related notions of poetics and drama.
Vico's *New Science* (1744) proposed that human language began as poetic
activity. This theme is revisited in the dramatism of Burke and Goffman
(chapter 1). Play is an essential aspect of human interaction.

Play is in principle interactive, grounded in the local occasion, and patterned on nonplay. Anthropologist Gregory Bateson describes zoo animals
playing:

> I saw two young monkeys *playing,* i.e., engaged in an interactive sequence of
> which the unit actions or signals were similar to but not the same as those of
> combat. It was evident, even to the human observer, that the sequence as a
> whole was not combat, and . . . that to the participant monkeys this was "not
> combat."
>
> Now, this phenomenon, play, could only occur if the participant organisms
> were capable of some degree of metacommunication, i.e., of exchanging signals
> which would carry the message "this is play." (1972, p. 179)

Bateson argues that playing animals must imitate some "primary activity,"
such as combat. Play-combat mimes combat, or re-encodes combat's activities
using signals that are in some sense not serious, or fictional or metaphoric (p.
183). Bateson labels such signals "metacommunicative" (p. 190) because they
frame interaction—or instruct partners how to interpret messages.

Bateson offers two analogies for frame: First, the picture frame.

> The frame around a picture . . . says "Attend to what is within and do not attend to what is outside." . . . The picture frame tells the viewer that he is not to use the same sort of thinking in interpreting the picture that he might use in interpreting the wallpaper outside the frame. (pp. 187-88)

Bateson's second analogy for frame is the mathematical set. Bateson admits that the analogy of the picture frame is too concrete to account for metacommunication, but the mathematical analogy is too abstract. This admission helps us notice that "frame" in Bateson is an idealized conceptualization, not a communicative phenomenon. What are the communicative phenomena in which we frame play? How do monkey, otter, dolphin, and *homo ludens* achieve framing messages?

In *Frame Analysis*, Goffman argues that communicators use framing messages, or *keys*, to help each other define communication situations. A key is

> the set of conventions by which a given activity, one already meaningful in terms of some primary framework, is transformed into something patterned on this activity but seen by the participants to be something quite else. (1974, p. 43)

Keys transform primary activity to play. Goffman widens the notion of framing to include theatrical conventions such as an initial curtain going up, radio announcers' techniques for announcing station breaks, orators' ploys for disattending to hecklers, and bridge players' alternation of bidding with interpersonal gossip. He argues that each act of framing is accomplished by a key, or framing message indicating "when the transformation is to begin and when it is to end" (p. 45).

A key brackets a *strip* of activity that happens in one setting at one time, and transforms that strip. Like brackets in mathematics, keys

> establish the boundaries of a strip of any length, all items in which are to be transformed in the same way and at the same time, and a place next to and on the outside of the left-hand bracket, the operator slot, in which any mathematical expression there inserted determines what the transformation will be. (p. 254)

As the "a" in the expression $a(x + y)$ transforms both items inside the bracket, the keying of a "drama" frame by a raised curtain transforms each actor's speech during a theatrical performance. Likewise teasing and fantasy are accomplished by keys placed at the "opening bracket" of the strip:

> the bracket initiating a particular kind of activity may carry more significance than the bracket terminating it. For . . . the beginning bracket not only will establish an episode but also will establish a slot for signals which will inform and define what sort of a transformation is to be made of the materials within the episode. (pp. 255-56)

To summarize Goffman's position: a strip of play activity is transformed by keyings that occur just before the framed activity or at its first act and function like a multiplier at the front bracket of a mathematical expression. The transformation accomplished by the key applies to each message in the transformed strip.

Basso (1979) describes play episodes among Western Apaches in ways that align with Goffman's approach. Basso suggests that play episodes in which Apaches ridicule "Whitemen" are keyed at their onset by a language-switch to English—a language that Apaches rarely use among themselves—and by stock phrases lampooning Anglo conversation openings (p. 29). Here is one instance: The scene is the home of J, K, and their children. J and K are speaking Apache when L, a clan brother of J, comes to the door. J says:

> J: Hello, My friend! How you doing? How you feeling, L? You feeling good?
> ((J now turns to K and addresses her.))
> J: Look who here, everybody! Look who just come in. Sure, it's my Indian friend, L. Pretty good all right!
> ((J slaps L on the shoulder and, looking him directly in his eyes, seizes his hand and pumps it wildly up and down.))

As this episode continues, K laughs at J's keying actions, and J remarks, in Apache, about the stupidity of Anglos. J keys his playful intention by speaking in semi-grammatical English and by using stock phrases to lampoon Anglo greetings. Are these the front bracketing keys for a play episode?

To answer that question we must ask how much of the work of framing appears at the very start of this interaction? J speaks two lengthy turns, each composed of multiple turn-constructional units. The clearest grammar error ('look who here') occurs in the second utterance indicated on this transcript. J accompanies his long spate of talk—all in English—with overbuilt dramatic gestures. The friend, L, presumably responds in ways that ratify the play frame, and the spectators to the event may show appreciation by means of laughter. Each of these cues raises the possibility of play, but these cues are located throughout the passage, and no one cue or set of cues seems to indicate play more than any other.

May we distinguish between framing done at the front bracket and activities that sustain a state of play?[2] For most instances of telephone speech play, it seems misleading to claim that a keying message signals a frame beginning for play. For ten years, my colleagues[3] and I have searched for the elusive beginning bracket carrying the message "this is play." Instead of clear front-bracket signals, we find instances like this one:

UTCL D8

CAROL: Have you *ate* t'day?
          (0.5)
CAROL: *Eaten?*=

RICK:	**=eh heh heh=**
CAROL:	**=day hay huh huh** *eated.* **·hhhh=**
RICK:	**=No** *I- I- I-* **already** *ea*ted heh heh heh

In this segment Rick and Carol begin to play. But where is the front bracket keying "this is play"? Play-relevant keying is displayed throughout the episode. Three kinds of keying seem especially important to this fragment:

(1) a speech error.
(2) laughter.
(3) repetition.

Each of these three keying-criteria locates different front bracketing of the play frame. The speech error occurs in this segment's first line. Laughter occurs after the error is corrected, and repetition occupies the following two turns. The play frame is created and sustained through each of these interactive details. There is no single front bracket for play in this episode, but rather play's interactive management occurs across this entire fragment.

Is there some feature that all play-keying has in common? After considering several descriptions of "games," the philosopher Wittgenstein asks whether there are any characteristics shared by all instances of games. "Don't think," he cautions us, "look!" Don't think that just because there is a word, "game," that all games have something particular in common. Rather, there seem to be clusters of *family resemblances* tying certain instances of games to others in networks of similarity (1953, paragraphs 64-66). Could this be any less true for the notion of play which animates games and other interactional events? Don't think, listen!

We may, by repeated listening, transform the question: "How do speakers begin playing?" into the question: "How do telephone partners interact to play?" Bateson anticipates this reframing of the question in his essay, "A theory of play and fantasy":

> In the Andaman Islands, peace is concluded after each side has been given ceremonial freedom to strike the other. This example, however, also illustrates the labile nature of the frame "This is play," or "This is ritual" . . . [T]he ritual blows of peace-making are always liable to be mistaken for the "real" blows of combat. In this event, the peace-making ceremony becomes a battle. . . . [T]his leads to recognition of a more complex form of play: the game which is constructed not upon the premise "This is play" but rather around the question "is this play?" (1972, p. 182)

In this instance keying raises a question: "Is this play?" rather than establishing a proposition "This is play." Such interrogative keying invites a partner's agreeing or disagreeing alignment. Play is accomplished in slots within trajectories. Any marking of a single turn may raise the question: "Is this play?" Parties must then work out the course of play-in-progress.

Drew's study of the sequential environment of teasing (1987, chapter 7) aligns with Bateson's suggestion that play keying raises a question. Drew notes that teasing utterances may be followed by straight (po-faced) responses. Alternately, a tease might be followed by a counter-tease, or by a show of amusement. There are also other alternatives, such as responding with anger, asking "are you kidding?" or ignoring the possible tease. A teasing utterance raises a question—Is this play? Is this teasing? Metacommunicative framings come about not through individual message units that accomplish bracketing, but by interactive displays across speakers' turns. Each such indication of play's possible relevance may be confirmed, denied, ignored, or transformed by what happens next.

With the issue posed this way we may reconsider keyings that mark possible play: error, laughter, and imitation.

Speech Errors and the Keying of Play

The speech error aids description of the poetics of ordinary talk because errors "provide a break in the conversation's surface which permits easy observation of the phenomena" (Jefferson, 1977, pp. 2-3). This imagery suggests ocean waves that break upon beaches. These are spectacular phenomena in their own right. However, they also indicate subsurface phenomena—waves work in the ocean even when no breaks appear on the surface. Jefferson suggests studying speech errors to discover poetic devices in conversation because errors show workings of conversational structuration that operate all the time—but usually remain unnoticed.

For instance, Jefferson argues that certain speech errors occur due to the speaking of a "sound-row." The sounds in a row are marked with square brackets.

> Super Bowl XI
>
> **Gowdy:**   **[Fore]man stopped at the [for]ty, *thir*ty yard line.**

> SBL:1:1:9:1:R
>
> **Audrey:**   **And I: *I:* [w]ill uh be: up that [w]ay [W-] (.) uh Thursday.**

Jefferson argues that these errors occur within a run of similar word-initial sounds leading a speaker to choose an incorrect item from the desired category (i.e., Wednesday not Thursday, or forty instead of thirty). These errors occur because alliteration's poetic force momentarily supersedes a rational course of talk.

The performer of an error may experience a comic pratfall, a moment of broken surface, a glimpse of life's impossible complexity. Actors sometimes orient to errors in celebratory playful ways.

Jefferson, 1987, p. 87

PAT: ...the Black Muslims are certainly more
        provocative than the Black *Muslims ever* were.
JO: The Black *Pan*thers.
PAT: The Black *Pan*thers. What'd I
JO: You said the Black Muslims twice.
PAT: *Did* I *really?*
JO: Yes you *di:*d, but that's alright I forgive you,

In this case, the error and the subsequent correction occur in the first two turns. The other four turns in the segment show aftershocks orienting to this break in conversation's surface. Jefferson describes Jo's first utterance 'The Black Panthers,' as an *exposed correction,* or a turn that has no other business than to do correction. Exposed corrections trigger further repetitions, laughter, and accounts. These may chain out into extended play episodes. This speech error and its subsequent correction may be taken (in retrospect) as a front bracket for an episode of play.

Jefferson, 1987, p. 97

CHARLES: ... gyrate- not gyrate- is gyrate the right
            word?
LEE: Gravitate.
CHARLES: *Gra*vitate! heh gyrate hehh
LEE: hehh

To blatantly correct an error in the prior utterance breaks the plane of language, or claims that the prior error has already done so. Exposed correction calls attention to the form of talk itself: "Is this metacommunication?"

To summarize: errors may trigger corrections, aftershocks, and other celebrations. Posterror interaction may key the question, "Is this play?" The keying is distributed across turns containing the error, the correction, and subsequent aftershock activity. This telephone instance occurs ten minutes into a hilarious encounter (see duet before this chapter).

UTCL D8

RICK: Have you had dinner yet?
           (0.4)
CAROL: No I haven't.
CAROL: ⌈Have you.⌉
RICK: ⌊I- I'm   ⌋ so h(h)ungr(h)y,
CAROL: Are you starving?
RICK: ↑Ye:s
           (0.3)

⇒   CAROL: Have you *a*te today?
                   (0.4)
     CAROL: *E*aten
     RICK: *h*eh heh ⌈heh huh   ⌉
     CAROL: ⌊heh hueh⌋ I said *e*ated ·*h*hh=
     RICK: =No I- I- I already *e*ated *h*hhih

This speech error (arrow) becomes a focus for playful celebration. The error is at first corrected by its speaker, but the correction contains another error ('I said eated')—possibly showing ceremonial self-deprecation. Rick then laughs and ridicules the error by repeating: 'I already eated.' Carol shares the laughter and adds another mistaken verb form—is this slapstick? Rick picks up the mistake theme by repeating "eated" in a turn that *could* answer a question:

               D8 detail ((idealized))
     CAROL: **Have you ate today?**   [eaten]
     RICK: **No, I already eated.**   [ate]

But as a monkey's "playful nip" does not denote a "bite," Rick's is a fictional (probably false) answer. The answer makes a tense-mistake on the same verb as the question's error, which may point the earlier error. Is this ridicule? Much teasing, laughter, and repetition follow, allowing us to see, in retrospect, that this speech error triggers aftershock "fantasizing" (Bales, 1969; Bormann, 1972).

The speech error may be seen to act as a front-bracket key in Goffman's approach to framing. It certainly is the moment from which this episode, viewed in retrospect, became playful. However, numerous speech errors are ignored, and others are corrected without play or comment. It is not just the error by itself that keys play, but also its subsequent corrections and the co-celebrations. These celebrations are marked by shared laughter.

Shared Laughter and the Keying of Play

Laughing's distinctive nonverbal vocalization is a sign of play. Quintilian notes that laughter often seems trivial but

> has a certain imperious force of its own which is very hard to resist. It often breaks out against our will and extorts confession of its power, not merely from our face and voice, but convulses the whole body as well. (p. 443)

Laughter is a sort of involuntary, vocal exhalation that signals amusement, farce, or the unexpected. When laughter occurs, it ties itself to the last thing said (Sacks, Fall 1967, lecture 14, pp. 15-18), and celebrates that prior event by inviting play keying.

Jefferson's transcription system has produced a revolutionary break-through in the study of laughter. Whereas previous researchers and tran-scribers have indicated the occurrence of laughter only in vague terms, Jefferson transcribes its actual syllables: i.e., hah hah hah (1985). These transcriptions reveal startlingly precise patterns in laughter, including the patterns by which two parties *share* laughter. Conversation participants offer each other opportunities to laugh, primarily by laughing during or after a speaking turn—marking that turn as a candidate laughable, and inviting playful keying—in shared laughter.

Jefferson, 1979, p. 81

ELLEN:	*I am cheap* he said, ·hh about the b*i*g
	things. he says but not the *li*ddle
	things, hhhHA⌈HA HA HA
BILL:	⌊heh heh heh

In this instance, Ellen invites Bill to laugh by laughing after her own utter-ance. Bill accepts the invitation and the two speakers overlap their shared laughter. To describe Ellen's laugh tokens as "inviting laughter" rather than simply as "keying" is to situate in dialogue the achievement of play framing. The first laugh raises the question: "is this play?" and the second laugh ratifies play as a live possibility. The play frame is keyed not by just the first laugh, but by the shared laughter of two speakers.

Once laughter raises possible play keying, the frame must periodically be resustained by further shared laughter. The relevance of an invitation to laugh is cancelled if the next speaker talks without laughter.

Jefferson, 1979, p. 84

JAMES:	...dat *nee*dle's what I can't stand
	HAH⌈
VIC:	⌊Use- Tellim *ga*:s.

James stops laughing as soon as Vic shows (by talking) that he has declined the invitation to laugh. The keying of play is interactive. Jefferson also illustrates instances in which speakers of the laughable turn display equivo-cal signals that might be laughter—that raise the question: "is this laughter?"

GTS, Jefferson, 1979, p. 89
((FACE TO FACE, GROUP SETTING))

ROGER:	*You*:: are what dey refer to in rougher
	circles as a chick'n shit=
ROGER:	=hhh ⌈hhehh
KEN:	⌊heh:heh heh

Following his possible witticism, Roger makes an out-breath noise that might become laughter. This seems to invite Ken's laughter, but only when Ken laughs does Roger more clearly laugh. Where is the keying of play here? In interactive patterning coperformed by two speakers.[4]

Shared laughter in telephone conversation rarely begins with both parties commencing laughter at the same moment. Rather, one party more-or-less invites the other one to laugh by laughing during or after an utterance. Glenn (1989) cites Ella Wheeler Wilcox's poetic proverb "laugh and the world laughs with you" to illustrate laughter's orientation toward becoming shared. Glenn defines shared laughter as transcribable laugh tokens occurring in adjacent turn units by different speakers:

> Charles: *Gra*vitate! heh gyrate hehh
> Lee: hehh

or occurring in overlap:

> RICK: *h*eh heh ⌈heh huh   ⌉
> CAROL: ⌊heh hueh⌋ I said *eat*ed ·*h*hh

Laughter, unlike speech, thrives in lengthy overlap. In fact, play may drive speech from the floor while partners share severe giggles. Laughter's overlap-ability makes it useful for extending play's relevance. In the D8 segment shared laughter binds the play episode together by repeatedly ratifying play's continued relevance. Each arrow here indicates an instance that fits Glenn's criteria for shared laughter.

> UTCL D8
>
> | | CAROL: | Have you *a*te today? |
> |---|---|---|
> | | | (0.4) |
> | | CAROL: | *Ea*ten |
> | ⇒ | RICK: | heh heh ⌈heh huh   ⌉ |
> | | CAROL: | ⌊heh hueh⌋ I said *eat*ed ·*h*hh |
> | | RICK: | No I- I- I already *eat*ed ⌈*h*hhih |
> | | CAROL: | ⌊You already *eat*ed? |
> | | RICK: | Yes |
> | ⇒ | CAROL: | What did you eat at *h*h ⌈↑hih= |
> | | RICK: | ⌊But I'm going to go- |
> | | | I'm gonna go- r*an* now .*h*h *h*h *h*h |
> | | CAROL: | You gonna go r*an* |
> | | RICK: | I'm gonna go ran |
> | ⇒ | CAROL: | nh *h*ah *h*ah *h*ah hah |
> | | RICK: | ·*h*h |

⇒ CAROL: Fuck you. ·*hhh* *hah* hah hah hah hah He's gonna go
          r*a*n now eyahuh huh hih *huh* *h*uh huh huh huh
          ·*h*h ⌈↑Leave me al↑o:ne.
   RICK: ⌊and the- and then- and then I'm gonna-
          and then I'm gonna *go*:n to a movie *h*hh
   CAROL: Gonna g*o*ne to a movie?
⇒ RICK: Gonna g*o*ne to a mov⌈(h)ie.
   CAROL: ⌊ehhih hih hnh hnh hnh
   CAROL: ·*h*hh *Ar*e you gonna gone to a movie?
   RICK: Yeah,
                (0.2)
   RICK: ⌈You wanna c*o*med? *h*no(h)o,
   CAROL: ⌊(You)
   CAROL: I wanna c*a*me.
⇒ RICK: ·*h*hh Wanna c(h)ome
   CAROL: hnh huh You wanna came ↑hnh hnh hhn ↑hnh
          hnh hnh (0.4) ·*h*hhh heh Leave me al↑o:ne.
⇒ RICK: ·*h*hh
                (0.5)
   CAROL: uhh (.) *h*eh I'm gonna went home Lee Anne
          says huh huh hûh (0.3) ·*kh*hh
                (0.2)
   CAROL: *R*ick l*a*ugh.

Especially at the seven locations marked by arrows in this transcription, shared laughter extends play from turn to turn. The players provide booster laughter every three to five seconds, reindicating a continuing positive answer to the recurrent question: "Is this still play?" As long as the laughter recurs, participants play, but the state of play ends when a partner fails to share laughter. Then the other party says, 'Rick, laugh!' These partners orient to shared laughter's absence as well as its presence.

Two-party versus Multi-party Shared Laughter

Glenn (1989) contrasts shared laughter's initiation in two-party and multi-party conversations. In two-party conversations, such as most telephone encounters, the speaker of the laughable is also the first person to laugh about two thirds of the time.

⇒ RICK: ·*h*hh Wanna c(h)ome
   CAROL: hnh huh You wanna came ↑hnh hnh hhn ↑hnh

But in multi-party conversations eighty percent of first laughs are by somebody *other* than the speaker of the laughable turn.

UTCL A30

SAM: *But. (.) if I dri:ve up (0.4) in my: (1.2)*
        s::::ixtee:n ninetee:n.
        ⌈get out and *push*: so ⌈help me:
LIL: ⌊heh hih heh hih   ⌊hih

⇒   LIL: ⌈ihh ih*eh* heh *heh* h*a*h hah hah huh
    JON: ⌊ih ih ih ih ih ih

In this instance, from a three-party telephone conversation, Sam speaks the laughable line about driving an old car in order to show himself as a man of the people. Lil begins to laugh in overlap with this utterance, and the third speaker, Jon, joins Lil's laughter: The shared laugher is therefore between two listeners. Spectatorship is a common ingredient in play. Recall Basso's instance, in which speaker J relies upon an audience in his keying of play. Group settings might be the most natural play settings. The telephone dyad is a special case because there is ordinarily only one primary recipient, hence the speaker of the laughable must play roles of both speaker and cocelebrant.

Whatever the reason for the contrast, multi-party telephone conversation has a different sound in its play episodes than does the telephone dyad. Contrast this three-party telephone instance with the instance from D8, above:

UTCL A30

JON: **But wh*a*t cars do businessmen dri:ve. They**
        drive C*ou*gars and Merc*e*deses they don't drive
        uh (0.2) nineteen *ei*ghty one uh Chevrolets
SAM: **ehh huh=**
JON: **=Gray M*a*libu:s and**
LIL: *h*hh
⇒   SAM: ⌈↑hih hih heh heh heh
    JON: ⌊**And u::h and P*o*ntiacs that- that do*n*'t work**
SAM: hih ⌈hih hih hih
JON: ⌊**and need radiators it-**
SAM: hih huh
JON: **Nineteen** ⌈**fifty D*a*tsuns that need new brake=**
SAM: ⌊i*h*ih   ehih hih
⇒   JON: **=(dances)** ⌈*hhh* ↑hu:h ↑hu:h huh-h
    SAM: ⌊hih hihuh
JON: ⌈*hh h*h huh huh   ⌈huh
SAM: ⌊**Well hey ma:n just a** ⌊**part a gittn (0.8)**
        that's right there hey (0.2) majority people
        in this world not driving Bee Em Dubyuhs
            (0.8)

SAM: And they gonn say I'm working di*rect*ly with
        the people

LIL: R*i:* ⌈ght.

JON: ⌊ehhh *hu*nuh

SAM: Suppo*rt* the p⌈*eo*ple

LIL: ⌊ih hih hih=

SAM: =Dr*i*vin the c*a*r- ↑like the people.

⇒ LIL: ⌈hih heh heh

   JON: ⌊ehhu huh ↑hih huh huh-uh huh huh
               (0.4)

LIL: euh hu:↑:h

JON: ·hhh So, I wo⌈uld

SAM: ⌊I would- I wouldn't want my
        *fe*llow const*i*tuents.

JON: ↑uh ⌈*h* h h h   ⌈huh- ahh

SAM: ⌊to *fee*l *ou*t of pl⌊*a*ce. When *I* dr*i:*ve *u*p
        (0.8) in what *East Au*stin.

⇒ LIL: Eh ⌈*he*h h*a*h hhh

   SAM: ⌊In muh- *Per* se? (0.2) *Benz.*

SAM: And what they gonn say this « uppity mobile
        *pe*rson. » want a- wants to come t*e*ll me what- .
        wh*a*t could he tell me. eh- loo- lo*o*k at him,
        he- (0.3) s*hi*t he alr*e*ady up in the hierarchy
        so sh*i*t (0.4) why should I l*i*sten to *hi*m he
        duh- you know he can't help me
               (0.4)

SAM: *But.* (.) if I dr*i:*ve up (0.4) in my: (1.2)
        s::::*i*xtee:n ninetee:n.
        ⌈get out and p*u*sh: so ⌈*he*lp me:

LIL: ⌊heh hih heh hih   ⌊hih

⇒ LIL: ⌈ihh ih*e*h heh *he*h h*a*h hah hah huh

   JON: ⌊ih ih ih ih ih ih

SAM: everb*o*dy else in the ↑neighborhoo:d car.

⇒ LIL: ↑eh eh ⌈eh eh ehh-eh.

   JON: ⌊*u*hh hh*â*h hy*u*h

SAM: This d*u*de will pro'ly call well hey this is a
        individual probly who- you know, (0.2) who's
        gonna share somethin- of c*o*mmon *i*nterest with
        me

This instance illustrates shared laughter in multi-party conversation.[5] The
arrows designating shared laughter show different formats than occur in

two-party laughter. Most often, two listeners share the laughing, and sometimes the speaker himself laughs after a listener laughs. In two-party telephone conversation the speaker most often provides the first laugh (Glenn, 1989).

It is not clear in this three-party instance that further speaking cancels the relevance of laughter, as it does in two-party calls. This question deserves further attention.

These differences inform us both about the nature of play and about the importance of the variable *number of participants* in telephone conversation. In play episodes the number of participants affects the forms for eliciting and sharing laughter. Perhaps the three-party setting is more vulnerable to marked play-episodes.[6] Telephone talk is presently moving beyond the dyad. Many telephones now allow three parties to be connected at once, and if this feature comes into routine use, it could bring dramatic changes to telephone speaking.

To summarize: Laughter, especially shared laughter, keys the continuing relevance of play in an encounter. Laughter ratifies that play is in progress, or raises the question: Is this play? Speakers deploy laughter to invite others to join in celebrating. Laughter extends play.

Repetition and the Keying of Play

> Play . . . renews itself in constant repetition.
> Hans-Georg Gadamer

Aristotle defined all poetic activity as imitation. Bateson writes that play emerges in imitation of combat. In telephone play partners do considerable verbal imitation—especially repeating things said shortly before. For repetition to occur, there must first be some model to repeat, then miming of that model. A repetition locates the model, which allows repetition to serve backward-listening discourse functions, such as repair initiation, metacommunication, and play keying. Any repetition may do all of these at the same time.

In the D8 example the partners feature the repetitions of four verbs: eat, run, gone, and come. The playful possibilities of this scene unfold first in repetition of "eaten/eated," then run through four cycles of four repetitions each. Each of these cycles turns around comic mistakes in verb tenses. This play episode displays such rich poetic structure in rhythm, rhyme, lexicon, and stanza that we may set it as a traditional poem:

C:	**Have you ate today?—eated**
R:	**No I already eated**
C:	**You ready eated?**
R:	**Yes**
C:	**What did you eat at?**

R:	But I'm going to go ran now
C:	You gonna go ran?
R:	I'm gonna go ran
C:	Fuck you, gonna go ran now
C:	Leave me alo:ne.
R:	And then I'm gonna gone to a movie
C:	Gonna gone to a movie?
R:	Gonna gone to a movie
C:	Are you gonna gone to a movie?
R:	Yeah. You wanna comed? no
C:	I wanna came
R:	Wanna comed?
C:	You wanna came?
C:	Leave me alo:ne.

Setting the lines this way shows the play episode as a poem of four stanzas. Each stanza displays four repetitions of a verb error. At the end of the second and fourth stanzas is a repeated refrain: 'Leave me alone.' These repetitions outline the episode's dramatic structure.

Within this repetitive dramatic structuring, these partners play a delicate game focused around two framing questions: (1) is this play? and (2) is this courtship?

The courtship reading shows not only in play keying, but also in the pre-sequential organization of this same episode. In the first, third, and fourth stanzas the players advance pre-invitations to dating activity: going to supper, going to a movie. The segment that contains the first 'eated' speech error displays a probable gambit toward arranging for a meal together.

RICK:	Have you had dinner yet?
	(0.4)
CAROL:	No I haven't.
CAROL:	⌈Have you.
RICK:	⌊I- I'm so h(h)ungr(h)y,
CAROL:	Are you starving?
RICK:	Ye:s
	(0.3)
CAROL:	Have you *ate* today?

Just when the pre-invitations have come to the point at which an invitation would be most relevant, the speech error occurs. In fact the turn with the error 'Have you ate today' occurs when Carol, having announced that she has not eaten, could be fishing for Rick to invite her on a date.

The topic of going to a movie, which follows, is another matter that could grow interactively into a date proposal. The parties play upon this issue with a set of "to come" verbs—a verb used in date invitations ('wanta come?'), and also a verb with sexual associates. These pre-invitation sequences revel in sexual double-entendre on topics that are standards for romantic celebration: inviting, eating, movies, and sex.

Consider the refrain following stanzas two and four: 'leave me alone.' This phrase's uses include: "stop pestering me," "leave me without a date," and "give me a break." 'Leave me alone' literally asks the other to stop a line of action; but its ironic use celebrates those very playful actions (e.g., tickling, foreplay, pranks). Like the playful nip Bateson describes in animal play, these instances of 'leave me alone' do not denote what they literally denote.

Play deepens in repetition. The second 'leave me alone' is more obviously playful than the first. The fourth set of stanzas with verb errors is more obviously playful than the first—although it still preserves the ambiguity that it *might* get transformed into an actual date invitation.

A broader sense of repetition might be grossly measured by how much repeating has already happened in the whole encounter. The 'eated' instance occurs ten minutes into an encounter (see duet before chapter). Below are the first lines spoken by the parties to each other during the encounter:

UTCL D8.2:1

	RICK:	YE::ES? *h*eh *h*eh heh
	CAROL:	Rick?
	RICK:	·*h*hh Ye(h)e:(h)s?
⇒	CAROL:	(h)You qu*ee*:r w(h)at're you doin
		(0.4)
⇒	RICK:	U:h I dunn*o* what're you doin you queer bait

Note the repetitive symmetry of Rick's response to Carol's marked initial inquiry. He repeats and transforms her term 'you queer,' into 'you queer bait.' This symmetrically returns the initial inquiry, retaining-by-repeating its special marking: 'queer.'

Carol's initial inquiry uses the format of a possible pre-invitation; and Rick's response parries this possibility while at the same moment celebrating its occurrence. The patterning of repetition-in-play stems from the earliest moments of this encounter. This is part of the background for the subsequent 'eated' episode.

Repetition and Metacommunication

These players' poetic repetitions co-occur with another indication of heightened message awareness: *meta-talk,* or explicit commentary on conversational form. Repetitions, by locating prior items, display metalinguistic awareness. All question-repeat repair initiation partakes of this property (see Schegloff et al., 1977). The heightened awareness spawned by any repetition may provide apt openings for explicit meta-talk. (See **m** notations below.)

		D8.2:1
	RICK:	What're *you* guys doin
		(0.3)
	CAROL:	*Well-* um we've been looking for: apartments all ↑da:y and no:w (.) we're (cooking)
	RICK:	you're- you're (punting)
	CAROL:	Cooking
		(0.2)
	RICK:	K*i*cking
	CAROL:	↑Cooking.
	RICK:	*Coo*king *h*h *h*h
	CAROL:	↑Ye::s.
	RICK:	Oh *ho* ho ho=
	CAROL:	=P*u*mping, we're p*u*mp*i*ng. *h*hh ↑huh huh huh=
	RICK:	=·*h*hh=
m	CAROL:	=·*h*hh huh, what could th*a*t mean
		.
		. ((about 10 seconds deleted))
		.
	RICK:	P*u*mp*i*ng?
	CAROL:	Pumping
		(1.2)
	RICK:	Puppy? or pumping.
	CAROL:	↑Pumping.
		(0.2)
m	CAROL:	Isn't that what you said?
	RICK:	Pumping?
		(0.2)
	CAROL:	Yeah
	RICK:	S*e*xually heh heh heh
m	CAROL:	Is that what you mea(h)nt
	RICK:	·*h*hh no(h) not at a(h)ll.
	CAROL:	O(h)h,
m	RICK:	·*h*hh Is that what *you* meant?
	CAROL:	↑No. not at ↑all.

This play episode is completed within the first minute of this telephone encounter. Its sexual innuendo culminates in the twin inquiries: 'is that what you meant?' and twin denials, followed by rhythmic heavy breathing and an abrupt topic shift. Each round of play is achieved in tit-for-tat dialogue, with uptake and response orientating to repetition frames.

Perhaps there is a family of speech objects that show: (1) repetition, and (2) going meta (Schiffrin, 1980; Simons, 1990). Formats for meta-talk specify an utterance and make some observation about it: e.g., 'Isn't that what you said?' These do not always contain repetitions (some of them do), but they do have the function of asking the other to recall what was said, which topicalizes it:

> CAROL: Pumping, we're pumping... what could that mean

or

> CAROL: Is that what you m(h)eant

Simons (1990) refers to instances in political discourse in which parties are "going meta," or moving out the ordinary forward-moving focus of talk to raising awareness of previous talk. The most useful part of Simons' formulation might be the word "going" which shows a shift of partners' attention to discourse details.

There is some principled connection between repetition and going meta. To repeat something is to fish up a previous bit of discourse by redoing it. Repeating promotes examination of the bit of talk as discourse. Next Turn Repair Initiation is done by a repeat of part of a prior utterance. Such turns have in common with exposed corrections that speakers take entire turns that do nothing but repair. Perhaps any turn that does nothing but repeat or near-repeat is a turn that asks a keying question: "Is this speaker going meta?"[7] Or "is this speaker marking this utterance?"

The Thick Guess

The 'pumping' instance displays another repetition-play form, a thick guess, or obviously-wrong repetition whose irony stimulates further play:

> RICK: *Pumping?*
> CAROL: *Pumping*
>   **(1.2)**
> ⇒   RICK: *Puppy? or pumping.*
>   CAROL: ↑**Pumping.**

Rick is acting thick here. He surely does not believe that Carol said 'puppy,' but his obviously-wrong repetition locates the former utterance and suggests humorous play in regard to it. The thick guess leads Carol to repeat

again—and her raised pitch shows uptake of Rick's thick guess. The thick
guess is itself a repeat, albeit one with a pratfall, and it elicits further
repetition.

> Glenn: Simons 2

> A: Who'd you(h) mea(h)n ba:d people
> B: Ba(h)- people
>   (0.8)

⇒   A: Bat people: ⌜or
>   B: ⌞Ba:d people.
>   ((further play))

The speaker of a thick guess does a mock repair, a repetition that asks for
another repetition. The thick guess invites the partner into a repetition game
in service to play.

In the 'pumping' instance, thick guesses braid with repetitions of 'kick-
ing/cooking' and of 'pumping.' The details of these beginnings are arranged
so that no speaker bears primary responsibility for initiating courtship-laden
foolishness. Meanwhile both partners use meta-talk to show that the other
party is primarily responsible for romance initiation.

Play Reframed

Repetition combines with shared laughter and speech errors in celebrating
play framing. Such keying does not cluster near the beginning bracket but
emerges throughout a play episode. The emergent productivity of play
grows from back-and-forth iteration across speaking turns.

Gadamer (1975) argues that play's back-and-forth motion is the ground of
being from which all artistic action flows. Playful interaction seems to flow
without effort, on its own momentum. The individual speaker recedes, and
we hear Whitman's America singing. Play episodes lift up a corner of the
universe to reveal the great Poem, speaking us.

We track the uses of play toward an esthetic ontology. The natural attitude
of everyday life includes orientation to interactive poetic play. Vico wrote
that "the world in its infancy was composed of poetic nations, for poetry is
nothing but imitation" (1744/1970, p. 33).

As telephone partners, let us attune ourselves to our most primordial
voice, the voice of poetry in conversation. Play—the moving back and forth
across speaker turns in repetitive and fictional structurating activity—is the
ground of being from which all speech communication emerges.

Play is, of course, foolishness, which is to say poetics. Like all art, foolishness develops projects. Our examples forward adolescent courtship and
ritual teasing. To speak playfully is to not foreground rhetorical purposes.
Playing does not rule out purposeful accomplishment, but rather puts it in

its place—within play. Poetic play exists before rhetoric, and rhetoric's purposeful speaking grows out of it. As Bateson writes:

> Poetry is not a sort of distorted and decorated prose, but rather prose is poetry which has been stripped down and pinned to a Procrustean bed. . . . (1972; p. 136)

Bateson argues that "where the systemic nature of the world has been ignored in favor of purpose" results have been tragic. If playful interaction is the natural state of conversational speaking, then we fall from this state each time we select and pursue certain (rhetorical) purposes for speech action. The modern telephone partner has thoroughly fallen into purposeful communication, except during those redemptive moments when something breaks the surface of our self-serving rut—a mistake, pratfall. Then we fantasize, we play.

This holds special relevance to telephone conversation because so much of that medium has become the especial carrier of purposes. The telephone invites the subordination of poetry to purpose. Perhaps investigation of the poetics of everyday talk can help restore a damaged performance ecology. Certainly the telephonic revolution, like the industrial revolution out of which it grew, brings ecological damage in its mixed bag of progress. We can best track these suspicions in the first seconds of telephone conversations, the moment of access, a moment that finds callers and answerers may be at cross purposes. This is the primary battlefield of the telephone access war.

```
                        (UTCL A24.1)
            SUE:        Hi. ( . ) You've reached four six fi:ve six
                        three three zero. (0.4) Sorry we can't
                        answer your call right now but if you leave
                        your name number (0.3) and a message we'll
5                       get back to you as soon as we can. (1.0)
                        Please leave your message at the sound of the
                        bee:p. Tha:nks
                            (2.0)
                        BEE::::::::::::::::::::P
10          JAN:        Hi Sue this Jan I just wanted to see: if
                        maybe you could bring ·hhhh some candles to:
                        um (0.6) pt Bato's beca:use ·hhhhhhhhhhh I
                        don't have ti:me. And I got the ca:ke ( . )
                        And its cute and dorable umkay bye
15                          # # (0.3) ((tones)) (1.3)
                        Ri::::::::::::::ng
                            (3.7)
                        Ri::::::::::::::ng
                            (3.0)
20                      BEEP ((CALL WAITING))
                        ## ((ANSWERER PICK-UP))
            JAN:        Hello?
            SUE:        Hi::.
            JAN:        Hold on.
25                          # ((SWITCHING))
            JAN:        Hello
                            (1.2)
            JAN:        Hel⌈lo
                           ⌊R::::::::::ng
30                          # ((SWITCHING))
            JAN:        You screening your calls
                            (0.4)
            SUE:        No why
            JAN:        ·hhhh Cu' I just ↑called you.
35          SUE:        Did you r(h)eally I'm not at home
                        ⌈hhhhuh Wha-
            JAN:        ⌊Oh huh huh I mean like I just hung ↑up.
```

```
        SUE:    What's up
        JAN:    ·hhhh Nothin I called to see'f you could
40              bring candl:es to Bato's
                    (0.4)
        SUE:    Candles
        JAN:    Yeah=
        SUE:    =Birthday candles
45      JAN:    Yeah
        SUE:    What kinda cake did you get ((baby voice))
        JAN:    I got- it- it's little.
                    (0.4)
        JAN:    Because it's so:- cute- and it's great.
50      SUE:    Okay hh
        JAN:    I went to Texas star it's like- almond and
                chocolate and shit.
        SUE:    ↑Yu:m.
        SUE:    Un⌈kay
55      JAN:        ⌊And- pra- amaretto or some'n.
        SUE:    That's cool five o'clock?
        JAN:    ·hhh U::m yeah ↑who's all goin ↑I want like a
                lot a people to ↑g⌈o::.
        SUE:                      ⌊I have no idea.
60      SUE:    I mean Leslie dund even know if she can go:
                and Julia's leaving town (0.3) I jus saw
                Julia she says she's called ub- every day
                this week ( . ) y'all hou- y'alls place and
                Mary won't call her back=
65      JAN:    =I've called her ten fuckin times she ain't
                called back
                    (1.6) / ((breathing))
        SUE:    Anyway where's Mary
        JAN:    ·hhhhhh She getting u:m bikini wax
70                  (0.4)
        SUE:    Oh is she
        JAN:    Yeah=
        SUE:    =Uhh (0.2) I wouldn't do that if you paid me
        JAN:    Uh huh huh huh ↑huh huh huh ·hhhhh
75      SUE:    Has she ever done it before
        JAN:    Uh uh
        SUE:    Oh my God ( . ) uh huh huh ·hhhh huh
```

		⌈huh huh
	JAN:	⌊I hope she had a dri:nk beforehand
80		(0.6)
	SUE:	Have you done it
	JAN:	Uh uh
	SUE:	·Aaaahh *o:*⌈::hh
	JAN:	⌊I won't do it=
85	SUE:	=I won't e:ither. I used to.
		(0.5)
	SUE:	⌈but
	JAN:	⌊I'm tryin to get hold of Pecan Street for
		Tracy's deal hh
90	SUE:	For Tracy- what Tracy's deal
	JAN:	She having a shower here hh
	SUE:	When
	JAN:	April som'n
		(0.3)
95	JAN:	You're *o*n the l*i*st ·hh
	SUE:	That's cool
	JAN:	*A*wright
	SUE:	·hhh U:m- well when's Mary gun be home.
		Do you know?
100	JAN:	O*h a*w
	SUE:	I talked to her mom this morning
	JAN:	Oh really
	SUE:	Called her mom to see if she wanted me to do
		anything special in Mexico
105	JAN:	What'd she say
	SUE:	Will I go by the store tomorrow she
		might have a little something for me give
		Mary uh- fact they're gonna take her out to
		dinner tomorrow night
110	JAN:	·hhhhhhh Awright=
	SUE:	=And we'll pro'ly take her out to dinner
		Sunday night.
	JAN:	·hhhhhhh ↑Alright well then I'll see you at
		fi:ve. I'll tell Mary to call you.
115	SUE:	pt ·h- W:ell- (0.2) when are you leaving are
		you at home for a while?
		(0.4)

	JAN:	Euh- I'm like in and out all day (.) but I'll
		pro'ly be home for like an hour and a half or
120		so.=
	SUE:	=We:ll- can I come by and say hello?
	JAN:	Yeah.
	SUE:	Okay.
	JAN:	*Byh*
125	SUE:	Bye

9

THE TELEPHONE ACCESS WAR

It is my heart-warm and world-embracing
Christmas hope and aspiration that all of
us—the high, the low, the rich, the poor, the
admired, the despised, the loved, the hated,
the civilized, the savage—may eventually be
gathered together in a heaven of everlasting
rest and peace and bliss—except the
inventor of the telephone.

Mark Twain, 1890

The telephone, for all its uses, conveniences, and joys, brings interpersonal complaints in its wake. Many complaints are about access to telephone partners.

In the duet before this chapter, Jan, with some edge to her voice, asks her friend Sue: 'You screening your calls.' Jan had just telephoned Sue and left a message on Sue's answering machine. Sue then called a moment later while Jan was trying to call somebody else!

Jan's question, 'are you screening your calls?' reminds us of one current use of the telephone answering machine. This chapter ties call screening to current conflicts over power relationships between telephone callers and answerers: the telephone access war.

The telephone's rise to popularity a century ago changed contemporary life in many ways, some of which were obvious at the time, and some of which are now becoming apparent. Telephony privileges projects of callers over those of answerers, and over those with whom answerers had previously been conversing.

North American telephony's technological advances have contributed spin-off technologies: switchboards, cables, long distance, microwaves, fiber optics, the transistor. Additionally, we now live in the age of telephone add-ons. The phone company has moved from POTS—plain old telephone service, to PANS—pretty amazing new services. We face a bewildering array of services: call waiting, conference calling, call forwarding, personalized ringing, phone shopping, and much more. Add-on vendors dazzle us with programmable telephones, answering machines, voice mail, computer modems, FAX machines, cellular and portable phones. The multi-party telephone conversation will become commonplace. We now may direct-dial world wide. We shall see increased video phoning.

The potential uses of new telephone services are staggering,[1] as is the recent growth of the industries touching telephony. In 1982 there were fewer than one million answering machines sold, but consumers purchased nearly 13 million in the first nine months of 1989. Cordless phone sales rose from 2 to 9 million annually during the same period (Hall, 1989).

Telephone expansion is not all good news. Why do many of today's telephone complaints echo Mark Twain's lament? Why should we curse the telephone and its inventor? How is it that certain problems of telephone life become increasingly evident in an age of unprecedented innovation? Perhaps a century of telephone use takes a cumulative toll, or new technological developments overload telephony resulting in catastrophic stresses.

The predominant telephone problems revolve around who gets to talk to whom and when. Recent complaints in the public press show a continuing fascination with telephone access:

> Many secretaries are so protective of their bosses that it's impossible to break the phone barrier. . . . When a secretary says in a very intimidating voice, "Mr Golson is in a meeting. May I inquire what you're calling about" I keep a list of responses on my wall which I refer to depending on my mood. . . . "Tell Mr. Golson we just got his tests back from the lab. . . . [or] I just wanted to tell him the fire has been put out." (Art Buchwald, 10-3-85)

This writer tells of a power-struggle between a caller and an answerer's stand-in. The caller adapts to this problem with innuendoes designed to break through this access barrier. As this caller strategizes against a stand-in for the answerer, the next instance expresses irritation with stand-ins for callers, or

> people calling you up without actually calling you up. Instead you pick up your phone to hear a secretary demand to know who you are, inform you that Mr. Wingdinger requires you and then order you to hold. For days. (Michael Kilian, 2-28-86)

Both callers and answerers are likely to complain about getting put on hold. The length of such a hold can be a source of anger, or humor—but always gives interpersonal offense.

These two complaints address struggles that have been going on for most of the telephone century. The next two items fret about new telephone technologies and therefore reveal themselves as artifacts of the late eighties and early nineties. However, these instances also show concerns of access:

> Today I want to CLICK. Excuse me. OK. Today I want to talk about CLICK. Excuse me again. OK, where were we? Oh, yeah, I was saying that CLICK.

Never mind, just ignore it. I was saying that I want to CLICK about this major stride forward in CLICK phone technology called "call waiting," which is such a big CLICKing CONVENIENCE that I'd like to find the CLICK who invented it and. . . . (Dave Barry, 1989)

Call waiting increases a caller's power to enact wanton interruptive disregard for events in progress. Call waiting, like the telephone itself, grants imbalanced powers to callers (see "Shoe" cartoon). By contrast, the answering machine grants power to the answerer. The "honesty" of this phone machine provides a brutal caricature of the powers that a machine's user may wield. These powers are the stakes in the telephone access war.

These journalists' laments take a humorous tone, but the anger behind the humor springs from systematic problems of access in telephone conversation. The privacy of our homes is increasingly under telephonic attack. The telephone overruns our cars, our patios, our airplanes. Soon, we may have the option to carry a telephone in a wristwatch. Is this an unmixed blessing? What are the prices of this progress?

The telephone has created interactive imbalances by interrupting other activities, tying purposeful pairs of people together, and privileging callers' projects. The phone's first hundred years have displayed almost unchecked caller hegemony.

Caller Hegemony

The telephone shifts power to the calling party, who knows what person is to be called, and why. The answering party takes a pig in a poke. This development, now a century old, creates media effects we are just beginning to evaluate. The ringing telephone may truncate virtually any ongoing activity. Consider the following scene: You and your best loved one are having the most difficult argument you can remember. S/he has just escalated the argument by calling you a terrible name. You ready a stinging retort, but just then the phone rings. Do you answer it? The overwhelming majority of the hundreds of individuals to whom I have posed that question indicate that they would answer the telephone even on such an extreme occasion.

Any activity in progress seems vulnerable to interruption by telephone. So we find these contemporary telephone pathologies: Sixteen customers stand in the department store line while the clerk stops waiting on them to answer the phone. The college student, in a twenty-minute interview with a professor, waits through four telephone interruptions. The suburbanite gets up from a family supper to hear a computer ask "Mrs. Behrens, how are you?" The programmer interrupts a debugging effort to answer the phone, then must start the task over. The shop supervisor stops instructing a worker when the phone rings; a lathe remains idle during the supervisor's phone conversation. The sleeper awakes at three AM to answer a call intended for the all-night restaurant with a similar phone number.

Figure 10: The Honest Answering Machine (Reprinted by permission: Tribune Media Services.)

These problems of access are as old as the telephone; they emerge directly from telephone use. Many of these features of telephony were apparent to observers in the phone's first generation, as illustrated three quarters of a century ago in Ruth Draper's monologue, "The Italian Lesson."[2] This half-hour sketch shows a tutorial on Dante interrupted four times by telephone calls.[3] Here is one instance:

> ((SCENE: THE ITALIAN STUDENT, A SUBURBAN
> HOUSEWIFE, BEGINS TO READ THE FIRST LINES
> OF DANTE TO HER TEACHER.))
> **Signorina, I think I'll just run through those**
> **beautiful li:nes aga:in, just to get in the spirit of it**
> **(1.0)**
> **·hhh Nell mezzo: (.) del camin: dee nostra: vita**
> **·hhh ↑Mi ritro va⌈ee: per: unas selva-**
> ⇒　　　　　　　　　⌊rin::::::::::::g
> **Excuse me this telephone is so maddening**
> **Hello?**
> **(0.4)**
> **I'm sorry, I'm afraid it's important or they**
> **wouldn't call me = hello who is it please.**
> **(0.7)**
> **↑Oh Miss Pounder.**
> **(0.3)**
> **Excuse me for being so fierce, Miss Pounder**

A telephone summons interrupts a speech event in progress. An oral reading of a line of poetry is occurring when the telephone rings in overlap with that line. The poetry reading continues about a second and a half, and is then cut off at the next to last word of a poetic line. The location of this cut off displays to the interrupted partner, the teacher, that the present encounter is being truncated. This cue is followed by an apology to the teacher paired with the justification that a phone call must be important. The face-to-face encounter is put on hold.

Draper's monologue portrays the telephone's power of access. Recall the nineteenth-century fiction cited in chapter 2 in which a telephone marriage proposal is accepted over a face-to-face one. Like the Draper monologue, that instance pictures a telephone intruder wresting access away from a face-to-face partner.

Both the "Italian Lesson" and the parable of the two suitors show the caller overpowering the answerer. In the earlier instance, the answerer accepts the telephonic marriage proposal. In the "Italian Lesson" the answerer apologizes to the caller for her 'fierce' mode of answering. These instances show the answerer's powerless position and illustrate that these problems are as old as the telephone itself. Caller hegemony comes with the telephone summons that calls us (1) away from other things, and (2) into asymmetries of relationship.

It is sometimes claimed that telephones are a social leveller because you can, in principle, use them to call anybody (Rakow, 1989). That is only one privilege that the telephone grants to a caller. The telephone also privileges the caller's projects over those of answerers.

How has caller hegemony interacted with socioeconomic privilege? From the early days of the telephone, certain (rich and powerful) people have purchased protection from the vulnerabilities of the answerer role. People high in hierarchies hire telephone answerers—servants at home, receptionists at work—to screen out unwanted intrusions. With these protections for some, we limp into the historical present nagged by imbalances of caller hegemony. We must reexamine the notion that the telephone provides social levelling.

Certain effects of telephone usage have been highlighted and extended in the last decade—since about 1984. That was the year that telephone call waiting first became commonplace in Austin, Texas. Numerous access conflicts emerge with current telephone innovations: telephone call waiting, telephone answering machines, mobile phones, multi-party calling, call forwarding, fax machines, and voice mail. More of these innovations are on the horizon including video phoning, conference calling, and ways to track the identity of callers. These innovations exacerbate properties of the telephone medium and affect the caller-answerer relationship.

We discuss these issues below in terms of three topics: telephone call waiting, telemarketing, and telephone answering machines. In each of these arenas callers and answerers struggle in a telephone access war.

Why I Cancelled Call Waiting

Historically, the telephone has been a medium built for two. Numerous recent innovations (e.g., the conference call, the triad connection) begin to extend telephone talk beyond the dyad. Call waiting is one such development. Its interaction is neither quite dyadic, nor triadic. Rather, the call waiting user waffles back and forth between two dyads. This service, almost unknown until 1980, has now swept to massive popularity.

A call waiting subscriber purchases the possibility to be summoned from one phone call to another—and to juggle the two callers—while speaking to one partner at a time. Call waiting intrudes into the telephone encounter much as the telephone itself intrudes in the rest of life. Therefore to examine call waiting conversations may help us understand the older medium it typifies, but whose phenomena we no longer hear in force of habit.

Call waiting interrupts an ongoing telephone call at a moment that cannot be predicted. Partners must manage the intrusion right on the scene of its occurrence. The trajectory of call waiting prefaces features a "hold on" sequence that begins with a BEEP intruding into a phone call and signalling that there is a new summons awaiting the call waiting subscriber. A subscriber may respond to this beep by placing the present partner on hold.

Each call waiting preface provides a case study in how parties to conversation adapt to a surprising intrusion:

Family Phone 2

	40	Partner:	**But y'know what?=**
	41	SUMMONS:	**# BEEP #**
⇒	42	Subscr:	*Ha*ng on I gotta call nthe other line.
	43	Partner:	**Kay,**
	44	SWITCH	**##**

A call waiting beep triggers a brief exchange to put partner on hold so that subscriber may switch partners. This switching activity is bounded by two electronic switching noises transcribed as lines 41 and 44.[4]

This call waiting preface unfolds quickly. From the caller's standpoint the summons at 41 is just an ordinary phone call, and presumably caller would allow subscriber four to six rings (20 to 30 seconds) to respond. Yet subscriber orients immediately to the beep and completes the switch within three seconds—which is the median length of call waiting prefaces.

When this call waiting beep occurs, there is already sequential business on the floor. Partner has just said, 'You know what?' a pre that anticipates a response like "What?" followed by some telling from the first speaker (Schegloff, 1968; Sacks, 1972; Nofsinger, 1975). This call waiting beep intrudes into this response-relevant moment, thereby presenting subscriber with simultaneous constraints to respond to two pieces of sequential business. Subscriber responds only to the beep, requesting that the partner 'hang on.' Partner says 'kay,' indicating alignment to the revised agenda—and agreeing to hold on. Subscriber instantly switches away, completing the call waiting preface.

To summarize: A call waiting preface consists of a beep, hold on, and okay. If the call waiting noise occurs when there is sequential business on the floor, this business is usually dropped.[5] Sometimes comedy occurs here, as in the duet preceding this chapter. Jan is placing a phone call when the call waiting beep occurs:

	R::::::::::::::ng	
	(3.0)	
	#BEEP#	((call waiting beep))
	##	((SWITCHING))
JAN:	Hello?	

SUE: Hi::.

JAN: Hold on.

Even though she is already waiting for somebody to answer her own phone call, Jan abandons this activity, clicks over to the new caller, and says 'Hello?' Caller Sue answers with 'Hi::.,' indicating a claim to intimacy and expectation that Jan will recognize her voice. Jan's response to this first greeting is not a return greeting, but an insertion sequence *in the middle of a greeting pair* to begin the call waiting preface. Greeting pairs are not ordinarily interrupted by insertion sequences, hence this is a marked occurrence indicating call waiting's priority.

Hold On Outside Call Waiting

To thicken description of how "hold on" turns suspend turn taking without closing a call, we examine this feature in non-call waiting telephone encounters. In these instances, "hold on" still requests a suspension of turn taking.

UTCL A10

D: *Ho*ld on okay?=

K: =Yeah.

These partners use 'hold on' because of interruptive activity at D's end of the phone call. As with call waiting, the request is immediately granted by 'yeah.'

That this is what 'hold on' speakers are trying to achieve can be shown in instances in which that outcome does not immediately occur. Participants recycle elements of the sequence.

UTCL D8.3

C: Lemme get a pencil, hold o:n

          (0.2)

C: Kay

          (0.8)

C: Kay?

          (0.4)

R: Ok*a*y

Carol says 'hold on,' then there is a pause, indicating there is a problem in eliciting Rick's 'okay.' Carol's next verbalization is another version of okay, which prompts her partner. Immediately upon receipt of Rick's 'okay,' speakers suspend turn taking.

Hold on sequences request a suspension of turn taking similar to those in call waiting. However, these non-call-waiting hold ons respect constraints of turn, sequence and episode. This becomes evident as we examine a bit more of an instance described above:

> UTCL A10
>
> **D:** **Eight thirty to twelv- (0.5) o:h shit.**
> **Hold on okay?=**
> **K:** **=Yeah.**

D's turn approaches a possible completion point, when its final syllable is cut-off ('twelv-'). After a pause D says: 'o:h shit. Hold on okay?' The speaker precedes 'hold on' with a cut-off, a pause, and the oh-prefaced expletive 'oh shit'—all of which project that what is to follow does not continue what has gone before (Jefferson, 1978, pp. 220-21). That is, this speaker of 'hold on' previews its appearance and places it near boundaries of turn constructional units.

'Hold on' occurrences also respect sequential units larger than a turn. In this next instance, the speaker of 'hold on' waits till an episode ends before requesting an interruptive time-out.

> UTCL A10.2 ((simplified))
>
> **JOAN:** **Seth says that the brownies were wonderful**
> **and he's eaten a whole lot of them**
> **PAT:** **Are *you seri*ous? They're *aw*ful**
> **JOAN:** **Robert said he *lo*ved them**
> **PAT:** **Oh heh my God they're some of the**
> ***wor*st brownies I've ever tasted**
> **JOAN:** **Well that=**
> **PAT:** **=And they *wer*en't supposed to be brownies anyway**
> **they were supposed to be chocolate chip *coo*kies**
> **JOAN:** **Hah hah well they *tur*ned out to be good brownies**
> **PAT:** **Hah *they*'re hah hah hah**
> **(0.3)**
> ⇒ **JOAN:** **Okay (.) would you hold on a second?**
> **PAT:** **Okay**

Joan compliments Pat's brownies, and he deflects the compliment amid laughter and joking. The after-compliment episode runs its course before the diplomatic 'hold on' turn, preceded by a disjunct marker—a pause-bracketed 'okay.' Joan thereby places 'hold on' at an episode completion.

To summarize: Many hold on turns in telephone conversation, like those in the call waiting preface, begin a two-part sequence that suspends turn taking without ending the phone call. However, speakers of non-call waiting hold ons respect turn units, sequences, and episode trajectories. When the call waiting beep summons its subscriber, hold on runs amok over these constraints.

Hold On and Telephone History

Call waiting prefaces are recent phenomena. Hold on turns have presumably occurred since telephone dyads became routine. Hence, the contrast between the call waiting preface and older uses of hold on may indicate consequences of call waiting upon patterns of telephone conversation.

The spread of telephone conversation a century ago elevated the dyad's importance and stimulated practices to carve dyads from larger communities—including 'hold on.' Telephone partners cannot see one another. Hence, occasions occur in which partners experience disruptions at one end of the connection and ask the other to "hold on." This phrase describes a phone partner left waiting, holding the unused phone.

Hold on sequencing becomes a resource applicable to new problems such as those of the telephone call waiting subscriber. But call waiting hold ons alter conversational ecology by trumping into sequential entities-in-progress. This development risks polluting our stream of consciousness. We cannot gauge the damage in these violations.

At the moment of the call waiting summons, subscriber falls victim to an institutional bind, a difficult choice due to a commercial arrangement with the telephone company. To subscribe to call waiting is to make oneself accessible to intrusion. Like the professor who leaves an office door open, the call waiting subscriber is obligated to receive summons objects. When the call waiting beep occurs, subscriber experiences obligation to speak with any individual who happens along. (People who invariably answer their phones experience a similar bind.)

The interactional price of call waiting accessibility is to ask your current partner to accept second-banana status. What happens at call waiting is like the TV show *Let's Make a Deal*, in which contestants are offered opportunities to trade items they have won for something unknown—something behind the curtain. The call waiting subscriber is offered a trade of the current conversation partner for an unknown caller. A TV contestant who already possesses something of value may bypass a suggested deal, and so may an interpersonally authentic subscriber who ignores the beep. But at the point of the beep a deal has been proposed (albeit by an offstage unknowing caller) and *either* its acceptance or rejection has been made relevant. Subscriber may at that point experience the beep as an inescapable constraint. Rare indeed is the subscriber who resists the beep—though many claim to do so.

Call waiting's intrusion is that of the telephone itself, writ small. To achieve a telephone dyad, a telephone caller asks the partner to put the rest of society into nonparticipant status: on hold. The one place where we had been safe from such telephone intrusion was, paradoxically, when we were on the phone! Call waiting destroys even that refuge.

Philosopher Henry Johnstone argues that putting another on hold is a violation against the human conversation (1982, p. 51).

> Among communicative acts most emphatically in violation of the ethics of communication is the act of putting another person on hold. To place another on hold is not only to treat him as an object incapable of making a creative response: it is to force him into a position in which he can make no response whatever.

To place others on hold is ethically questionable because the utterance "hold on" is such a strong first pair-part that its use approaches unilateral suspension of dialogue. "Hold on" asks the other to keep alive the obligations of dialogue while receiving none of its benefits.

If any use of "hold on" is questionable, some uses are more questionable than others. Perhaps one may excuse the telephone user who occasionally puts a partner on hold without violating turns and sequences. Perhaps there are also institutional extenuating circumstances, say at ticket agencies or information services, in which callers must be kept on hold to get access to a scarce interlocutor. The cost-cutting HMO and the toll-free service number routinely exceed the bounds of responsibility in limiting such access. Still, the worst of all hold ons may be the private personal purgatory of call waiting.

Telemarketing and the Eclipse of Privacy

Caller hegemony is dramatically illustrated in telemarketing calls. Marketers gain access to answerers using name lists, random dialing, and computer calling. Consumers complain that telemarketers invade their privacy. Citizen responses include an increase in unlisted numbers and the rise of machinery to identify a caller's number to a potential answerer. These developments grow as natural consequences of caller hegemony in telephone conversation.

These developments shift conversation's ecology toward callers' purposes and provide a niche for certain capitalists:

FN

Me:	Hello?
C:	Hello, Mr. Hopper?
Me:	Yes.
C:	This is Ty Eager from TeleSell how are you today

This caller uses the answerer's name to accomplish a degree of access. Since the name suggested by the caller is mine, it is difficult not to say 'yes.' The telemarketer thereby exploits caller hegemony to achieve named identification of a stranger. At next turn, caller self-identifies, then rushes to a phatic initial inquiry. A stranger who moves to initial inquiry without going through greetings cheats against the human conversation. This cheating resembles that described in chapter 4, in which a caller to a doctor's office greets the answerer—then asks for a special favor. But that was a single occurrence; the TeleSell instance occurs, by policy, thousands of times each day. Professional callers identify a stranger-answerer by name, and then launch inquiries that simulate acquaintance. The goal is to keep a potential consumer on the line against her will. If an answerer follows ordinary rules of the telephone opening—as in this next instance—the telemarketer may virtually force access:

> UTCL A35.24
>
> H: Hello
> D: Mister ↑Smalley
> H: Yes
> D: ↑This is Missy Weevil, sir I'm calling you
>   from the Ward Life Insurance Company in
>   Chicago?
> H: Uh huh
> D: ↑How do you do sir.
> H: Just fine.
> D: Great. How was your Christmas?
> H: Just fine,

This caller identifies the answerer with the try-marked term of address, 'Mr. Smalley?' From the answerer's standpoint, the task is simple: is it you? Given such a strong first pair part, it takes an act of will not to assent, although assent allows for the caller to self-identify. Caller then accomplishes self-introduction in a turn that ends with try-marked pitch, asking only for recognition of the company. The answerer responds with 'uh huh' which caller counts as permission to proceed. By this time, the caller has gained a footing for encounter by exploiting the topography of the identification/recognition slot. Telemarketers exploit a conversation systemics that normally forbids unwarranted access by strangers—to gain precisely that access!

This particular caller moves next to a preliminary initial inquiry—something that rarely occurs in stranger-stranger interaction (chapter 4). By sliding past the greeting, to which she lacks title, the caller does an action that may function as a substitute greeting (Sacks, 1964). (The form used here also recalls a format used in introductions: 'how do you do, sir.') When the answerer gives an unmarked answer 'fine,' the caller next presses an inquiry related to the current holiday. By the time answerer responds to this inquiry, these parties have fabricated an acquaintance. It would be futile for answerer to pretend that there is no encounter in progress. He consequently must listen to the following:

D: Great. How was your Christmas?

H: Just fine,

D: Good. ·hhh today we- we wanna tell y'about an important service I'll be real brief with you sir ·hhh uh- an important service that's being made available to you ·hhh our supplemental group accident hospital insurance pla:n? ·hhhh As a current policy holder you know Ward Life- pt ·hh- provides dependable coverage at very reasonable rates .hhh and this plan is no exception ·hh now, .h if you're between the ages of eighteen and sixty nine, it can provide you and your family with high benefits for death or injury from covered accidents ·hh daily payments to help cover hospitalization due to covered accidents ·hhhh and Mister Smalley because you *are* a loyal Ward Life customer ·hh your acceptance into this plan *is* guaranteed. .hhh And you don't even have to mail in a check or remember when ↑premiums are due:, .hhh We'll just begin automatically charging the monthly premium ↑for this coverage to your Montgomery Ward credit account .hhhh Mister Smalley ↑I have a program specialist right here ·hh and he or she would like to take ·hh a few minutes mo:re to give you the details would that be all right

⇒   H: We:ll I think I've got enough: hospi'lization an: and uh accidental

D: M:k⌈ay,

H: ⌊u:h coverage at the present time, I don't think I need any more

D: All Right. = Well Mister Smalley let me just say this one thing sir ↑most of our customers do have other coverage...

          ((call continues))

A sales pitch, like a storytelling, may stretch turn-taking procedures to grasp an extended turn. Once the pretense of encounter has been established, the telemarketer minimizes transition-relevance opportunities. These occur only when the right kind of answer moves towards a sale. If a resisting answer occurs (see ⇒) the caller's rejoinders aim to route the encounter toward a place where the answerer may not be able to resist.

We find ourselves held in thrall by such strategy because telemarketers exploit principles of encounter opening and adjacency sequencing to gain access to us. However, we should not unreflectively blame all professionals implicated in such activities. The telephone creates an evolutionary niche in semiotic ecology, a space for dialogue that privileges a caller's projects. Such projects then develop, as nature abhors a vacuum. In the wilderness, if erosion forms a crack in a rock, some plant will grow there. If a pond forms in the desert, predators will hunt there. Telemarketing occupies semiotic spaces entailed in the development of telephone conversation. The telemarketer adapts to the telephone's ecology somewhat as a lioness waits for lunch by the waterhole.

Telephone answerers are, if forewarned, not defenseless against attack-access. Answerers who study telephone openings may understand the points of vulnerability that telemarketers exploit: recognition/identification and initial inquiry. Within these opening-slots answerers may defend themselves. Here is one arguably successful sales-resisting opening:

> FN
> A: Hello?
> C: Hello Mister Allen?
>   (0.6)
> ⇒   A: What can I do for you.
>   C: Okay, this is Tracy from Carpet Colors
>   ((A hangs up))

In this instance the answerer balks at ratifying the caller's try-marked identification. Answerer's pause following this first pair-part prefigures disagreement, then answerer poses an insertion-sequence question: 'What can I do for you?' Thereby this answerer parries two of the caller's advantages: the identification-guess is not confirmed, and the answerer substitutes a first-pair part constraining caller to answer instead of asking. Additionally, the break in the rhythm of the opening shows caller that answerer regards the encounter as problematic. Therefore, this answerer is able to neutralize caller hegemony by verbal judo that builds a defensive posture within the resources of turn marking in the telephone opening—pausing, introducing an insertion sequence, and so on.

As this instance shows, such neutralization of caller hegemony is incomplete. The answerer must still be willing to exercise the hearably rude option of hanging up. That may be the appropriate response to a baldly intrusive sales call. An answerer not armed with knowledge of the telephone opening may be reluctant to hang up, or may feel guilty afterward. An informed caller recognizes this action as retaliation for abuse of cultural customs for encounter access.

Hegemonies may contain the seeds of their own deconstruction. Until the mid-eighties, the caller held most all of the advantages in the telephone opening. This balance may be changing today, partly due to growing answerer suspicions, but in larger part due to another machine that combines the tape recorder and the telephone.

Telephone Answering Machines: The Answerer Strikes Back

In the summer of 1989, I received a telephone call from a newspaper reporter who claimed that California's unlisted telephone numbers had increased by one third in the past year. The reporter sought my opinion on this statistic. I speculated that telemarketers were chasing telephone customers out of the phone book in pursuit of privacy. This reporter's question showed that caller hegemony was being contested—the telephone access war escalates when the answerer strikes back.

Today's answerers challenge caller hegemony in various ways. The increase in unlisted numbers protects answerers from some sales pitches, but it also screens out friends and family. It makes answerers into electro-hermits who are unavailable to respond to intimates or emergencies. Besides, some telemarketers respond with random-dialing technologies which reach even unlisted numbers. These innovations skirmish on the boundaries of telephone access.

In 1989 a device went on sale that provides an answerer a visual display of each caller's phone number. This information helps answerers decide whether to answer the telephone. This device has sparked an immense legal wrangle over whether a caller's privacy is invaded if an answerer learns his or her phone number. The argument seems especially acute for holders of unlisted numbers, who pay to keep their number secret only to have this secrecy violated by the new device. There is now a service in some places that allows a caller to "block" the access of an answerer's machine that might give away the caller's number. What is this wrangle about, and what explains its severity? One possibility is that the squabble is over a challenge to caller hegemony. The telephone caller protects his privilege with self-righteous squeals akin to the defenders of tax shelters.

The Bell System has introduced a related service, personalized ring, to solve some privacy problems. This option allows identification of an answerer's most frequent callers by assigning each caller's number a distinctive signature ring. This allows recognition of frequent and desired callers without invading any occasional caller's privacy. Personalized ring is also a much smaller challenge to caller hegemony.

These services bring to the fore scattered squabbles over caller hegemony. But meanwhile, the telephone answering machine dwarfs their impact. The telephone answering machine, like the telephone itself, is a simple machine whose consequences continue to evolve with its use.

It started innocently enough. As the eighties began, the answering machine became widely available in retail stores. It was designed to provide a convenience to people who wished not to miss phone calls when they were away from the phone.

The telephone answering machine, like this book, is built on an alliance between the telephone and the tape recorder. It is a tape recorder, connected to the telephone, that "answers" the phone, transmits a prerecorded message, and designates a slot for the caller to leave a message—which it also records. The answering machine thereby provides for an exchange of monologues: answerer's prerecorded message for the caller's fresh new one.

The first thing that I noticed about the telephone answering machine was that many callers objected to it. I objected to it myself, and perhaps the first twenty times I got connected to an answering machine I hung up without leaving any message. In the middle eighties, my students measured message-leaving rates around fifty percent. Half the callers left messages, the other half hung up.[6]

During this period I resisted purchasing a telephone answering machine, even though I was working on this book. It seemed wrong somehow to subject callers to the same trauma I had faced. I even relished fantasies that if I, and enough people like me, did not leave messages, people would stop using these vile machines.

Now I believe that this emotional reaction was a consequence of the answering machine's reversal of caller hegemony. In the premachine phone encounter, caller knows at the outset who is the target partner and the reason for calling. The answerer, who must say hello before learning who is calling, is at a disadvantage. The answering machine reverses this imbalance: the expected called party does not answer, but instead the caller's summons garners a mechanical response—a robot receptionist. The caller usually expects to speak only in response to some answer, but the machine turns the tables so that the caller must provide the first actual fresh speech in the encounter. Dialogue is not possible. The caller must identify himself or herself into a void that does not answer.

The telephone caller has been protected until the answering machine, but now the caller must state his or her identity and business. The machine commits to nothing. This is the most principled reversal of empowerment in telephone history. The answerer strikes back.

The telephone answering machine throws us a learning curve; and it eventually seduces most of us into using it effectively. The first time your call gets answered by a machine, you may hang up. At this point you may denounce the machine. But eventually, you come to a situation in which you benefit from leaving a message. Your first message may be halting and incomplete, but these patient machines keep offering opportunities to leave more effective and more complex messages.

Eventually, we discover that certain messages are best if done as monologue. The heroine in *Teenage Mutant Ninja Turtles* gets fired by machine; Brun-Cottan (1989) reports this instance:

> Hi: M:ama um:m wanted to tell you: that I've been meaning to tell you for a while ·h I broke my wa:tch an cause when I w:ent into the water when I first got he(.)re: it (0.2) got broken an:d ·hh I'm sorry en I'm kind of ma:d but I *h*ad te get it off my conscience. . . . .

By the time we discover that certain messages may be best treated as monologues, we are hooked on the answering machine. As we discover more and more uses for the machine, we eventually consider purchasing one ourselves. Once your machine is in use, it follows quite naturally that you may experience the answering machine's strongest reversal of caller hegemony: screening your calls.

What Callers Say to Answering Machines

Over its decade of widespread use in the USA, users of the telephone answering machine have developed formats for leaving messages. The order of things that callers say to answering machines parallels, in some respects, the canonical telephone opening (chapters 3 and 4). These issues may be illustrated with this instance:

> UTCL A24.1 ((see chapter beginning))
> **Hi Sue this Jan I just wanted to see: if maybe you**
> **could bring ·hhhh some *can*dles to: um (0.6) pt B*a*to's**
> **beca:use ·hhhhhhhhhhh I don't have ti:me. And I got**
> **the ca:ke (.) And its *cu*te and *d*orable um*k*ay bye**

The summons (ring) and the (mechanized) answer have already occurred. The machine answer exits the canon for telephone openings at the answering turn, but the caller is still faced with the issues to which canonical features of openings are addressed: such as recognition and greeting. In this instance the caller greets, specifies the recipient, and self-identifies by name. She then specifies a reason for calling.

This answering-machine message shows slots for (1) greeting, (2) self-identification, (3) stating business, and (4) saying goodbye. These slots get filled with items that mark situation and relationship in ways similar to the telephone opening. As in the canonical telephone opening, these forms entail previous acquaintance but not intimacy. The message below was left on a stranger's machine:

UTCL A13d.8 (N. Knapp)

Yes (.) my name's Robbie Crow (.) and I'm calling about the ad you had in the paper Sunday? today? ·hhhhhhh U::m u:h for- for housekeeper, for one day a week, (0.3) and I do have references if you li:ke a'n (.) or you can call me (0.2) u:m I'll be home later this afternoo:n ·hhhh 'S after six (.) and my number's four three one (.) oh three six eight (0.2) Thank you

The caller begins with "yes," the most frequent first word spoken by unacquainted callers in the telephone opening (chapter 4). The caller then states her full name, first and last, and moves to her reason for calling. She leaves her telephone number. Finally, this stranger's machine message concludes with 'thank you' rather than 'bye.' These contrasts between telephone messages of acquaintances and strangers are shown in Table 7 (Taylor, Thomason and Hopper, 1992). It shows a profile of slots for answering machine messages. Each slot's item claims (among other things) a particular relationship state. Acquainted callers greet the recipient, offer minimal self-identification, often delete such details as own phone number in favor of a request to return the call, and close with "bye." Strangers' messages open with "yes," state a full name, leave a phone number, and end with thanks.

Table 7
Answering Machine Messages of Acquaintances and Strangers

RELATIONSHIP →	ACQUAINTANCE (n=87)	STRANGER (n=85)
SLOT ↓		
FIRST UTTERANCE	'Hi' or answerer's name (85%)	'Yes,' or caller's name (61%)
SELF-IDENTIFICATION	First name or less (90%)	Full name or more (81%)
CALLER'S PHONE #	Absent (86%)	Present (96%)
CLOSING	Bye (87%)	Thank you (72%)

Intimacy may be marked in a machine message, as in the telephone opening, by minimalist messages featuring greetings:

UTCL A13e.6.

Hi it's me (0.2) Bye.

In this instance the greeting and goodbye appear, with only an implicit marking of self-identification: 'it's me.' Callers mark intimacy by retaining the greeting, but they may delete most everything else. Recognition is achieved in vocal recognition as a side-effect of greeting.

Telephone answering machines, when investigated further, may reveal further similarities to telephone conversation openings. The rhythmic patterns of pauses in these messages may also suggest locations for turns of the fictionalized other. But the most important impact of the answering machine is its evolution into a device for call screening—a development that flouts the reversal of caller hegemony.

Screening Your Calls

When I purchased an answering machine, I was immediately thunderstruck by this fact: telemarketers virtually never leave messages on it. The answering machine neutralizes the telemarketer's advantage, and screens out telephone junk mail. Once caller hegemony has been countered by the answering machine, the next step seems obvious, at least in retrospect. This is use of the telephone answering machine as a device for "screening" calls; or forcing any caller to self-identify to the machine—even when one could answer the phone. This commits the caller, not the answerer, to speak first. Based upon information gathered thereby, the answerer may decide whether to respond to the call.

Of course, the practice of screening has its own side effects. Some desirable callers may hang up as well as the ones a machine owner wishes to screen out. Other callers may express negative feelings about an answerer who screens calls. In the dialogue before this chapter, Jan leaves a message on Sue's machine; then Sue calls Jan right afterward. Jan, the answerer, asks Sue about this coincidence:

> UTCL A24
>
> JAN: **You screening your calls**
> **(0.4)**
> SUE: **No why**
> JAN: **·hhhh Cu' I just ↑called you.**
> SUE: *Di*d **you r(h)eally I'm not at ho**me
> ⌈*h*hhhuh Wha-
> JAN: ⌊**Oh huh huh I mean like I just hung ↑up.**
> SUE: **What's up**
> JAN: **·hhhh Nothin I called to see'f you could bring**
> **candl:es to Bato's**

Jan's first utterance 'You screening your calls' suggests that an explanation is in order for the coincidence that this return call comes right after she left a message on Sue's machine. Sue denies that she is call screening, and asks for explanation ('No why'). Jan explains that she just called, and Sue explains that 'I'm not at home.' By this account Sue shows that she hears Jan's possible accusation and denies it. Both parties now treat the situation as comedy; Jan persists through shared laughter to describe why she asked, and to celebrate the coincidence. This instance shows that call screening is an accountable answerer's practice.[7]

This instance also reveals some dynamics of caller-answerer power relations. Callers usually start the first topic in a call. However, this caller asks 'what's up' and then listens to Jan's message about bringing candles to Bato's—the same message Jan had left on Sue's machine. That is, these telephone partners, during the discussion of call screening, reframe this event from a call placed by Sue into, in effect, a return call. The business discussed first, and at length, is the birthday party about which Jan had left the previous message. Only much later in the call do we find indications of why Sue might have called in the first place. Sue never explicitly introduces her business, but instead employs a stepwise topic shift (see discussion of this instance in chapter 7) to ask to speak to Jan's apartment-mate, Mary. Sue's pursuit of talk about Mary may indicate that her original reason for calling was to talk to Mary. If that is not the case, Sue never does indicate her reason for calling—which is also a reversal of caller hegemony.

From this discussion we can draw no single lesson, except that there is no such thing as a free ecology. The answering machine empowers the answerer over the caller, striking back at imbalances of caller hegemony. However, in this particular instance, the tables turn once more and a caller (Sue) is made role-vulnerable by mention that a message has just been left on her machine. She then acts as if Jan had been the caller. These partners compute all this socio-algebra, and subsequent negotiation over topic transitions, in ways that advantage neither partner.

Many issues of telephone technology arise in this encounter, including the telephone answering machine, call waiting, and the statuses of caller and answerer in the telephone opening. We also hear instances of numerous practices, described throughout this book, including telephone opening, turn taking, and topic transition. That is typical of telephone conversation's rich and diverse semiotic ecology.

Telephone conversation displays the age-old technology of spoken interaction and also transforms it. Some practices of telephone conversation continue to evolve in response to technological developments such as call waiting, telemarketing, and the telephone answering machine. Hang on for further developments!

Yet let us remember that telephony and its cousin-technologies grow out of the richest subsoil of human civilization: the interaction order. They exemplify and reveal the human conversation at the same time as they transform it. Our ongoing conversation remains the primary spiritual environment to which our lives are brief visits. We are guests of the conversation.

ENVOI
The Interaction Order

This book only begins to describe telephone conversation. The teleconference, the 900 number, the fax machine, and electronic mail each require volumes on their own. So does the answering machine and its human cousin the telephone receptionist.

The beginning of telephony wrought changes in the ecology of speech communication by emphasizing the oral and by promoting the importance of the dyad steered by a purpose-centered caller. Much of twentieth-century scholarship, including the discoveries and philosophies of linguistic pragmatics, are built upon experiences of telephony. This development is fortunate to the extent that telephone conversations are like other conversations—and by and large they are. We can read the world of spoken interaction out of the telephone conversation. The study of telephone conversation may rebegin the science of speech.

We describe here only the beginnings of many events which demand description throughout their entire course: We treat telephone call openings, but not their closings, their main topics, and much else. We describe the beginnings of topics, stories, and pre-sequences, but leave aside the management of these matters through extended tellings while the other party says things like "uh huh" (Jefferson, 1981; Drummond, 1990). These beginnings entail an open-textured hope for work that may follow. Rather than bragging about how much we now know, let us take each description as an invitation to further inquiry. This book's importance can only be shown by subsequent researches. It should be utterly superseded by future writings—lost in interaction like individual achievements in the telephone opening.

Telephone conversation is unique in its limits to sounds, the dyad, and so forth. Further, the telephone itself wrings changes in the interaction order: caller hegemony, for instance, placing the other on hold, for instance. These changes amount to transformations of our stream of consciousness. The telephone and its relatives the tape recorder, the answering machine, and so on, carry importance comparable to mass media—yet we are just beginning to detect their effects one hundred years into the experience.

We have known that the telephone is important and that it is a communications medium. We have not thought to combine these two insights. Now none of us is old enough to remember the telephone's beginning. We must therefore reconstruct the archeology of the telephone era on sketchy evidence. The most important of such materials are audio recordings, the stuff out of which this book is fashioned. Historians should recover echoes of our prerecorded past through retrieving and recopying "old" recordings from the phonograph, the wire-recorder, and other ancestors of current audio techniques. Perhaps the most compelling unwritten chapter is the saga of the telephone operator, told from audio recordings of their interactions with consumers and each other. Early long distance calls, party line interaction, telephone calls of historical interest, and a good deal else should become the focus of archival research before remaining recordings are lost through ignorance of their value.

The telephone's history intertwines with the audio recorder, especially in what both these media teach us about ourselves. As the telephone holds up the sounded conversation for examination, the tape recorder makes replays possible. The telephone is a mirror for speech, and the tape recorder provides means to keep, replay, and analyze what the mirror shows us. Microanalyses of telephone conversation teach us not only about telephones but about the interaction order displayed therein.

"The interaction order" is the title of Erving Goffman's last written legacy, a speech his health did not allow him to deliver, in which he argues that interaction is a domain ordered beyond the wildest dreams of most investigators (1983). The interaction order pervades every message, every telephone opening, every turn at talk. In Sacks' words, "there is order at all points." In whatever place we sample the human conversation, orderings may emerge from description—less because our methods are so sophisticated than because the order is so pervasive that any sampling procedure is bound to find some of it (1984).

This book is about *both* telephone conversation and the interaction order. The primary orderings of telephone conversation are those of the interaction order. Speakers address one another one speaking turn at a time. The workings of speaking turns and their structures of alternation in two-party conversation are substantial objects in themselves. We are still just beginning to investigate turn taking, which provides the ordering rack of interaction, the primary engine for doing spoken being in time. The telephone provides a wonderful environment for investigating turn taking because of the medium's constraints to sounds, and to two speakers. Each of those limits emphasizes how turns work.

The telephone's number of participants is crucial, and we must not pretend that we understand everything about turn taking from studies of two-party conversation. Less clear is the importance of nonverbal communication to turn taking. Certainly its importance is substantial, but it may be substantial in ways that hang from and support the turn-taking system, rather than in ways that supplant it in favor of other systemics. Researchers who downplay the importance of turn taking to any aspect of interaction are factually incorrect. Turn taking frames all interactive signalling.

Turn taking, which is most easily studied in telephone conversation, is a systemics without meaning. To fathom what telephone partners do with turn taking we must consider more than one speaking turn. Speakers' turns have not, after all, evolved to be performed one turn at a time. Rather they appear in our experience embedded in what has gone before and bringing what comes next. Turns appear in sequences, and these sequences support larger entities like encounter openings, topic trajectories, story prefaces, and episodes of play. These are the units of accomplishment in which spoken interaction gets things done. Theories of communication based upon the meanings of words and individual sentences are interesting artifacts in postliterate society. But they may not provide the most important components of a theory of spoken action.

The interaction order displays communicative phenomena of various sizes. Some writers conceptualize these varied sizes as layers of order (Pearce and Cronen, 1980), though I remain agnostic about such a metaphor. For the moment let us describe phenomena. Lead us not into premature theory nor hasty data reduction.

We may expect systemic wisdom in the structurations of interaction order. This order may be so rich with the wisdom of evolution and the craft of human understanding that our best hope is to disturb it as little as possible. Our spoken ecology may be the most important artifact of socio-civilized existence. We disturb these systemics at our peril. Telephony reveals our nature to us as it transforms us into our future selves. Especially in its favoring of the caller, telephone technology seriously biases the interaction order toward purposeful manipulation. There is limited hope that recent devices (like answering machines) partially neutralize caller hegemony. But the telephone's marriage of communication to purpose goes beyond the telephone access war. In this wider sea of problems our best redemptive possibilities lie in deeper understanding of the interaction order, and in renewed appreciation of poetic orientations toward interactive being. In this sometimes harsh but always awesome school, the telephone may long remain our best teacher.

Practitioners' Epilogue

What are this project's practical implications for telephone speakers? The premature place of our science, and my own esthetic ontology, leave me reluctant to offer the following list. But here are some speculations about how you can increase your contentment, insight, and effectiveness in telephone conversation.

1. *Speak short turns* to promote dialogic interaction.
2. *Attend to rhythm* in telephone interaction, especially during the

telephone opening. Regular rhythm partakes of the canonical; irregular rhythm suggests the problematic.

3.   *Cherish small talk,* especially in openings. Small talk works many wonders, and the degree to which telephone partners align on small talk's rhythms and accomplishments goes before communicative effectiveness, formal elegance, and speaker satisfaction.

4.   *Work through problems* rather than investing heavily in a first guess about what is wrong. Begin by indicating uptake in your next turn, perhaps with a pause or a partial statement. Let trajectories emerge across speaker turns—like dramatic plots.

5.   *Spare excessive clarity and meta-talk.* Especially in the early portions of telephone conversation, suggest rather than state, lead rather than force. If you observe problems or breaks in the rhythm, merge toward dealing with them. "What do you mean?" is a problematic utterance—use it sparingly.

6.   *Keep interaction alive.* Often when you do not know just what to say, take a short turn, ask a projective question, engage your partner. Keep the encounter's rhythm, or mark a subtle alteration in it.

7.   *Keep calls to finite length.* Plan, in advance of calls, what a good length for the call might be. If you are ready to quit at the end of that time, use possible pre-closings like "I'll let you go now," to test the other's readiness to close.

8.   *Attend to partnering productivity,* rather than primarily to your individual self. Telephone conversations are team efforts. Take your eye off the I, put your ear to work for partnership.

9.   *Describe your practices of telephone conversation.* Tape record two to five of your own telephone calls. Choose the most mundane calls: calling out for pizza would be one instance of a useful but mundane call. Listen for moments when something goes well or badly in the call. Replay these parts of the recordings a dozen times to locate the precise word or phrase where things changed. Stay with each single instance, and dwell on its details. How does the next speaker react to this same moment? Most of us have trouble doing this. Stay descriptive for as long as possible. To focus your listening, transcribe a few lines, using the techniques from this book. Finally, make a list of problems you observe and write plans for self-improvement. Be patient with yourself; language change is, and should be, slow.

10.   *Use the skills developed in describing telephone conversation in the rest of your spoken interaction.* You may be surprised at how much of your conversational life works according to the principles you learn in describing telephone conversation.

11.   *Listen and respond with a poetic ear.* Listen for and cherish puns, figures of speech, rhyme, assonance, rhythm, allusion, and the like.

Follow Walt Whitman's advice: listen to our poetic voices. Put your ear on the line. Let me know what you discover.

Gail Jefferson developed the transcribing conventions used in this book.

Speaker is identified as on a play script, by a fictionalized name justified at the left margin. Conventionalized English spelling is supplemented by misspellings to show marked pronunciations. Certain nonword particles (uh huh, or hah hah hah) are spelled to indicate precise pronunciation.

Certain added transcription symbols help to show timing and emphasis within utterances. These include:

(1.7)	Single parentheses enclosing numbers indicate a pause in conversation. The numbers show pause duration in tenths of seconds.
(.)	Single parentheses with just a period between indicate a pause shorter than two-tenths of a second.
I ⌈do. ⌉ ⌊I do⌋	Brackets indicate overlapping utterances.
xxx= =yyy	Equal signs at the end of one utterance and the beginning of the next indicate closely contiguous utterances that do not overlap (latching).
b*a*d	Italics indicate pronounced vocal emphasis.
u::m	Colons indicate the stretching of the sound that each colon follows. More colons indicate longer stretching.
↑Oh	An arrow just before a sound indicates a rise in pitch (↓ indicates a fall in pitch.)
-	A hyphen following a sound indicates a cut-off of the speech stream (glottal stop).
?	A question mark indicates rising pitch at word or phrase ending, *not* necessarily a grammatical question.
.	A period indicates sliding or falling pitch at the end of a word or phrase.
,	A comma shows intonational completion too subtle to be indicated by a period or question mark.
I °do°	Superscripted degree signs bracket a word or phrase lower in volume than the surrounding talk.
hhh	h's indicate audible outbreaths, sighing, or unvoiced laughter. Duration is one-tenth of a second per "h."
·hh	A superscripted period followed by h's indicates audible inbreaths. These are a prominent feature of telephone conversations.
pt	This symbol indicates an audible lip smack that often precedes inbreath in telephone conversation.

y(h)es	(h) indicates laughter embedded inside a word.
» I see «	Chevrons indicate that a particular phrase is spoken faster than the surrounding talk. Reversed [« I see »], these show slowed speech.
*	An asterisk indicates a gravelly voice, or break in pronunciation.
((noise))	Actions and noises are described within double parentheses.
#	Indicates electronic noises.

1. The People of the Phone

1. Edward Said distinguishes beginnings from origins: Origins are "divine mythical and privileged," but beginnings are "secular, humanly produced, and ceaselessly re-examined" (1975, xiii).

2. Although telephone calls may now include multiple parties, most encounters still occur between two parties.

3. There are more long pauses in face-to-face conversation than on the telephone. Telephone speakers may cleanse "dead air" as radio broadcasters do. However, even in the ways they pause, telephone speakers and face-to-face speakers are more alike than different (Thomason and Hopper, 1992).

4. Utterances must display sequential appropriateness as well as grammaticality. Chomsky (1965) describes sentences of a language (usually one at a time) in terms of grammar. But speakers who only select grammatical utterances, without attending to the sequence, cannot converse.

5. With certain limitations, especially those touching culture and language, one ought to be able to find any conversational phenomenon in operation in these instances. Exemplars in the chapters are often taken from these duet-transcriptions so that you may examine more details of the events in which they occur. The phenomena thereby demonstrated have been replicated in other materials.

6. There have been several stage productions based upon just such materials as the duets and trios presented here (Stucky, 1988; Hopper, 1988; Crow, 1988).

7. For introductory treatments see Nofsinger, 1991; Hopper, Koch, and Mandelbaum, 1986; and Levinson, 1983, chapter 6. See also Schegloff, 1987a; Zimmerman, 1988; Jacobs, 1988, 1990; Jackson, 1986; Mandelbaum, 1990; Beach, 1989, 1990; Hopper, 1988, 1989a; Heritage, 1984b, chapter 8; Heritage, 1989; Pomerantz, 1990.

8. Of course no absolute standard of naturalness is attainable, and there is also no hard-and-fast criterion for labeling speech natural. But being recorded does not necessarily induce artificiality. People quickly forget they are being recorded (Wiemann, 1981).

9. A problem in this facile alliance is covert wiretapping. We obtained written permission from the person at whose telephone the recordings were made. Whenever practicable we obtained written releases from all participants. We disguise names and other identifying features in all transcriptions.

10. Conversation analysts may use phonetics. Kelly and Local (1989) argue that no one system of transcription does justice to the richness of conversational data. They show analytic leverage that may be gained by phonetic transcription (see also Fitch, 1988; Modaff, 1988), though these authors admit that phonetic transcription is too laborious to attempt with large sets of data. Phonetic transcriptions should be undertaken when the investigator describes features illuminated by this transcription. Jefferson (1985) argues that some phonetic variation may be shown with creative misspellings of words that show special emphases of pronunciation. I use more standard spellings and fewer stress markings than Jefferson. We insure empirical reliability by adjudicating each transcription with multiple cotranscribers. A number of people have helped me in this task. Gail Jefferson and Richard Frankel have been

generous with valuative feedback concerning transcriptions. The transcriptions of Ray Thomason and Jennifer Mandelbaum have been notable in quantity and quality. Samuel Lawrence and Nathan Stucky designed cloze-procedure tests of intertranscriber reliability. Phillip Glenn worked on transcriptions of laughter.

11. Equations about motion and inertia work perfectly only when extraneous factors are controlled, as in a vacuum or a sterile lab solution. Water boils at 100 degrees centigrade only when it is free of impurities and located at sea level.

12. Many analytical claims are advanced in terms of exceptions: one often finds that the participants note the exception and, in fact, treat it as exceptional. One finds of rules for describing conversation, in Sacks' words, that "even when it does not work, you can see it working" (1987, p. 59).

2. The Rediscovery of Speaking

1. Ronell (1989) argues that Bell was obsessed with the absence of the intimate other: (a) his brother, Melly, died young after promising Aleck to contact him after death; (b) his intimate relationships to deaf women, including his mother, his wife, and Helen Keller; (c) his intense desire to attain personal solitude—he usually worked alone at night in his house in the country, and he allowed no telephone in his office.

2. Later, when Bell was beset by patent fights from Elisha Gray and others, his oratorical skills served him well. He was perhaps the most commercially successful courtroom witness in history (Bruce; Boettinger).

3. Many telephone demonstrations had amusing results, as when a scientist tested the phone by saying:

> "Hey diddle diddle—follow that up." He rapidly put the telephone up to his ear and announced with much glee, "He says the cat and the fiddle." Fifty miles away my assistant was answering the question. I asked him next day if he understood "Hey diddle diddle." He said "No." "What did you say?" "I asked him to repeat!" (Prescott, p. 85)

Early telephony produced modest fidelity, but the recognizability of absent voices matched a yearning of the human spirit.

4. I owe this observation to Madeline Maxwell.

5. Marvin, 1988, p. 196, quotes from "From an admirer of the telephone," *Electrical Review*, Nov. 23, 1888, p. 6.

6. There are certain sounds, e.g., the sounds of the instruments of an orchestra or singers making harmonies, that are combined, but these strike most ears as singular phenomena: the orchestra plays, the barbershop quartet sings.

7. "A telephonic conversation," first published in *The Atlantic* in 1880, is reprinted in *The $30,000 Bequest and Other Stories*, New York: Harper, 1905.

8. In fact there are benefits to *not* orienting to the message status of actions. See Garfinkel's (1967, pp. 7–9, 20) discussion of "let it pass."

9. The 1888 *Electrical Review* reprinted this story from *NY Sun*, according to Marvin (1988) p. 72.

10. Dramatists consistently use interruptive telephone calls as Geritol for tired plots. For an early version of this, see Chekhov's (1903) play, *Three Sisters*.

11. Ronell critiques Heidegger's phenomenology: Heidegger's ear, Ronell argues, was trained on the telephone, especially in the role of answerer. Unlike Husserl, who had his office telephone disconnected in 1920, Heidegger answered the call—ultimately, from the Nazis. (Heidegger admitted to *Der Spiegel* that the Nazis delivered demands to him by telephone. Ronell admits that he refused those demands, but still he answered the call.) This tragedy, Ronell argues, shows in *Being and Time*, in which

"the call of conscience—is shown to possess the character of a telephone call" (p. 29). Ronell quotes Heidegger's *Being and Time* (1962), pp. 276–77):

> The caller is Dasein in its uncanniness: primordial, thrown Being-in-the-world as the "not-at-home". . . it is something like an *alien* voice.

The call of conscience has the very role-asymmetries of the telephone call. To Heidegger, an authentic response to the alien voice is the response-ability to answer. To render oneself answerable, one drops what one is doing and becomes indebted to the caller. Unfortunately, Ronell continues, Heidegger did not notice the telephonic resemblance in his notion of answerability, leaving vulnerable both his theory and his practice (pp. 29–33).

12. Conversely, such reader's experiences reveal lapses in verisimilitude. At the end of the 1986 film *Stand by Me* the narrator keyboards the final sentence to his story, then turns off the IBM-PC computer without saving the file.

13. Marvin p. 30.

14. Schegloff's model also motivates noticing that the probable first utterance of the call, the answerer's "hello," is not shown in the fictional instance.

15. Given the centrality of "speaking" to contemporary theory, it seems worth noticing that Saussure, Austin, Wittgenstein, and Sacks advanced their most revolutionary insights in lectures, not writings.

16. This is my translation, in collaboration with Nada Doany, who has retranslated much of the *Cours* to restore its oral flavor. Baskin (p. 11) translates this passage as: "We must examine the individual act from which the speaking-circuit can be reconstructed." Harris (1987, p. 11) translates: "We must consider the individual act of speech and trace what takes place in the speech circuit." Both translators retain the circuit trope only as a dead metaphor. These translators also abandon the pre-phenomenology in Saussure's phrasing. Our translation attempts to keep the metaphor alive and provisional.

17. Lakoff (1987) notes that the Japanese classifier *hon*, which applies to long thin objects (sticks, rolls of tape) and to linear trajectories (baseball hits) also applies to phone calls. The Japanese language classifies the phone call as linear (104).

18. E.g., from those cited above to Chomsky, to Brown (1973), and the varieties of sociolinguists in Gumperz and Hymes (1972), or Baugh and Sherzer (1984).

19. See Nofsinger, 1975; Jackson and Jacobs, 1980; Gumperz, 1982; Giddens, 1979; Thompson, 1984; Haslett, 1987; McLaughlin, 1984; Levinson, 1983; Heritage, 1984b, Zimmerman, 1988; Hopper, 1988, 1989a; Beach, 1989; Wootton, 1989; Schegloff, 1991.

20. Volosinov critiques Saussure's linguistics as failing to account for the dialogic nature of discourse. His notions of dialogue, like his coauthorship with Bakhtin, are heteroglossic. Dialogue is alternately a property of fictional characters' conversations, or a braiding of an author's voice with characters' voices, or resonances of reported speech, and the polyphony of works speaking to each other (Bakhtin, 1986). In the current work, we use the term dialogue primarily for two-party encounters— in contrast with monologue.

21. P. 19. Higgins played Pygmalion to Doolittle's Galetea on Wimpole Street, just a few doors away from the house in which the Bells, father and son, gave speech lessons to young ladies and demonstrations to philologists. An added note: the machine-sexuality nexus in the phrase "turn her on as often as you like" deserves psychoanalytic attention.

3. Telephone Openings

1. The canonical telephone opening *is* written down in *this* telephone book. Analogously, the words 'The Lord be with you' were spoken many times before they

were written down. All these formats ultimately derive from the human conversation. Heaven forbid that this volume should become a book of common prayer, but whenever the spoken gets written, strange powers are summoned into play.

2. But at the same time, answerer's action follows the associative thread: violin → cello → hello.

3. Passing strangers do not ignore each other completely—they rarely bump into one another, but pretend not to look at the other. Visual regard remains furtive. A dance of not-quite-meeting gazes is timed so that observational gazes are non-simultaneous. If walking-toward-each-other parties classify each other as unacquainted, they display civil inattention most markedly at about six to ten feet apart by moving gaze conspicuously toward the ground: they "dim their lights" (Goffman, 1963). These actions avoid the possibility of mutual gaze, which could lead to speaking or be perceived as rude (Gardner, 1980).

There are failsafes in face-to-face speaking against strangers' becoming embroiled in undesired encounters. If strangers do speak to one another, these events, marked by absence of greeting tokens, do not ordinarily lead into further talk. Thereby strangers are doubly sealed off from entering into sustained interaction. Sacks (1964) confirms this view in his description of an airport scene: A man asks a woman a series of questions, and after each of the first three questions she turns her gaze away. After a later question, she produces a cigarette, which he lights; she then turns to faces him. This illustrates the sort of interaction required to override fail-safes against continued interaction with strangers.

4. One exception to this generalization is a second encounter within a few minutes.

5. Sacks also argues that greetings pairs are rarely separated by insertion sequences (Winter 1970. lecture 4, p. 3). Many adjacency relationships may be temporarily suspended by a range of other activities, especially insertion sequences:

> A: May I have a bottle of Mich?
>   B: Are you twenty one?
>   A: No
> B: No   (Merritt, 1976, 333)

B does not initially answer the question, but disrupts the adjacency relation to insert a question. This insertion is hearable as relevant to the original question—that is, as seeking information relevant to the granting of the request.

Sacks claims that such insertion is unlikely to separate pairs of greetings. In chapter 9 we show a violation of this principle in call-waiting prefaces.

4. Situational Variations in Telephone Openings

1. Here is a place in discourse in which sexist practice supplies interactive convenience. Most receptionists are females, most executives are males. Since male and female voices may be reliably distinguished from brief telephone answers, this provides a notification to any caller that the desired party has not answered.

2. These openings included fifteen at a help-line operated by the National Cancer Institute's Cancer Information Service, twelve calls to two radio talk shows, five to a doctor's office, and two to telephone operators. Findings have since been replicated at a title agency and a messenger service.

3. The radio talk show is an environment in which acquaintance-like augmentations are commonplace. Most callers are probably listening to the show before they call, so like participants in traffic court (see Pollner, 1987) radio callers may develop some sense of how openings get spoken in this environment.

4. For detailed consideration of Moerman's contribution, see the essays edited by Hopper (1991a).

5. How Do I Know When It's My Turn?

1. Or like type 1 and type 2 error in classical statistics.

2. Frankel (1982) reports that an autistic child who rarely spoke nevertheless showed knowledge of transition-relevance by shifting his gaze to a probable next speaker at a TRP, but before speaker change.

3. Patterns of breathing may be implicated in transition-relevance, in a way that shows in the Aggie joke. Often, people trying to say "timing" early sort of breathlessly croak their answer, with little air behind it. A speaker must breathe before an ordinarily-cadenced turn-beginning. Our verbal habits are calibrated to breathe when TRP's approach, and this habit must be over-ridden to breathe early.

4. Only 26 of 420 telephone pauses (6 percent) were over one second in length; but over 100 of 420 of face-to-face pauses (24 percent) were longer than one second. (See also Short et al., 1976.)

5. Figure 7 is adapted from Jefferson (1986) and Schegloff (1987b). The notion of transition relevance comes from Sacks et al. (1974). The terminology of "current/next" is taken from Schegloff (1979b, p. 267). The diagram's format owes Drummond's (1989) diagram describing interruptive speech overlap, which appears in chapter 6. Figure 7 depicts turn taking as a relay race. One runner holds the baton at a time. The runners must pass the baton from the current incumbent to the next beginner, with a premium on passing the baton as smoothly as possible. This metaphor implies turns of prespecified lengths, like relay laps of 400 meters. To adapt the relay race analogy to telephone conversation we must imagine a relay event in which competitors improvise turn length. It is difficult to conceive a relay race in which turns could be of almost any length, and in which the next runner must manage turn transfer from any place on the track.

6. Sacks et al. choose the term transition-relevance place to refer to both a point and/or an opportunity space. We emphasize the latter in this treatment. It would be attractive to posit that to begin at point #1 would produce a one-syllable overlap, at #2 would produce a latch, and at #3 would produce an unmarked next transition. However, this presupposes a fixed ending-point for the prior turn, which speakers may not do.

7. Wilson and Zimmerman present some evidence for this claim, and the intervals they suggest are very brief. Their evidence conflates transition-relevance and speaker change. We interpret limited evidence from Sacks et al. (1974, note 30) and from our own study of turn-beginnings as suggesting that, when there is a transition-relevant pause and prior speaker then continues, the pause is longer than when the other speaker breaks the silence. This might indicate a cycling of the rules from (b) to (c) that takes about a third of a second.

8. I presume Jefferson tabulated instances of all three kinds of completion intonation.

9. The procedure: (1) to select, by number, one phone call from each of seven collections in UTCL, so that no speaker appears more than once; (2) to sample the turn-transitions on the second page from each encounter (range eleven to twenty transitions per encounter); (3) to delete from consideration simultaneous starts and shared laughter instances (Glenn, 1989), which are difficult to classify as turns and/or to codify for speaker-change. Contiguous turns separated by (.) were coded as smooth transitions (Walker and Trimboli, 1982).

10. Includes three latches (=), since these prove very similar to overlaps of a syllable or less.

11. Auer (1990) labels sentences' recurrent vulnerability to leftward expansion "the neverending sentence."

12. We limit our sample to pauses of two tenths of a second and above because (1) listeners do not "perceive" inter-turn pauses of less than two tenths of a second, but rather perceive such transitions as smooth (Walker and Trimboli, 1982); and (2) forty percent of inter-turn pauses are "micro-pauses" that appear to operate as markers of emphasis. Therefore (in the USA) a pause becomes perceptible *as a pause* at about two tenths of a second.

A note on pause measurement: We used Jefferson's subvocalization procedure to measure pause length. Thomason (1990) tested this method for clock-time accuracy against an expert-operated stopwatch and Macintosh Soundcap. Against those who argue that subvocalized pause lengths represent members' time, a metric perhaps related to speech rate as well as clock time, we attend to measuring primarily the latter. This decision is empirical to this degree: we started measuring our pauses against Macintosh Soundcap suspecting that we would find our measurements inconsistent and that these inconsistencies might be related to speech rate. However, our measurements, and Jefferson's, were as good or better than stopwatch timings!

13. The distributional "fact" that one sixth of pauses following TRPs were first pair-parts may have relevance for how we think about adjacency pairs. No scholar has ever estimated the frequency of utterances that are part of adjacency pairs, and this figure provides one rough estimate—for the limited environment of turns with pauses between them. If roughly one of six TRP pauses follows a first pair-part, would it follow that one utterance out of six is a first pair-part?

14. We also sought, and did not find, relationships between these variables and pause duration.

15. In our data, the construction [TRP + conjunction + pause] leads to the current speaker continuing in over ninety percent of all cases. To pause right after the conjunction provides a hitch that allows the other to repair the previous turn unit or offer other business urgent enough to override the current speaker's expectation to continue (Schegloff, 1979b; see his note 22).

16. Heritage (personal communication) notes that, whereas "Oh" at the start of an utterance like Lottie's would be a self-attentive response-cry, Lottie's turn-initial 'Hey' is specifically other-attentive and therefore marks the turn that follows as competitive and requests that Emma attend to it rather than to the development of her own turn.

17. Related instances occur when a speaker whose question does not elicit an answer takes a next turn to add more specifics to the inquiry.

> NB:II:1:R:3
>
> E: Oh no. They drag it out so THAT'S WHERE THEY WE
>   TOOK OFF on ar chartered flight that same spot
>   didju see it?
> ⇒   (0.7)
> E: ·hh when they took him in the airplane

Here E, after the pause, makes a further attempt at achieving recognition of the spot she mentions prior to the pause (Pomerantz, 1984b).

18. In our sixty clean-transition cases, there were also two flat-out disagreements and two agree-disagree second pair-parts. We do not argue that disagreers inevitably delay their disagreeing tokens. But since the current data contain twelve delayed disagreements and two to four immediate ones, we suggest that a majority of disagreements are expressed with delay. Perhaps disagreement flip-flops preference

systemics: that is, the unmarked case of disagreement is a delayed second, and an immediate disagreement would be marked.

19. This decision to combine the two newsmarks with three NTRIs in the present data is undoubtedly premature. But it is a curious thought that the two particles may share some slots of occurrence.

20. Another reading for this instance: NTRP speaker change (in the environment of pauses) most frequently follows a conjunction and a pause. This instance follows a pause and then Mimi continues with a free-standing conjunction. After the conjunction Mimi says 'u:m' which delays the content of the turn. This vocalized pause provides a hitch for Pam to speak, after all, if she wishes (Schegloff, 1979b, p. 270). Pam does so, beginning with a smooth turn-transition. This instance illustrates how speaker change is possible without *either* transition relevance or a pause.

21. It also seems that these violations occurred in competitive episodes, at moments in which speakers had been disagreeing across multiple turns.

6. Turn Beginnings, Speech Overlap, and Interruption

1. See Table 6 in chapter 5 for details. Overlaps occur less than half as often as inter-turn pauses in telephone conversation. Thus the one-in-three ration in "Vote for the devil" is above average.

2. Evidence on this topic was provided in an unpublished study by Lewis (1984) who compared two weeks of scripts obtained from the producers of a network daytime soap opera with the videotaped performances of the programs. The most frequent change from the scripted material was the addition by a speaker of a pre-positioned appositional such as "Well." Presumably actors in these dramatic programs, who must learn their parts quickly and perform live, use these pre-placed appositionals to prevent "dead air." Ordinary speakers, in less dramatic circumstances, also make use of these devices.

3. Is K's turn beginning just a late but unmarked start, with vulnerabilities described by Jefferson; or does K pause because the question was difficult to answer due to its presuppositional error, and then recognize after the new turn unit begins that it will not correct the presuppositional error?

4. Goodwin's (1980) and Schegloff's arguments about utterance restarts run parallel in that in each case the restarts pursue evidence of listeners' attentiveness. Each restart repeats information that may have not gained attention at first, either through lack of recipient gaze (Goodwin) or by the beginning of a turn having occurred in overlap (Schegloff).

Goodwin's and Schegloff's findings, however, differ in their applicability to telephone conversation. Since telephone recipients do not gaze at one another, Goodwin's description cannot apply to telephone conversation. Recycled beginnings do occur in telephone conversation. However, in telephone conversation there are many restarts that are not described as recycles due to having begun a turn in overlap. What are speakers doing with these; and are these acts related to listener attentiveness? One tentative answer: speakers restart to seek attention for topic-initial utterances.

5. Other investigators (Roger, 1989; Kennedy and Camden 1983) report interruptions more equally distributed between men and women.

6. Although certain overlaps that Jefferson (1986, p. 168) labels as "recognitional" do not fit this description.

7. Another problem of tabulating such artifacts shows up if you notice what happens next. Pam seemingly wins the competitive face-off at the simultaneous start; however, her turn unit subsequently suffers a deep overlap. Who wins the conflict may depend on what you count. Like most struggles, this one has two parties who keep on striving.

8. One reason to be pessimistic about counting simultaneous starts after pauses is that a great many instances involve one speaker uttering an "acknowledgment token," such as "oh" or "yeah." These speakers usually drop out of the turn-contention begun by the overlap, but is this because they had, in the first instance, only projected a short turn?

UTCL A21:7

PAM: ·hhh And then just make it like a:- a- workout room
         or whatever
                  (0.3)
⇒   GLO: [O:h
     PAM: [Steve's gonna- put all of his *free* weights in there

UTCL A35C.1:3

B: small amount ch you know because cause most of it would
        be interest [anyway]
A: [Right]   right
                  (0.4)
⇒   H: [Yeah
     A: [So I figured it'd keep it- (1.0) oh little ...

7. Beginning Discourse Episodes

1. Paul Gray and James van Oosting are presently writing a performance of literature textbook in which this duet between mother and daughter is the focus of their first chapter. These authors argue that this passage constitutes literature-in-performance.

2. Personal communication.

3. M's "resource" utterance is apparently intended as a joke, though D's response is "po faced" (Drew, 1987) or serious-sounding.

4. See Jefferson (1981) for some ways around this problem—ways that do not count topic units, but consider how topic talk is maintained by means of acknowledgement tokens.

5. Once a topic (or story) is begun, the recipient's work does not end, as the literature on *back-channels* indicates. Furthermore, it is sometimes only after a partner aligns as a recipient of a story or a topic-elaboration that topicalization can be shown to have taken place. On the differential role of back channels and assessments in the maintenance of topic, see Jefferson (1981); Schegloff (1982); Wootton (1989); and Drummond (1989). This substantial literature is not treated in this book because it is about *continuing* and extending trajectories and bringing them to ends, not about beginnings. This is of course an artificial distinction.

6. For related observations about the pre-invitation status of 'What are you doin' see Schegloff (1972, p. 109).

7. Pres lead toward future actions in a manner that some investigators label as "indirect," because the pre utterances perform more action than their literal meaning denotes. The characterization of these turns as *preliminary* is stronger than the characterization as indirect in at least two ways. First, the characterization covers a larger set of cases than that proposed by Searle (1975) for indirect speech acts. Second, the characterization may be offered on textual evidence. The indirect characterization becomes cumbersome when applied to extended instances of invitations. For more extended comparison of the pre-sequence explanation with the "indirect speech act" account see Levinson (1983, chapter 6) and Heritage (1984b, chapter 8).

8. Beginning to Play

1. As in previous chapters, we profit from limitation to spoken materials. Some accounts of play turn upon nonverbal activities such as smiles, visual double-takes, and movement (Glenn and Knapp, 1987). When we limit ourselves to sound, however, the phenomena of play become accessible to description.

2. For related examples see Glenn and Knapp, 1987.

3. Especially Mary Lynn Damhorst, Sandra Ragan, G. H. Morris, Phillip Glenn, J. K. Alberts.

4. Another example of the relation between laughter and play appears in the film *Quest for Fire*, which depicts members of two tribes in interaction. The more advanced tribe displays several technologies that the primitives lack: fire technology, face-to-face sex, and derisive laughter in the face of misfortunes. When the primitive hero tries to sneak into the advanced village, he sinks into quicksand. His cries for help bring dozens of spears thrown by laughing, masked villagers. Is this play? Yes, it turns out, it is initiation. The invoking of a comic frame in this scene transforms misfortune to membership.

Subsequently, members of the advanced tribe teach the primitives that play must be accomplished interactively. Early in the film, the woman from the advanced culture tries to invite the primitives to laugh after a rock accidentally falls on a man's head. She becomes convulsed with laughter, while intermittently looking at each other to pursue sharing of the laughter. They will not laugh. It is a painful scene, and she finally gives it up. In the next scene, she deserts her new boyfriend. He first mourns her absence, then pursues her to her home, leading to the scene reported at the beginning of this note. In a mirroring scene late in the movie, the primitives show that they have learned interactive laughter. In the very next scene the primitive hero finally learns face-to-face sex.

5. This instance appears to be a man-of-words duel between the two male speakers with the female speaker playing mainly a spectator-support role. In this segment the nonspeaking male joins the primary audience member, who celebrates both men's attempts at humor. Here is a location worthy of feminist analysis of laughter.

6. The role of spectators seems important here. This issue may even have relevance to the D8 flirtation-call; for there were roommates at both ends who had begun the encounter by "fixing up" these telephone partners. There is evidence that these overhearers were attending at each end of the call.

7. Repetition-laden turns are perhaps less meta, or more subtly meta, than 'Is that what you meant.' That theoretical melon may be indicated here, but cannot be sliced: some meta-messages may be more meta than others.

9. The Telephone Access War

1. In this spirit we hear today optimistic forecasts that every U.S. citizen may soon be guaranteed telephone access. Eventually, this may become a right of everyone on the planet, though progress toward this goal remains slow (Hudson, 1982).

2. Ruth Draper performed dramatic monologues for forty years until her death in 1957. The present transcription is taken from one of her recordings. In recent years, Patricia Norcia has revived much of Draper's material, and I was led to the present recording by Norcia's performances and by her gracious, lively discussion of the issues touched on here.

3. A total of seven telephone calls appear in this half-hour monologue; five of them (four incoming calls) interrupt the lesson itself. Two of the incoming calls are return calls, which shows this character already engaging in telephone tag.

4. Line 41 is two electronic noises [#] with a BEEP between. The partner does not usually hear the beep, but usually hears some interruption of sound during it.

5. Many informants claim to be rude to call waiting subscribers. I treat these

reports with skepticism, like reports of people who claim to have told off a bully. Of course partners have right of refusal, as with any request or proposal or order. Frequently people tell me that they refuse 'hold on' requests. However, our corpus has no recorded instances of partner refusal.

6. I believe that most new answering machines do not record "hang ups," so this statistic is presently hard to compute. Of course, what most of us want to know is how many calls that we wanted to receive were truncated by the caller's reaching a machine. I would predict that these will slowly decrease in number as the machine seduces more of us into using it. I also predict that in a generation the majority of stationary phones will be connected to answering machines.

7. Ironically, the instance occurs while Jan is already waiting for another person to answer a new call, which connects answering machine technology with call waiting, and suggests an increasingly crowded telephone conversationscape.

REFERENCES

Atkinson, J. M. (1984). *Our masters' voices*. London: Methuen.

Atkinson, J. M., and Drew, P. (1979). *Order in court: The organisation of verbal interaction in judicial settings*. London: Macmillan.

Atkinson, J. M., and Heritage, J., eds. (1984). *Structures of social action*. Cambridge: Cambridge University Press.

Auer, P. (1990). The neverending sentence. Paper presented at the International Pragmatics Association, Barcelona, Spain, July.

Austin, J. L. (1962). *How to do things with words*. Cambridge, MA: Harvard University Press.

Bach, K., and Harnish, R. (1979). *Linguistic communication and speech acts*. Cambridge, MA: MIT Press.

Bakhtin, M. M. (1981). *The dialogic imagination*. Trans. C. Emerson and M. Holquist. Austin: University of Texas Press.

Bakhtin, M. M. (1986). *Speech genres and other late essays*. Trans. V. McGee. Austin: University of Texas Press.

Bales, R. F. (1969). *Personality and interpersonal behavior*. New York: Holt Rinehart.

Barry, D. (1989). Who even asked for call waiting? Knight-Ridder Newspapers, May 15.

Basso, K. (1979). *Portraits of "the Whiteman."* Cambridge: Cambridge University Press.

Bateson, G. (1972). *Steps to an ecology of mind*. San Francisco: Chandler.

Baugh, J., and Sherzer, J. (1984). *Language in use: Readings in sociolinguistics*. Englewood Cliffs: Prentice-Hall.

Beach, W. A., ed. (1989). Sequential organization of conversational activities. Special issue of *Western Journal of Speech Communication, 53, 2,* 85–246.

Beach, W. A. (1990). Orienting to the phenomenon. In J. A. Andersen, ed., *Communication Yearbook 13* (pp. 216–44). Beverly Hills: Sage Publications.

Beach, W. A. (1991). Searching for universal features of conversation. *Research in Language and Social Interaction, 24,* 349–66.

Bennett, A. (1981). Interruptions and the interpretation of conversation. *Discourse Processes, 4,* 171–88.

Benson, T., and Anderson, C. (1990). The ultimate technology: Frederick Wiseman's *Missile*. In M. J. Medhurst, A. Gonzalez, and T. R. Peterson, *Communication and the culture of technology* (pp. 257–85). Pullman, WA.: Washington State University Press.

Berger, C., and Bradac, J. (1982). *Language and social knowledge*. London: Arnold.

Berlo, D. (1960). *The process of communication*. New York: Holt, Rinehart, and Winston.

Bitzer, L. F. (1968). The rhetorical situation. *Philosophy and Rhetoric, 1,* 1–14.

Blake, W. (1982). *The complete poetry and prose of William Blake*. Ed. D. V. Erdman. Los Angeles: UCLA Press.

Boettinger, H. M. (1977). *The telephone book*. New York: Riverwood Publishers.

Bormann, E. G. (1972). Fantasy and rhetorical vision: The rhetorical criticism of social reality. *Quarterly Journal of Speech, 58,* 396–407.

Bridgman, R. (1966). *The colloquial style in America*. New York: Oxford.

Brooks, J. (1975). *Telephone: The first hundred years*. New York: Harper and Row.

Brown, R. (1973) *A first language*. Cambridge, MA: Harvard University Press.

Bruce, R. V. (1973). *Alexander Graham Bell and the conquest of solitude*. Boston: Little, Brown.

Brun-Cottan, F. (1989). Answering machine messages. Conference on Ethnomethodology and Conversation Analysis, Calgary, Alberta, August.

Buchwald, A. (1985). There are ways to break through the secretary telephone barrier. *Austin American Statesman*. October 3, p. A17.

Burke, K. (1935/1984). *Permanence and change*. Berkeley: University of California Press.

Burke, K. (1941/1973). *The philosophy of literary form*. Berkeley: University of California Press.

Burke, K. (1945/1969). *A grammar of motives*. Berkeley: University of California Press.

Burke, K. (1966). *Language as symbolic action*. Berkeley: University of California Press.

Button, G., and Casey, N. (1984). Generating topic: The use of topic initial elicitors. In J. Atkinson and J. Heritage, eds., *Structures of social action* (pp. 167–90). Cambridge: Cambridge University Press.

Button, G., and Lee, J. R. E., eds. (1987). *Talk and social organisation*. Avon: Multilingual Matters.

Cappella, J. N. (1979). Talk-silence sequences in informal conversations. *Human Communication Research, 6,* 3–17.

Cappella, J. N. (1990). The method of proof by example in conversation analysis. *Communication Monographs, 57,* 236–41.

Carbaugh, D. (1988). *Talking American: Cultural discourses on Donahue*. Norwood, NJ: Ablex Publishing.

Carroll, R. (1987). *Cultural misunderstandings: The French-American experiences*. Trans. C. Volk. Chicago: University of Chicago Press.

Casson, H. H. (1910). *The history of the telephone*. Chicago: A. C. McClurg and Co.

Chomsky, N. (1965). *Aspects of the theory of syntax*. Cambridge, MA: MIT Press.

Compton-Burnett, I. (1938). *A family and a fortune*. London: Gollancz.

Cook, M., and Lalljee, M. G. (1972). Verbal substitutes for visual signals. *Semiotica, 3,* 212–21.

Crawley, C. (1931). *From telegraphy to television*. London: Warne.

Crow, B. (1988). Conversational performance and the performance of conversation. *The Drama Review, 32* (T119), 23–54.

Dance, F. E. X. (1972). The centrality of the spoken word. *Central States Speech Journal, 23,* 197–201.

Derrida, J. (1967). *Of grammatology*. Trans. G. Spivak. Baltimore: Johns Hopkins University Press.

Dilts, M. M. (1941). *The telephone in a changing world*. New York: Longmans.

Dindia, K. (1987). The effects of sex of subject and sex of partner on interruption. *Human Communication Research, 13,* 345–71.

Doany, N., and Hopper, R. (1989). Donner la parole à Saussure. Paper presented at annual meetings of the Speech Communication Association, November.

Drew, P. (1984). Speakers' reportings in invitation sequences. In J. M. Atkinson and J. Heritage, eds., *Structures of social action* (pp. 129–52). Cambridge: Cambridge University Press.

Drew, P. (1987). Po-faced receipts of teases. *Linguistics, 25,* 219–53.

Drew, P. (in press). Interaction sequences and "anticipatory interactive planning." In J. Vershueren, ed., *Searle on conversation: Pragmatics and beyond*. Amsterdam: Benjamins B. V.

Drummond, K. (1989). A backward glance at interruptions. *Western Journal of Speech Communication, 53,* 150–66.

Drummond, K. (1990). Back channels revisited. Dissertation, Texas.

Duncan, S., and Fiske, D. W. (1977). *Face-to-face interaction: Research, methods and theory*. Hillsdale, NJ: Erlbaum.

Fishman, P. (1983). Interaction: The work women do. In B. Thorne, C. Kramarae, and N. Henley, eds., *Language, gender and society* (pp. 89–103). Rowley, MA: Newbury House.

Fitch, K. (1988). Uses of phonetics in conversation analysis. Speech Communication Association, November.

Frankel, R. (1982). Autism for all practical purposes: A micro-interactional view. *Topics in Language Disorders*, 33–42.

Frankel, R. (1989). "I wz wondering—uhm could *Raid* uhm effect the brain permanently d'y know?": Some observations on the intersection of speaking and writing in calls to a poison control center. *Western Journal of Speech Communication, 53*, 195–226.

Freimuth, V. S., Stein, J. A., and Kean, T. J. (1989). *Searching for health information: The Cancer Information Service model*. Philadelphia: University of Pennsylvania Press.

Freud, S. (1930/1961). *Civilization and its discontents*. Trans. J. Strachey. New York: Norton.

Gadamer, H. G. (1960/1975). *Truth and method*. New York: Continuum.

Gardner, C. B. (1980). Passing by: Street remarks, address rights and the urban female. *Sociological Inquiry, 50*, 328–56.

Garfinkel, H. (1967/1984). *Studies in ethnomethodology*. Englewood Cliffs, NJ: Prentice-Hall; Cambridge: Polity Press.

Garfinkel, H., and Sacks, H. (1970). On formal structures of practical actions. In J. C. McKinney and E. A. Tiryakian, eds., *Theoretical sociology* (pp. 338–66). New York: Appleton-Century-Crofts.

Giddens, A. (1979). *Central problems in social theory*. London: Macmillan.

Glenn, P. J. (1989). Initiating shared laughter in multi-party conversations. *Western Journal of Speech Communication, 53*, 127–49.

Glenn, P. J., and Knapp, M. L. (1987). The interactive framing of play in adult conversations. *Communication Quarterly, 35*, 48–66.

Godard, D. (1977). Same setting, different norms: Phone call beginnings in France and the United States. *Language and Society, 6*, 209–19.

Goffman, E. (1959). *The presentation of self in everyday life*. New York: Doubleday.

Goffman, E. (1963). *Behavior in public places*. New York: Macmillan.

Goffman, E. (1964). The neglected situation. *American Anthropologist, 66*, 133–36.

Goffman, E. (1971). *Relations in public: Microstudies of the public order*. New York: Basic Books.

Goffman, E. (1974). *Frame analysis*. New York: Harper and Row.

Goffman, E. (1978). *Forms of talk*. Philadelphia: University of Pennsylvania Press.

Goffman, E. (1983). The interaction order. *American Sociological Review, 48*, 1–17.

Goodwin, C. (1980). Restarts, pauses, and the achievement of a state of mutual gaze at turn-beginning, *Sociological Inquiry, 50*, 277–302.

Goodwin, C. (1981). *Conversational organization: Interactions between speakers and hearers*. New York: Academic Press.

Goodwin, C. (1984). Notes on story structure and the organization of participation. In J. Atkinson and J. Heritage, eds., *Structures of social action* (pp. 225–46). Cambridge: Cambridge University Press.

Goodwin, C. (1986). Between and within: Alternative treatments of continuers and assessments. *Human Studies, 9*, 205–17.

Goodwin, M. H. (1991). *He-said-she-said: Talk as social organization among black children*. Bloomington: Indiana University Press.

Grimshaw, A. D., Ibrahim, and Bird, C. S. (1984). Greetings in the desert. In *Language as social resource: Essays by Allen D. Grimshaw* (pp. 128–75). Palo Alto: Stanford University Press.

Gumperz, J. J. (1982). *Discourse strategies*. Cambridge: Cambridge University Press.

Gumperz, J. J., and Hymes, D., eds. (1972). *Directions in sociolinguistics*. New York: Holt, Rinehart, and Winston.

Gurwitsch, A. (1964). *The field of consciousness*. Pittsburgh: Duquesne University Press.

Hakulinen, A. (1990). Utterance syntax and conversation analysis. Paper presented at International Pragmatics Association, Barcelona, Spain, July.

Hall, T. (1989). With phones everywhere, everyone is talking more. *The New York Times*, October 11, pp. 1, 20.

Harris, R. (1987). *Reading Saussure*. Lasalle, IL: Open Court.

Haslett, B. (1987). *Communication: Strategic action in context*. London: Erlbaum.

Heidegger, M. (1962). *Being and time*. Trans. J. Macquarrie and E. Robinson. New York: Harper and Row. (Originally published in German, 1927.)

Heidegger, M. (1962). The fundamental question of metaphysics. In W. Barrett, ed., *Philosophy in the twentieth century*, vol. 3 (pp. 219–50). New York: Random House.

Henning, M., and Jardim, A. (1977). *The managerial woman*. New York: Doubleday.

Heritage, J. (1984a). A change-of-state token and aspects of its sequential placement. In J. M. Atkinson and J. Heritage, eds., *Structures of social action* (pp. 299–345). Cambridge: Cambridge University Press.

Heritage, John (1984b). *Garfinkel and ethnomethodology*. Cambridge: Polity Press.

Heritage, J. (1989). Current developments in conversation analysis. In D. Roger and P. Bull, eds., *Conversation* (pp. 21–47). Avon: Multilingual Matters.

Heritage, J. (1991). Intention, meaning and strategy: Observations on constraints on interaction analysis. *Research in Language and Social Interaction*, 25, 309–30.

Hopper, R. (1988). Speech, for instance. *Journal of Language and Social Psychology, 7*, 47–63.

Hopper, R. (1989a). Conversation analysis and social psychology as descriptions of interpersonal communication. In D. Roger and P. Bull, eds., *Conversation* (pp. 48–66). Avon: Multilingual Matters.

Hopper, R. (1989b). Speech in telephone openings: Emergent interaction v. routines. *Western Journal of Speech Communication*, 53, 178–94.

Hopper, R. (1989c). Sequential ambiguity in telephone openings: 'What are you doin.' *Communication Monographs*, 56, 240–52.

Hopper, R., ed. (1991a). Ethnography and conversation analysis after *Talking culture*. Special section in *Research in Language and Social Interaction*, 25, 159–68.

Hopper, R. (1991b). Hold the phone. In D. Boden and D. Zimmerman, eds., *Talk and social structure* (pp. 217–31). Cambridge: Polity Press.

Hopper, R., and Doany, N. (1988). Telephone openings and conversational universals: A study in three languages. In S. Ting-Toomey and F. Korzenny, eds., *Language, communication and culture* (pp. 157–79). Newbury Park, CA: Sage.

Hopper, R., Doany, N., Johnson, M., and Drummond, K. (1991). Universals and particulars in telephone openings. *Research in Language and Social Interaction*, 25, 367–85.

Hopper, R., Koch, S., and Mandelbaum, J. (1986). Conversation analysis methods. In D. Ellis and W. Donohue, eds., *Contemporary issues and discourse processes* (pp. 169–86). New York: Erlbaum.

Horenstein, G. A. (1985). Intimacy in conversational style as a function of the degree of closeness between members of a dyad. *Journal of Personality and Social Psychology, 49*, 671–81.

Houtkoop-Steenstra, H. (1991). Opening sequences in Dutch telephone conversation. In D. Boden and D. Zimmerman, eds., *Talk and social structure* (pp. 232–50). Cambridge: Polity Press.

Hudson, H. (1982). The role of telecommunications in development. In O. Gandy, P. Espinoza, and J. A. Ordover, eds., *Proceedings from the tenth annual telecommunications policy research conference* (pp. 291–307). Norwood, NJ: Ablex.

Hudson, H. (1984). *When telephones reach the village*. Norwood, NJ: Ablex.

Huizinga, J. (1944/1955). *Homo ludens: A study of the play element in culture.* Boston: Beacon Press.

Jackson, S. (1986). Building a case for claims about discourse structure. In D. Ellis and W. Donohue, eds., *Contemporary issues and discourse processes* (pp. 129–48). New York: Erlbaum.

Jackson, S., and Jacobs, S. (1980). Structure of conversational argument: Pragmatic bases for the enthymeme. *The Quarterly Journal of Speech, 66,* 251–65.

Jacobs, S. (1988). Evidence and inference in conversation analysis. In J. A. Anderson, ed., *Communication Yearbook 11* (pp. 433–43). Beverly Hills: Sage.

Jacobs, S. (1990), On the especially nice fit between qualitative analysis and the known properties of conversation. *Communication Monographs, 57,* 241–49.

Jameson, F. (1972). *The prison-house of language.* Princeton: Princeton University Press.

Jefferson, G. (1977). On the poetics of ordinary talk. Paper presented at Second International Institute on Ethnomethodology and Conversation Analysis, Boston.

Jefferson, G. (1978). Sequential aspects of storytelling in conversation. In Jim Schenkein, ed., *Studies in the organization of conversational interaction.* New York: Academic Press, 219–48.

Jefferson, G. (1979). A technique for inviting laughter and its subsequent acceptance/declination. In G. Psathas, ed., *Everyday language: Studies in ethnomethodology* (pp. 79–96). New York: Irvington.

Jefferson, G. (1980). On 'trouble-premonitory' responses to inquiry. *Sociological Inquiry, 50,* 153–85.

Jefferson, G. (1981). "Caveat speaker": A preliminary exploration of shift implicative recipience in the articulation of topic. Final report to the (English) Social Science Research Council. London: Mimeo.

Jefferson, G. (1984). Notes on some orderlynesses in overlap onset. In V. D'Urso and P. Lombardi, eds., *Discourse analysis and natural rhetorics* (pp. 11–38). Padua, Italy: Cleup Editors.

Jefferson, G. (1985). An exercise in the transcription and analysis of laughter. In T. van Dijk, ed., *Handbook of discourse analysis,* vol. 3 (pp. 25–34). London: Academic Press.

Jefferson, G. (1986). Notes on 'latency' in overlap onset. *Human Studies, 9,* 153–84.

Jefferson, G. (1987). On exposed and embedded correction in conversation. In G. Button and J. R. E. Lee, eds., *Talk and social organisation* (pp. 86–100). Avon: Multilingual Matters.

Johnson, W. (1953). The fateful process of Mr. A talking to Mr. B. *Harvard Business Review, 31,* 49–56.

Johnstone, H. W., Jr. (1982). Communication: Technology and ethics. In M. Hyde, ed., *Communication, philosophy and the technological age* (pp. 38–53). University, AL: University of Alabama Press.

Katriel, T., and Philipsen, G. (1981). 'What we need is communication': Communication as a cultural category in some American speech. *Communication monographs, 48,* 301–17.

Kelly, J., and Local, J. K. (1989). On the use of general phonetic techniques in handling conversational material. In D. Roger and P. Bull, eds., *Conversation* (pp. 197–212). Avon: Multilingual Matters.

Kendon, A., and Ferber, A. (1973). A description of some human greetings. In R. P. Michael and J. H. Crook., eds., *Comparative ecology and behavior of primates* (pp. 591–668). London: Academic Press.

Kennedy, C., and Camden, C. (1983). A new look at interruptions, *Western Journal of Speech Communication, 47,* 45–58.

Kilian, M. (1986) Telephone-based civilization (as we know it) faces an insidious evil. *Austin American Statesman,* Feb. 28, A15.

240   References

Knapp, M. L. (1978). *Social intercourse: Greeting to goodbye.* Boston: Allyn and Bacon.
Lakoff, G. (1987). *Women, fire, and dangerous things: What categories reveal about the mind.* Chicago: University of Chicago Press.
Lakoff, G., and Johnson, M. (1980). *Metaphors we live by.* Chicago: University of Chicago Press.
Lerner, G. (1989). Notes on overlap management in conversation: The case of delayed completion. *Western Journal of Speech Communication, 53,* 167–77.
Lévi-Strauss, C. (1962). *The savage mind.* University of Chicago Press.
Levinson, S. C. (1983). *Pragmatics.* Cambridge: Cambridge University Press.
Lewis, L. (1984). Scripts and performances in televised soap opera. Unpublished paper, University of Texas.
Local, J., and Kelly, J. (1986). Projection and 'silences': Notes on phonetic and conversational structure. *Human Studies, 9,* 185–204.
Mandelbaum, J. (1987a). Couples sharing stories. *Communication Quarterly, 35,* 144–70.
Mandelbaum, J. S. (1987b). Recipient-driven storytelling in conversation. Dissertation, University of Texas.
Mandelbaum, J. (1989). Interpersonal activities in conversational storytelling. *Western Journal of Speech Communication, 53,* 114–26.
Mandelbaum, J. (1990). Communication phenomena as solutions to interactional problems. In J. A. Anderson, ed., *Communication Yearbook, 13* (pp. 255–67). Newbury Park, CA: Sage Publications.
Mandelbaum, J. (1991). Beyond mundane reasoning: conversation analysis and context. In *Research in Language and Social Interaction, 24,* 331–48.
Marvin, C. (1988). *When old technologies were new.* Oxford.
Maynard, D. W. (1980). Placement of topic changes in conversation. *Semiotica, 13,* 263–90.
Maynard, D. W. (1989). Perspective-display sequences in conversation. *Western Journal of Speech Communication, 53,* 91–113.
Maynard, D. W. (1990). On the interactional and institutional basis of asymmetry in clinical discourse. Paper presented at International Pragmatics Association, Barcelona, Spain, July.
McLaughlin, M. (1984). *Conversation: How talk is organized.* Beverly Hills, CA: Sage.
McQuail, D. (1990). Telephone research and communication science. Paper delivered at International Communication Association, Dublin, Ireland, June.
McTear, M. (1985). *Children's conversation.* Oxford: Blackwell.
Mehan, H., and Wood, H. (1975). *The reality of ethnomethodology.* New York: John Wiley and Sons.
Meltzer, L., Morris, W., and Hayes, D. (1971). Interruption outcomes and vocal amplitude: Explorations in social psychophysics. *Journal of Personality and Social Psychology, 18,* 392–402.
Merritt, M. (1976). On questions following questions (in service encounters). *Language in Society, 5,* 315–57.
Modaff, J. V. (1988). Speech melody, why leave it out? Paper presented at meetings of the Speech Communication Association, November.
Modaff, J. V., and Hopper, R. (1984). Why speech is 'basic.' *Communication Education, 33,* 37–42.
Moerman, M. (1977). The preference for self-correction in a Tai conversational corpus. *Language, 53,* 872–82.
Moerman, M (1988). *Talking Culture. Ethnography and conversation analysis.* Philadelphia: University of Pennsylvania Press.
Motley, M. T. (1985). The production of verbal slips and double entendres as clues to the efficiency of normal speech production. *Journal of Language and Social Psychology, 4,* 275–93.

Naremore, R., and Hopper, R. (1990). *Children learning language*. New York: Harper and Row.

Nofsinger, R. E. (1975). The demand ticket: A conversational device for getting the floor. *Speech Monographs, 42,* 1–9.

Nofsinger, R. (1991). *Everyday conversation*. Newbury Park, CA: Sage.

Oakeshott, M. (1967). The voice of poetry in the conversation of mankind. In *Rationalism in politics and other essays*. London: Methuen.

O'Barr, W. M., and Atkins, B. K. (1980). "Women's language" or "powerless language?" In S. M. McConnell-Ginet, R. Borker, and N. Furman, eds., *Women and language in literature and society* (pp. 93–110). New York: Praeger.

Ong, W. (1982). *Orality and literacy: The technologizing of the word*. London: Methuen.

Pearce, W. B., and Cronen, V. (1980). *Communication, action and meaning*. New York: Praeger.

Pollner, M. (1987). *Mundane reason*. Cambridge: Cambridge University Press.

Pomerantz, A. (1980). Telling my side: Limited access as a fishing device. *Sociological Inquiry, 50,* 186–99.

Pomerantz, A. (1984a). Agreeing and disagreeing with assessments. In J. M. Atkinson and J. Heritage, eds. *Structures of social action* (pp. 57–101). Cambridge: Cambridge University Press.

Pomerantz, A. (1984b). Pursuing a response. In J. M. Atkinson and J. Heritage, eds., *Structures of social action*. (pp. 152–63). Cambridge: Cambridge University Press.

Pomerantz, A. (1988). Offering a candidate answer: An information seeking strategy. *Communication Monographs, 55,* 360–73.

Pomerantz, A. (1990). Conversation analytic claims. *Communication Monographs, 57,* 231–35.

Pool, I. de S., ed. (1976). *Social uses of the telephone*. Cambridge, MA: MIT Press.

Pool, I. de S. et al. (1977). Retrospective technology assessment of the telephone, vol. 1. Report to National Science Foundation, Washington, D.C. (Project report #ERP75–08807).

Prescott, George B. (1972/1884). *Bell's electric speaking telephone: Its invention, construction, application, modification and history*. with 330 illustrations. New York: D. Appleton and Co., 1884. Reprinted by Arno Press, Technology and Society, New York, 1972.

Quintilian (1921). *Institutes of oratory*, vol. 2. Trans. H. E. Butler. London: Loeb Classical Library.

Rakow, L. F. (1988). Women and the telephone: The gendering of a communications technology. In C. Kramarae, ed., *Technology and women's voices* (pp. 207–28). London: Routledge and Kegan Paul.

Reddy, M. (1979). The conduit metaphor. In A. Ortony, ed., *Metaphor and thought*. Cambridge: Cambridge University Press.

Roger, D. (1989). Experimental studies of dyadic turn-taking behaviour. In D. Roger and P. Bull, eds., *Conversation* (pp. 75–95). Avon: Multilingual Matters.

Ronell, A. (1989). *The telephone book: Technology, schizophrenia, electric speech*. Lincoln: University of Nebraska Press.

Rorty, R., ed. (1967). *The linguistic turn: Recent essays on philosophical method*. Chicago: University of Chicago Press.

Rutter, D. R. (1987). *Communicating by telephone*. Oxford: Pergamon Press.

Rutter, D. R. (1989). The role of cuelessness in social interaction: An examination of teaching by telephone. In D. Roger and P. Bull, eds., *Conversation* (pp. 294–312). Avon: Multilingual Matters.

Rutter, D. R., and Stephenson, G. M. (1977). The role of visual communication in synchronising conversation. *European Journal of Social Psychology, 7,* 29–37.

Sacks, H. (1964—1972). Unpublished lectures. Transcribed and edited by G. Jefferson, mimeograph. To be published as *Lectures on conversation*, ed. G. Jefferson with introductions by E. A. Schegloff, 2 vols. Oxford: Blackwell.

Sacks, H. (1972). On the analyzability of stories by children. In J. J. Gumperz and D. Hymes, eds., *Directions in sociolinguistics* (pp. 325–45). New York: Holt, Rinehart, and Winston.

Sacks, H. (1974). An analysis of a joke's telling in conversation. In R. Baumann and J. Sherzer, eds., *Explorations in the ethnography of speaking* (pp. 337–53). Cambridge: Cambridge University Press.

Sacks, H. (1975). Everyone has to lie. In Ben Blount and Mary Sanches, eds., *Sociocultural dimensions of language use* (pp. 57–80). New York: Academic Press.

Sacks, H. (1984). Notes on methodology, in J. M. Atkinson and J. Heritage, eds., *Structures of social action* (pp. 21–27). Cambridge: Cambridge University Press.

Sacks, H. (1987). On the preferences for agreement and contiguity in sequences in conversation. In G. Button and J. R. E. Lee, eds., *Talk and social organisation* (pp. 54–69). Avon: Multilingual Matters.

Sacks, H. (1989). Harvey Sacks—Lectures 1964–1965. Ed. G. Jefferson. *Human Studies*, 12, 3–4. 183–410.

Sacks, H., and Schegloff, E. A. (1979). Two preferences in the organization of references to persons in conversation and their interaction. In G. Psathas, ed., *Everyday language* (pp. 15–22). New York: Irvington.

Sacks, H., Schegloff, E. A., and Jefferson, G. (1974). A simplest systematics for the organization of turn-taking for conversation. *Language, 50*, 696–735.

Said, E. W. (1985/1975). *Beginnings: Intention and method.* New York: Columbia University Press.

Saussure, F. de (1985/1915). *Cours de linguistique générale*. Publié par C. Bally et A. Sechehaye, Édition critique préparée par T. de Mauro. Translations: *Course in general linguistics*, tr. W. Baskin (1959), New York: McGraw-Hill; and R. Harris (1986), LaSalle, IL: Open Court Publishers.

Schegloff, E. A. (1968). Sequencing in conversational openings. *American Anthropologist, 70*, 1075–95. (Reprinted in J. J. Gumperz and D. Hymes, eds., *Directions in Sociolinguistics* (pp. 346–80), New York: Holt, Rinehart, and Winston, 1972.)

Schegloff, E. A. (1972). Notes on a conversational practice: Formulating place. In D. Sudnow, ed., *Studies in social interaction* (pp. 75–119). New York: Free Press.

Schegloff, E. A. (1979a). Identification and recognition in telephone conversation openings. In George Psathas, ed., *Everyday language* (pp. 23–78). New York: Irvington.

Schegloff, E. A. (1979b). The relevance of repair to syntax-for-conversation. *Syntax and semantics, volume 12: Discourse and syntax* (pp. 261–86). New York: Academic Press.

Schegloff, E. A. (1980). Preliminaries to preliminaries: "Can I ask you a question?" *Sociological Inquiry, 50*, 104–52.

Schegloff, E. A. (1982). Discourse as an interactional achievement: Some uses of 'uh huh' and other things that come between sentences. In D. Tannen, ed., *Analyzing discourse: Text and talk* (pp. 71–93). Washington, D.C.: Georgetown University Press (Georgetown Roundtable on Languages and Linguistics).

Schegloff, E. A. (1984). On some questions and ambiguities in conversation. In J. M. Atkinson and J. Heritage, eds., *Talk and social structure* (pp. 28–52). Cambridge: Cambridge University Press.

Schegloff, E. A. (1986). The routine as achievement. *Human Studies, 9*, 111–52.

Schegloff, E. (1987a). Between micro and macro: Contexts and their connections. In J. C. Alexander, B. Giesen, R. Munch, and N. J. Selzer, eds., *The micro-macro link* (pp. 207–34). Berkeley: University of California Press.

Schegloff, E. A. (1987b). Recycled turn beginnings: A precise repair mechanism in conversation's turn-taking organisation. In G. Button and J. R. E. Lee, eds. *Talk and social organisation* (pp. 70–85). Avon: Multilingual Matters.

Schegloff, E. A. (1990). Where does theory come from? More rules of turn taking. Paper delivered at Speech Communication Association, Chicago.

Schegloff, E. A. (1991). Reflections on talk and social structure. In D. Boden and D. H. Zimmerman, eds., *Talk and social structure* (pp. 44–71). Cambridge: Polity Press.

Schegloff, E. A., Jefferson, G., and Sacks, H. (1977). The preference for self-correction in the organization of repair in conversation. *Language, 53,* 361–82.

Schegloff, E. A., and Sacks, H. (1973). Opening up closings. *Semiotica, 7,* 289–327.

Schiffrin, D. (1977). Opening encounters. *American Sociological Review, 44,* 679–91.

Schiffrin, D. (1980). Meta-talk: Organizational and evaluative brackets in discourse. *Sociological Inquiry, 50,* 199–236.

Schramm, W., ed. (1954) *The process and effects of mass communication.* Urbana: University of Illinois Press.

Schwartz, T. (1973). *The responsive chord.* New York: Anchor.

Searle, J. (1975). Indirect speech acts. In P. Cole and J. L. Morgan, eds., *Syntax and semantics, Volume 3: Speech acts* (pp. 59–82). New York: Academic Press.

Selting, M. (1990). Aspects of prosody in question-answer sequences in German conversation. Paper presented at International Pragmatics Association, Barcelona, Spain, July.

Shannon, C. E. (1948). A mathematical theory of communication. *The Bell System Technical Journal, 27,* 379–423.

Shaw, G. B. (1913 /1983). *Pygmalion.* London: Penguin.

Short, J. A., Williams, E., and Christie, B. (1976) *The social psychology of telecommunications.* Chichester: Wiley.

Sifianou, M. (1989). On the telephone again! Differences in telephone behaviour: England versus Greece. *Language in Society, 18,* 527–44.

Simons, H. (1990). Going meta. Lecture at University of Texas at Austin, November.

Streeck, J. (in press, a) The dispreferred other. In J. Vershueren, ed., *Searle on conversation: Pragmatics and beyond.* Amsterdam: Benjamins B. V.

Streeck, J. (in press, b) On projection. in E. Goody, ed., *The social origin of intelligence.* Cambridge: Cambridge University Press.

Stucky, N. (1988). Unnatural acts: Performing natural conversation. *Literature in Performance, 8,* 28–39.

Suchman, L., and Jordan, B. (1990). Interactional troubles in face-to-face survey interviews. *Journal of the American Statistical Association, 85,* 231–41.

Taylor, E., Thomason, R., and Hopper, R. (1992). Hello answering machine this is Darryl. *Western Speech,* Feb.

Terasaki, A. (1976). Pre-announcement sequences in conversation. *Social Sciences Working Paper No. 99.* University of California at Irvine.

Thomason, W. R. (1990). The relationship between transition relevance and speaker change in two conversational pause environments. Paper presented at annual meetings of Speech Communication Association, November, Chicago.

Thomason, W. R., and Hopper, R. (1992). Pauses, transition-relevance and speaker change. *Human Communication Research, 18,* 429–44.

Thompson, J. (1984). *Studies in the theory of ideology.* Cambridge: Cambridge University Press.

Thoreau, H. D. (1845; 1962). *Walden and other writings.* Ed. J. W. Krutch. New York: Bantam.

Tsui, A. B. M. (1989). Beyond the adjacency pair. *Language in Society, 18,* 545–64.

Vico, G. (1744/1970). *The new science of Giambattista Vico.* Abridged translation of third edition (1744) by T. G. Bergin and M. H. Fisch. Ithaca: Cornell University Press.

Volosinov, V. N. (1930/1973). *Marxism and the philosophy of language*, Trans. L. Matejka, and I. R. Titunik. New York: Seminar Press.

Walker, M. (1982). Smooth transitions in conversational turn-taking. *Journal of Psychology, 110*, 31–37.

Walker, M., and Trimboli, C. (1982). Smooth transitions in conversational interactions. *Journal of Social Psychology, 117*, 305–306.

Walker, M., and Trimboli, C. (1984). The role of nonverbal signals in co-ordinating speaking turns. *Journal of Language and Social Psychology, 3*, 257–72.

Watson, T. A. (1913). The birth and babyhood of the telephone. Address delivered to third annual convention of the Telephone Pioneers of America. Chicago: A T & T.

West, C. (1979). Against our will: Male interruptions of females in cross-sex conversation. In J. Orsanu, M. Slater, and L. L. Adler, eds., *Language, sex and gender: Annals of the New York Academy of Sciences, 327*, 81–97.

West, C., and Garcia, A. (1988). Conversational shiftwork: A study of topical transitions between women and men. *Social Problems, 35* , 551–73.

West, C., and Zimmerman, D. (1983). Small insults: A study of interruptions in cross-sex conversations between unacquainted persons. In B. Thorne, C. Kramarae, and N. Henley, eds., *Language, gender and society* (pp. 103–18). Rowley, MA: Newbury House.

Whalen, M. R., and Zimmerman, D. H. (1987). Sequential and instititutional contexts in calls for help. *Social Psychology Quarterly, 50*, 172–85.

Whitman, W. (1855). *Leaves of grass*. Brooklyn. (Reissued, 1959, Viking Press.)

Wieder, D. L. (1988). From resource to topic: some aims of conversation analysis. In J. A. Anderson, ed., *Communication Yearbook 11* (pp. 444–54). Beverly Hills: Sage.

Wiemann, J. (1981). Effects of laboratory videotaping procedures on selected conversation behaviors. *Human Communication Research, 7*, 302–11.

Wiens, A. N., Thompson, S., Matarazzo, J. D., Matarazzo, R. G., and Saslow, G. (1965). Interview interaction behavior of supervisors, head nurses, and staff nurses. *Nursing Research, 14*, 322–29.

Williams, C. (1930). *War in heaven*. London: Gollancz. (Reprinted, 1949, Erlman's Publ., Grand Rapids, MI.)

Williams, F., and Dordick, H. (1985). Social research and the telephone. Research report: Annenberg School of Communications, University of Southern California.

Wilson, T. P., and Zimmerman, D. H. (1986). The structure of silence between turns in two-party conversation. *Discourse Processes, 9*, 375–90.

Wittgenstein, L. (1953). *Philosophical Investigations*. Trans. G. Anscombe. London: Macmillan.

Wolfe, T. (1987). *The bonfire of the vanities*. New York: Farrar Straus and Giroux.

Wootton, A. J. (1989). Remarks on the methodology of conversation analysis. In D. Roger and P. Bull, eds., *Conversation* (pp. 238–58). Clevedon: Multilingual Matters.

Zahn, C. (1984). A re-examination of conversational repair, *Communication Monographs, 51*, 56–66.

Zimmerman, D. H. (1988). On conversation: The conversation analytic perspective. In J. A. Anderson, ed., *Communication Yearbook 11* (pp. 406–32). Beverly Hills: Sage.

Zimmerman, D., and West, C. (1975). Sex roles, interruptions and silences in conversation. In B. Throne and N. Henley, eds., *Language and sex: Difference and dominance* (pp. 105–29). Rowley, MA: Newbury House.

Znaniecki, F. (1934). *The method of sociology*. New York: Farrar and Rinehart.

INDEX

ROBERT HOPPER is Charles Sapp Centennial Professor of Communication, Department of Speech Communication, The University of Texas at Austin. His most recent books are *Children Learning Language* (with R. C. Naremore) and *Between You and Me*.